SECOND LANGUAGE DISCOURSE:
A Textbook of Current Research

SECOND LANGUAGE DISCOURSE:
A Textbook of Current Research

edited by

Jonathan Fine

Bar-Ilan University

P
53
.S39
1988

Ablex Publishing Corporation
Norwood, N.J. 07648

Copyright © 1988 by Ablex Publishing Corporation.

Printed in the United States of America

Library of Congress Cataloging-in-Publication Data

Second language discourse: a textbook of current research/edited by Jonathan Fine.
    p.   cm.—(Advances in discourse processes; v. 25)
  Bibliography: p.
  Includes index.
  ISBN: 0-89391-413-4
  1. Language and languages—Study and teaching. 2. Second language acquisition.
I. Fine, Jonathan. II. Series.
P53.S39 1987   87-19702
481 '.007—dc19   CIP

Ablex Publishing Corporation
355 Chestnut St.
Norwood, New Jersey 07648

Contents

Preface to the Series

Roy O. Freedle,

Series Editor

This series of volumes provides a forum for the cross-fertilization of ideas from a diverse number of disciplines, all of which share a common interest in discourse—be it prose comprehension and recall, dialogue analysis, text grammar construction, computer simulation of natural language, cross-cultural comparisons of communicative competence, or other related topics. The problems posed by multisentence contexts and the methods required to investigate them, while not always unique to discourse, are still sufficiently distinct as to benefit from the organized mode of scientific interaction made possible by this series.

Scholars working in the discourse area from the perspective of sociolinguistics, psycholinguistics, ethnomethodology and the sociology of language, educational psychology (e.g., teacher–student interaction), the philosophy of language, computational linguistics, and related subareas are invited to submit manuscripts of monograph or book length to the series editor. Edited collections of original papers resulting from conferences will also be considered.

Volumes in the Series

Preface

The field of discourse analysis is at once an old field stretching back to antiquity and a relatively new field of about thirty years. In even this later period of a few decades there have been several different approaches and changes of approach to studying connected language, whether spoken or written. It is the aim of this volume to bring some of the diverse theoretical approaches, methods, and findings of discourse analysis to bear on second language teaching and learning.

My strategy has been to present current, original research as both substantive papers for the specialist and as examples of the field for the learner. Learning by reading original sources is important to understand the strengths and limitations of the research. Introductions have been provided to the individual chapters to highlight certain themes and to draw some of the connections that exist among the chapters. The most basic theme is the simultaneous use of several approaches or methods of analysis.

Second language discourse has many dimensions. The chapters include both oral and written language, theoretical and applied perspectives, experimental and descriptive studies, sociolinguistic and psycholinguistic considerations, classroom and real life discourse, teaching and evaluation. These dimensions are not oppositions but complement each other to describe a field. Each chapter cuts across a number of these dimensions and thus demonstrates part of the interaction of dimensions in second language discourse. Detailed appendices of results and research instruments have been included to aid both research and practical applications of these papers.

I am indebted to Andrew Cohen for discussions at the planning stage of this volume and to Joel Walters for various advice along the way. They share no blame for the shortcomings. I would like to thank all the authors for their patience in writing and rewriting their chapters and revising once more.

My family has endured the preparation of this volume with patience. Their assistance is greatly appreciated.

Jerusalem   Jonathan Fine

August 1987

CHAPTER 1

The Place of Discourse in Second Language Study

Jonathan Fine

Bar-Ilan University

What is discourse analysis? Why is it important in second language teaching and learning? This chapter addresses both these questions, often simultaneously, to give a background for the following chapters and to raise specific issues for the application and theory of second language discourse analysis. The plan of the chapter is as follows: a brief description of what discourse analysis is with suggestions of its connections to and importance for second language teaching, a review of some factors that cause variation in discourse, a specific examination of the relationship between the content of what is said in conversation and the conversational structure that expresses it, a brief discussion of some issues in nondialogue forms of discourse, and finally a discussion of context in second language discourse.

Discourse is generally taken to mean the organization of stretches of language greater than a sentence (the usual upper limit for grammatical analysis). Thus, discourse analysis can focus on conversation, monologue, or written language, when searching for the patterning of the language (see Freedle, 1977, 1979; Grimes, 1975 for some of the fundamental studies and concepts). Discourse analysis must determine the units of these larger stretches of language, how these units are signaled by specific linguistic markers, and/ or the processes involved in producing and comprehending larger stretches of language.

The word *process* is important especially for second language discourse. Discourse is produced by speakers or writers for other people. The psychological steps or processes involved in producing and comprehending discourse are related to the patterning of the discourse. For example, some passages are easier to remember, easier to learn, or forgotten in predictable ways (Freedle, 1977, 1979; Fine & Freedle, 1983). The analysis of discourse offers a method of investigating these psychological processes of language production and comprehension. In second language learning and teaching it is particularly important to be able to view the processes involved. Much of second language teaching and learning is undertaken with specific objectives and with quite limited amounts of time and materials. Under these conditions, there is every incentive to develop the most efficient methods and materials. Understanding the psychological processes of the second language learner is a step toward more efficient second language teaching.

Aside from the cognitive or psycholinguistic connection with discourse, second language discourse is crucially related to the culture and situation of the second language. Not only is a student learning a new language but he is also learning how to use that language in the appropriate situations. These situations are, in turn, defined by the culture that specifies, for example, that there are social superiors and inferiors who should speak to each other in certain ways or that on given culturally determined occasions certain formulae are appropriate (Gleason & Weintrab, 1976). Discourse rather than syntax or phonology, for example—is particularly influenced by differences between cultures. For example, the degree of politeness and where politeness is appropriate is specific to each culture. That is, not only the words for saying polite things differ from language to language but where, when, and to whom they are spoken. The importance of context to discourse studies and to second language learning will be discussed more fully towards the end of the chapter.

As well as context, there are two other major factors to be considered in second language discourse. First, there is the difference between oral and written language. Each of these two modes of language has its own patterning at the level of discourse. Second, language behavior involves both production and comprehension. Longer stretches of language, in particular, can show how the processes of production and comprehension proceed (see, for example, Nix, 1983; Graesser, Robertson & Clark, 1983; Morrow, 1985).

The importance of the study of discourse for second language teaching stems from the role of discourse as operating as communicative units in context and as indicators of comprehension and production processes. Second language teaching and learning have as their objectives (except for the limited cases of learning only to read a language) the appropriate use of the language in real situations. At the early stages of second language learning the correct sounds and grammar are constantly stressed. However, at later stages, second language learning must focus on issues such as the appropriateness of saying x or y on a particular occasion. At this stage of language acquisition, what makes an utterance more or less appropriate is less likely to be the exactitude of the phonology and more likely to be the proper arrangement of one sentence or clause in its context.

Second language learning can be viewed as the acquisition of the appropriate comprehension and production processes. Given this perspective, the importance of discourse becomes clear. Through examining longer stretches of language, cognitive processes of language use have been outlined (for early work, see, Freedle, 1977, 1979; for more recent work, Chafe, forthcoming). By examining discourse in second language acquisition, crucial information about the ordering and integration of specific cognitive processes in second language acquisition can be obtained. This understanding of cognition can be used to efficiently design materials and teaching programs.

As mentioned, there are several influences on discourse patterns. In examining second language discourse, we will describe three of these influences: the situation of language use, the context of the discourse, and the patterning deriving from the conversations. The last of these will be examined in some detail. Interactions between discourse patterns and the speaker's knowledge of situations have been clearly shown. Rintell (1981) studied Spanish speakers speaking both Spanish and English, and addressing both older and younger listeners. Requests to older addressees were more deferential than to younger addressees. Although in English there was no effect based on the sex of the addressee, in Spanish, speakers were more deferential when requesting from the opposite sex compared to the same sex. She concludes: "While in both languages an older listener seemed to elicit a rise in the level of deference of requests, none of the other effects or interactions (e.g., length of utterance, sex of addressee, age of speaker) were the same for both languages."

For language learners, Scarcella and Brunak (1981) differentiate the acquisition of language forms (specifically, politeness forms) and the learning of when to use these forms. They found that second language speakers do not vary politeness features (such as address forms) as much as first language speakers and the second language speakers use some linguistic features inappropriately. For example, they use declarations such as "You can come along" to superiors whereas native speakers use them only to equals. In both the above studies of second language speakers it is the assessment of the situation that is important for the second language speakers. They must determine which features of the situation are relevant to adjustments in politeness. Furthermore, they must then learn which features of the second language are to be adjusted for changes in politeness. Politeness and similar concepts such as authority, social distance, and purpose of communication tend to influence not a single language variable but a set of language features which together create distinctive patterns in larger stretches of language. Politeness, for example, is created by a series of features including terms of address, choice of sentence types, intonation, and verb modality. It is together that such features form discourse which is interpreted as polite. If only some of the appropriate features are present, the listener may not be able to form the proper interpretaion of the language and may even guess that the speaker is using a second language because the total pattern of discourse does not fit with the pattern expected of a native speaker for the particular situation.

Besides assessing the situation to determine the proper discourse form, the second language speaker must also consider the content of what is to be said and how it influences the pattern of discourse. Halliday (1973:485 and elsewhere) develops the concepts of a "can mean" potential and a "can say" potential in language behavior. As a second language learner becomes more familiar with the culture and discourse patterns of the new language, he or she learns what the possible meanings are for the culture. For example, one cannot name a ship or pass a sentence in a court of law if the necessary institutions and customs do not exist in a particular society. Even in less institutional frameworks, meaning potentials can vary from culture to culture, say, for example, in the categories of chastisement. The second language learner must learn the meaning potentials that derive from the culture and which are then mapped onto specific linguistic structures. The "can say" potential consists of the options provided by the linguistic system, in our case, the second language. The learner's task is to make the appropriate choices from the options of the language (at sentence level, for example, to appropriately choose active or passive in a language which has those options). The choices in the language system, though, derive from the possibilities presented by the "can mean" potential given by the culture. Thus the content itself is a result of the set of choices established by the culture and in turn constrains the choices that can be made from the specific set of linguistic structures and patterns of the language (see, for example, the structure of British legal texts, Kurzon, 1984).

A substantial shaping of discourse derives not only from the situation of the language use and the content, but from the use of language in conversation as well. Much of second language teaching focuses on conversation with adequate conversational skills being a major objective of most programs. Conversation is also the usual stimulus for first language learning. Given the importance of conversation in language learning and as an influence on discourse, several aspects of conversation will be dealt with in detail. As outlined earlier, the content of utterances can affect discourse patterning. Here we will deal with the discourse patterning in conversation with respect to (a) the specification or generality (in artificial intelligence terms, the relative packing and unpacking) of lexical concepts, and (b) the effect of lexical choices on turn-taking and the interaction with social relationships.

In dealing with utterance-to-utterance relationships in conversation, a number of researchers have found it necessary to examine the content of utterances (often conceptualized as propositions). Schegloff, Jefferson and Sacks (1977) list some devices for checking understanding in conversation (see also Pica & Doughty, this volume). The form *Y'mean X*? can be used by a speaker to verify a prior utterance. The content of *X* must be a plausible interpretation of the prior utterance given the social and situational circumstances, otherwise the device of correction can become rude, satirical, or accusatory. For example,

A: *Linda decided to move to Agincourt.*
B: *Y'mean she couldn't take Bob anymore?*

Similarly, Labov and Fanshel (1977) note that their rule of confirmation (If A makes a statement about events assumed to be known by B, then it is heard as a request for information) depends on classifications of social facts by the speakers. There must be a roughly equivalent understanding of the propositional content of utterances and, considerably beyond this, the content must be categorized into social facts in similar ways by the speakers. An utterance intended as an insult must be so understood by the addressee. Another example of this linking of the content of the utterance to their role in conversation is the conditional relevance of negative statements. Labov and Fanshel (1977) summarize the relationship as: "An assertion that X has not occurred presupposes that someone expects (for some reason) that X would occur." In a conversation, the utterance "I am not a thief" suggests that the speaker is denying the expectations of at least some of the addressees. The second language learner must learn the categorization of social facts as expressed by the language being acquired and also the specific linguistic devices for indicating understanding of those social facts. Learning to express content in the second language is the beginning of the overall processes of learning language for social purposes.

The patterning of discourse can involve the choice of lexical items in conversational structure. Lexical packing refers to the amount of semantic information that is conveyed by a word. If a speaker says "ball" instead of "toy" in a given situation, he is "unpacking" or displaying more semantic information and making it available to the listener. In conversation there is very often a choice of relatively unpacked lexical items (e.g., chair, table) or a relatively packed lexical item (e.g. furniture). The level of lexical packing or unpacking in a conversation can be dependent on social relations.

A: *We just added a new piece of computer equipment. It cost something like $2,000, so take good care of it.*
B: *We just added a new Apple disc drive II and Minx. It cost something like $2,000, so take good care of it.*

A is appropriate for a custodian who sweeps around the lab but would be odd addressed to a systems programmer. B, which is more unpacked relative to A, would seem to have the reverse appropriateness conditions.

Conversation and the choices of the amount of information to be given to a listener can be seen as a specific use of a more general notion: the specificity of scripts that people use and display to others. Following Schank and Abelson (1977), a script is taken as "a structure that describes appropriate sequences of events in a particular context." It is composed of slots and requirements of what can fill the slots. For example, buying a magazine may be a script, some of whose slots are: entering a store, finding the magazine title, checking the date, paying an employee, possibly receiving change, leaving the store. In speaking, it would be inappropriate to specify all the slots in a script for someone who knew the script well. In second language learning, or, perhaps more particularly, second language teaching, the choices of linguistic features that construct the pattern of conversation (by lexical choices or otherwise) must be carefully specified with respect to the target language.

The power relationships between speakers and the perceived information states of listeners are closely related to the content of utterances in conversations. Gunter's (1974) analysis of dialogue points to the relations between interaction, intonation, and lexical unpacking. With the context utterance given below, the accent can fall on a number of words, as indicated by the emphasis shown in the response statement (assuming falling intonation in all cases).

> Content: The man can see the boy.
> Response: The man can *see* the boy.
>   The man *can* see the boy.
>   The man can see the *baby*.
>   The man *can* see the baby.

Gunter argues that if there is repetition of the vocabulary of the context statement, the second utterance will have the meaning, "I agree that your context statement is true, given that it contains the items under my accent." In cases of replacement of lexical items, the second utterance will convey the interpersonal message of: "Your context statement is true only when the item under my accent replaces the corresponding item in your context." That is, the sentence stress usually covers new information. However, Gunter also notes that the speaker can de-emphasize new information by not accenting the replacement. Thus the level of lexical unpacking (*boy* compared to *baby* in the above example) can be either brought to attention by placing the replacement under accent or de-emphasized by not being accented. In the latter case, the change in the level of unpacking can be challenged by the first speaker if it is seen as socially relevant. The first speaker may have to judge which is the more important change in lexical unpacking, as in the following sequence:

> The man can see the *boy*.
> The man *can* see the baby.

To extend the analysis to conversational sequences beyond statements, consider the following situation: a university secretary is speaking to her employer, a junior member of the faculty.

Your note said to invite the faculty.
Does that include the teaching assistants/the dean/your father-in-law (who both speakers know is the dean)?

The use of "the teaching assistants" and "the dean" may be appropriate attempts of clarification by unpacking "the faculty." However, "your father-in-law" may be inappropriate because it points out a socially relevant (too relevant?) fact. The secretary will be aware of a script involving the influence that can be used by an older family member to get a job for another (younger, less powerful) family member. The script usually carries with it a negative evaluation from someone outside the family circle—especially if that person is not in a position to engage in the same kind of activity.

The social structure and lexical relationships in the above example also interact with the sequencing of utterances. If there is no prior mention of "faculty," if the utterance stands independent of other utterances, "Do you want your father-in-law invited?" can be quite appropriate, perhaps even suggesting solidarity between the speakers. The conversational dependence among utterances (e.g., question-answer, request-compliance) and the social roles they are linked to impose constraints on the propositional content of utterances and on the relation between the propositional contents of different utterances.

The expected norms in these cases are clearly set by the cultural situation and depend on sociolinguistic knowledge of the community. In a more detailed way, other linguistic dimensions may be affected by cultural knowledge. Sherzer (1981) reports how different levels of telling and retelling of information in different situations determine the levels of embedded speakers in a Kuna narrative. A speaker may reformulate a narrative to achieve quotation within quotation to the point of ambiguous reference. However, the reformulation device is a part of the patterning of cultural tellings and retellings. It is the linguistic reflex of a specific set of cultural interaction patterns. These patterns must be recognized by competent (and especially, artistic) speakers and audiences. Speakers must understand their cultural situation of telling or retelling as they create their discourse.

Scripts can be a way of conceptualizing adult-child and child-child dialogues. Adults must adjust their language to the more limited social knowledge of children. Children may not realize that a certain action is a departure from a script (for example, tendering a very large bill to pay for a small item) and so may not understand the language used in context (for example, shopkeeper: "You must be crazy; I don't have change for that.") Teachers, in particular, must adjust to children's knowledge of scripts as well as their linguistic level of development. On the other hand, children need exposure to different scripts and departures from standard scripts in order to learn what is appropriate in dialogue.

The relative packing of lexical concepts can interact with the social relationships through the interpretations of scripts. Consider:

A. You make the salad and I'll do the casserole.
B. You cut the salad.
C. Cut, toss, and arrange the salad.

Utterance C can be interpreted less as a personal instruction than as an unpacking of some prior statement such as: "Let's share making dinner." On the other hand, the unpacking of lexical concepts in signaling a script can be intended or interpreted as specifically relevant to the hearer. If less unpacking is normal in a given situation (if A is typical), then unpacking can be intended and/or interpreted as criticism with the assumption that a hearer does not know what should be known. If too much detail is given (by lexical unpacking, or over specification of the details of the script), a hearer can respond: "Just because I'm an X (typist, lawyer, chimney sweep) doesn't mean that I can't/won't Y (make a salad, drive a car, stand on my head)."

Scripts and social relationships are closely related and the mutual negotiation of a social relationship is dependent on this interaction and on the conversational structure of the dialogue. Take, for example, the following exchanges:

A (1) You make the salad and I'll do the casserole.
   (2) You cut up the salad.
B (1) Should I cut the ends off the carrots?
   (2) Should I cut the carrots lengthwise?
   (3) Do you want the carrots julienne or brunoise?
   (4) I'll julienne the carrots.

In a busy kitchen, B (1) is liable to be a frustrating answer for the speaker of A (1). A speaker of A (1) would probably be more frustrated with B (1) than a speaker of A (2). Furthermore, B (1) is more frustrating an answer to hear than B (2) or B (3). These latter two responses indicate a lexical unpacking of "make" or "cut up" which is appropriate and confirms that the speaker of A could have assumed that the other speaker understands what is to be done.

The statement of B (4) (with falling intonation) may have the pragmatic force of seeking confirmation, but assumes that the speaker has more confidence in the appropriateness of the action than does a speaker of B (3).

That is, the differences among B (1) - B (3) which reflect social relationships and appropriateness of actions, are also affected by conversational structure. B (4) may not require the speaker of A to answer at all, whereas B (1) - B (3), being surface questions, require a conversationally adjacent and relevant answer. B (4) requires a remark by the speaker of A only to repudiate the statement (expecting sarcastic comments like "of course," "what else").

One can further work out how the assumptions of social relationships and actions vary depending on who the speakers of A and B are in the above example. The social relationships of chief chef to sous chef, spouse to spouse, or one new roommate to another new roommate give different appropriateness values to possible sequences of utterances. The following table gives an approximation of these values.

This table, however, collapses a number of different variables. For example, A (1) - B (3) is probably inappropriate between spouses if there is a tacit sharing of responsibility. B (3) may assume a power relationship not

	chief chef to sous chef	spouse to spouse	new roommate to new roommate
appropriate	A (1) - B (3)	A (1) - B (4)	A (1) - B (2)
inappropriate	A (1) - B (1)	A (1) - B (3)	A (1) - B (1)

existing between the spouses. On the other hand, the inappropriateness or anomaly of the sequence A (1) - B (2) between new roommates may indicate a gap between the speakers in the basic cultural scripts that they have available.

This outline of social relationships and scripts suggests the delicate interaction of social systems, knowledge systems, and linguistic systems that face the learner in acquiring a second language. The task is not just the mastery of each of these systems but it is crucially the interaction of the systems that leads to the native-like behavior in the second language situation.

In Wasco-Wishram, Silverstein (1981) reports the use of augmentative and dimunitive forms (involving sound features of consonants and some vowels) is a signal of the speaker's attitude towards what is talked about:

"in using such an augumentative or dimunitive (vs. neutral) form, the speaker communicates his attitude towards the hearer, and this attitude becomes a contextual reality with effects on how the interaction then proceeds. [For example]: you don't tell a salacious story about someone who has just been referred to dimunitively, at the risk of offending the prior speaker!"

This situation in Wasco-Washram demonstrates how social relations, the content of a message and, in fact, the phonological realization of the language can combine to determine how a stretch of language is interpretated.

A case of the meaning content of language interacting with situational and circumstances is given by Silverstein (1981) from the work of Dixon on Djirbal. This Australian language has two nonoverlapping vocabulary sets, an everyday set and a set for use when certain relatives (a classicatory mother-in-law) are present. Thus, vocabulary items carry information of word-sense and also "a context-dependent 'indexical' value, that indicates whether or not a classificatory mother-in-law is present as an audience in the speech event" (Silverstein, 1981). Thus, the choice of vocabulary set is determined by the social (familial, in this case) relations of the speaker to the members of the audience, as well as by the more usual constraints of choosing items for their word-sense. Whereas in English the role of social relationships in constraining lexical choices may seem minor (forms of address, politeness, deference, and so on), such relationships can affect the choice of all lexical items in each situation of language use.

A detailed study of the relation between propositions in utterance must take into consideration the social relationships among speakers, the circumstances of the interaction, and conventional sequencing of utterances (including repairs, question-answer-confirmation patterns). Scripts are seen as conceptual entities which influence speakers' interpretations of utterances and the predictions of a speaker about the intentions, attitudes, and speech of the interlocultor.

Nelson and Gruendel (1979) have started this type of analysis from a developmental perspective and their conclusions are illuminating. They reason that preschool children have acquired few scripts and so may have few in common with other speakers. Children may also not recognize the signs of others' misunderstandings. Nelson and Gruendel interpret the latter type of difficulty as leading to a display of egocentrism. "Sharing social scripts for how things are done, what to expect next, who plays what role, can serve to overcome this apparent egocentrism, and we therefore believe that learning scripts provides an essential foundation for much of the child's social, cognitive, and linguistic development" (Nelson and Gruendel, 1979:91). The parallel here between children's acquisition of scripts both in production and comprehension and that of the second language learner should be clear. Scripts organize long stretches of language behavior such that selecting the script guides the production of utterances and recognizing the script guides the interpretation of another's discourse. As with children, the early second language learner could be expected to have few shared scripts with native speakers and perhaps not to recognize misunderstanding when it occurs.

The organization of propositional information in utterances and the conversational organization of utterances are related to the interpersonal "moves" one can make in dialogues. An example is the use of narratives to represent affective propositions, with the requirement that the affective propositions (e.g., "Let me tell you something exciting...") must be reportable (Labov & Fanshel, 1977). By reportable, we mean that the event in the narrative is "different from ordinary experience, and in itself justifies holding the listener's attention" (Labov & Fanshel, 1977:105). The propositional content determines the type of move which is being made. A nonreportable event (e.g., "Your blood is flowing") in most everyday contexts would be regarded as irrelevant and perhaps as an attempt to ignore an earlier utterance or to change the topic. The following constructed conversation gives the flavor of such nonreportable events and how they would be regarded as irrelevant, diversionary, or rude in terms of conversational moves:

Father: So why don't you go out and rake the leaves. It's a nice day and they
say it might rain tomorrow. I'll help you when I finish the car.
Son: ......Actually I was going to see Bob now. Did you know that your
blood is flowing?

Similarly, Nelson and Gruendel's (1979) characterization of a dialogue as "an extended series of turns during which a single topic or set of related topics is sustained or changed according to conversational rules" requires that speakers are in approximate agreement over what is a single topic or related topics. That is, their structuring of content must reasonably coincide. The second language learner is again in a parallel position to young first language learners in learning agreement about topicalness and the discourse pattern of dialogue.

Conversely, a speaker's knowledge of conversational structure provides the information to direct the interpretation of content. There are a number of pairs of turns which are closely dependent on each other; generally the use of one turn (the first pair partner) invites and raises the expectation that the second turn (the second pair partner) will be contributed by the second speaker. Conversational first pair partners such as greetings, invitation, questions, and the first turn of telephone conversations direct the interpretation of the turn which follows as, respectively, another greeting or acknowledgment, an acceptance or refusal, an answer and a word of acknowledgment. For example, the turn after "Can you come over for coffee on Saturday night?" (in a conversation between friends) will be interpreted as relevant to the issuance of an invitation. Utterances such as "The kids have colds," "Have you learned to make decent coffee yet?" "Any chance of leaving before dawn?" will be interpreted in terms of the prior turn. The propositional content scarcely has independent effect. The conversational sequencing and the identity of the speakers have overriding importance. Put another way, Grice's (1975) rules of conversational implicature, which lie behind some of the more surface level dependencies between turns, direct participants in dialogue in interpreting utterances (cf. Rommetviet, 1974). The directions can be violated but even the violations are recognized as violations with respect to the norms.

The preceding review focused on some of the influences on the discourse of conversations. Much of the work reviewed deals with first language discourse. However, the studies point to the variety of influences on conversational discourse and some of the interactions of those influences. Lexical concepts can be expressed in greater or lesser detail. The content of what is said and various social facts shape discourse. Sequences of events seen as organized groups (in scripts) affect both the production and comprehension of discourse. Cultural knowledge at various levels (for example, at the level of scripts "how to buy a lottery ticket" or at the level of social relations "who is deferred to and how much deference is appropriate") is important in constructing and interpreting discourse. All these influences on discourse can be seen as areas in which the second language learner must develop competence. To reiterate a point made earlier, the patterning of language in larger stretches is particularly connected to the formation of discourse. As the examples show, discourse is constituted to actualize the social use of language. Elements of the social use of language thus contribute specific influences on the form of discourse. The case of second language discourse must then be seen not just as the acquisition of a set of linguistic patterns but rather as the acquisition of the relation between social uses of language and the discourse patterns that result from those uses in the specific second language context.

Although conversation is often the focus of second language programs, a consideration of second language discourse must also include monologues, mainly narratives, and written language—longer stretches of language by one person. This section will review some of the kinds of patterning in connected discourse found in different languages and the connections among speakers, context, and discourse. Unlike conversation, connected discourse is more under the control of one speaker or writer. Although the speaker or writer must consider the listener or reader, there is less active negotiation of the content and structure of the discourse. The influences on discourse structures are therefore of a more general linguistic, contextual, and cultural nature than is the case with conversation. What are some of these influences and how do they affect comprehension and production of discourse and what then are the issues for second language learning and teaching?

Simply in terms of linguistic resources used to indicate discourse units, languages differ widely. For example, in Longuda (a language spoken in Nigeria) a special suffix -wa is used to signal the thematic character in folk tales and is attached to characters to indicate both the status of the character and the relation of the character to the action and locale in the tale. Furthermore, in first person narratives the speaker has the status of thematic character and the suffix is attached to the speaker's location (Newman, 1978). Many such discourse markers are documented in Grimes (1978). Longacre (1968) discusses cases of more common linguistic devices being used to mark discourse structures. Frequently, tense sequences, length of sentences, or repetition serve to indicate the beginnings or ends of units in the stories he examined. For example, in Waffa legend narratives, the tense changes from a "far past" to a "near past" in the denouement and then back to the "far past" in the next section (the closure) of the narrative. Although examples from unusual languages may seem extreme, they draw attention to the range and subtlety of the linguistic markers of oral discourse.

The production and comprehension of written discourse is also influenced by several factors. Even in a first language, school children develop increasingly sophisticated connections and series of connections in their writing. Patterns of conjunction and reference establishing different meaning relations in the students' writing. These meaning relations and how they are expressed change as writing ability increases (Bracewell, Fine, & Ezergaile, 1980; see also Canale, Frenette, & Bélanger, this volume). McClure, Mason, and Williams (1983) provide evidence that cultural differences were associated with different preferred orderings of sentences. In this case, the subjects were Black, Hispanic and Anglo students who all spoke English. That is, cultural influences helped shape the overall structure of the stories being considered, although all three sets of subjects dealt with the same information in the same language.

With such a range of differences in extended discourse from the productive point of view it can be expected that comprehension process also follow the structure of discourse. Stein and Glenn (1979), in a pioneering study, showed that different parts of a story (analyzed into categories such as major setting, minor setting, initiating event, and so on) have different likelihoods of recall. The structure of a story is not just a matter of how material is organized to constitute the story but also bears on what is recalled. As spoken or written discourses differ from language to language and even culturally within a language the expectations of the listener or reader can be assumed to vary. Thus when studying a second language, learners can be faced with discourse structures that do not fit with the expectations brought from familiarity with the discourse structures of the first language. For example, it may be difficult to understand a story that does not begin with introductory material about the major characters if parallel stories in the first language typically begin that way. In a study of Hebrew-speaking university students, Cohen and Fine (1978) found that these students did not follow the pattern of English-speaking peers in trying to process the text structure of English academic discourse. In particular, the non-native speakers had difficulty organizing material found in different paragraphs. Thus both the structure of discourse viewed as semantic categories (the Stein & Glenn study) and the specific kinds and patterns of discourse markers (the Cohen & Fine study) must be seen as part of the processing task to be acquired by second language learners.

The learning of second language discourse is the consequence of skills and patterning from several sources. On the simplest level there is the new set of high level discourse structures and their markers. These structures may be organizing content that may never have been expressed at all in the first language (for example, consider various ritual formulae or cultural and commercial transactions). The content may in turn derive from social meanings found in one society and not in another—this being a more specific case of diverging recurrent and more or less standardized situations found in different cultures. From a cognitive point of view the preceding social facts and linguistic patterns must be parsed, organized, and translated. The second language situation as a locus of discourse production and comprehension involves the operation of cognitive processes and the social patterning that influences the discourse patterning. The actual language to be produced or comprehended, with its own structures and markers, is but a part of the cognitive task at hand.

The preceding discussion has hinted at the role of situation, or situations, in the production and comprehension of discourse. This notion needs further exploring to show its special importance for second language discourse (the problem of "context" or "situation" is an important issue in itself in linguistic theory; see, for example, Hasan, 1985). Let us take *situation* to be the nonlinguistic factors that have a bearing on linguistic forms and *context* to be the verbal part of situation, that is, the linguistic forms in a situation that bear on the production of further linguistic forms. For production in a second language, the proper understanding of the situation and context must be obtained. For comprehension, similarly, it is interpretation with the constraints of situation and content that is the sign of proper second language use. Of course, all levels of language can be affected by situation and context. What then is the special role of discourse? Language use means language operating in situation. It is rare that language in situation consists of simple sentences. Rather, language is strung together in ways that make it appropriate to the situations of use. The sentences so strung together have characteristics that form the sentences into text (see Halliday & Hasan, 1976, Chapter 1); that is, the language is made to operate as a semantic unit in situation. "Texture" or the character of being a text is thus built by the relationship of language in longer stretches. For example, in the conversation, "Have you seen John lately?" "No, he must be in the other class," *you* connects the language to an addressee in the situation, *lately* connects the language to some period of time just before the act of speaking (that is, to another part of the situation), *he* connects the answer to the question by referring to a participant mentioned in the question, and *another* connects the language to the situation by the assumption that both speakers are in the same class, or that there is an explicit connection to some earlier stretch of language (the context) in which a class was mentioned by one of the speakers. Without such connections to context and situation, stretches of language seem to be constructed examples rather than language in use. Compare extremes such as "A cow saw a horse," "A boy was not seen in class," and "Tables should be kept clean" with the example of dialogue given earlier. Without connections to context and situation, language does not sound like natural language. It is this "sounding like natural language" that must be the goal in second language teaching and learning. Thus it is discourse in particular that must be taken into account in second language teaching.

The general approach that emerges from the preceding evidence and discussion of second language discourse is that a focus on one part of language or of language separated from its social and psychological bases will not reveal the interdependencies of those factors. It is in the interaction of language, situation, and psychological processes that discourse emerges. There is now sufficient detailed information to at least start the charting of these interactions in second language discourse and to use that information in constructing materials and programs.

Bibliography

Benson, J.D.; W.S. Greaves, ed. (1985) *Systematic perspectives on discourse, Volume 1: Selected theoretical papers from the 9th International Systematic Workshop.* Norwood, N.J.: Ablex.

Bracewell, R.; J. Fine; L. Ezergaile (1980) Cohesion as a guide to the writing process. Paper presented to the American Educational Research Association, annual meeting, Boston.

Chafe, W. (forthcoming) Cognitive constraints on information flow, to appear in R. Tomlin, ed., *Coherence and grounding in discourse.* Amsterdam: J. Benjamins.

Cohen, A.D.; J. Fine (1978) Reading history in English: Discourse analysis and the experience of native and non-native readers, *Working Papers in Bilinguilism,* 16: 55-74.

Fine, J.; R.O. Freedle, ed., (1983) *Developmental issues in discourse.* Norwood, N.J.: Ablex.

Freedle, R.O. (1977), ed., *Discourse production and comprehension.* Norwood, N.J.: Ablex.

Freedle, R.C. (1979), ed., *New directions in discourse processing.* Norwood, N.J.: Ablex.

Gleason, J.B., & S. Weintraub (1976) The acquisition of routines in child language, *Language in Society,* 5: 129-136.

Graesser, A.C.; S.P. Robertson; L.F. Clark (1983) Question answering: A method for exploring the on-line construction of prose representations. In Fine & Freedle (1983).

Grice, H.P. (1975) Logic and conversation. In P. Cole, J. Morgan, ed., *Syntax and semantics, vol. 3.* New York: Academic.

Grimes, J.E. (1975) *The Thread of Discourse.* The Hague: Mouton.

Grimes, J.E. (1978) ed., *Papers on discourse.* Dallas: Summer Institute of Linguistics.

Gunter, R. (1974) *Sentences in dialog.* Columbia, S.C.: Hornbeam.

Halliday, M.A.K. (1973) *Explorations in the functions of language.* London: Edward Arnold.

Halliday, M.A.K.; R. Hasan (1976) *Cohesion in English.* London: Longman.

Hasan, R. (1985) Meaning, context and text- Fifty years after Malinowski. In Benson and Greaves (1985).

Kurzon, D. (1984) Themes, hyperthemes and the discourse structure of British legal texts, *Text,* 4: 31-55.

Labov, W.; D. Fanshel (1977) *Therapeutic discourse: Psychotherapy as conversation.* New York: Academic.

Longacre, R.E. (1972) *Hierarchy and universality of discourse constituents in New Guinea languages.* Washington, D.C.: Georgetown University Press.

McClure, E.; J. Mason; J. Williams (1983) Sociocultural variables in children's sequencing of stories, *Discourse Processes,* 6:131-143.

Morrow, D.G. (1985) Prominent characters and events organize narrative understanding, *Journal of memory and language,* 24: 304-319.

Nelson, K.; J.M. Gruendel (1979) At morning it's lunchtime: A scriptal view of children's dialogues, *Discourse Processes,* 2:73-94.

Newman, B. (1978) The Longuda verb. In Grimes (1978).

Nix, D.H. (1983) Links: A teaching approach to developmental progress in children's reading comprehension and meta-comprehension. In Fine & Freedle (1983).

Rintell, E. (1981) Sociolinguistic variation and pragmatic ability: A look at learners, *International Journal of the Sociology of Language,* 27:11-34.

Rommetveit, R. (1974) *On message structure.* London: Wiley.

Scarcella, R.; J. Brunak (1981) On speaking politely in a second language, *International Journal of the Sociology of Langue,* 27: 59-75.

Schank, R.C.; R.P. Ableson (1977) *Scripts, plans, goals and understanding: An inquiry into human knowledge structures.* Hillsdale, N.J.: Erlbaum.

Schegloff, E.A.; G. Jefferson; H. Sacks (1977) The preference for self-correction in the organization of repair in conversation, *Language,* 53:361-382.

Scherzer, J. (1981) Tellings, retellings and tellings within tellings: the structure and organization of narratives in Kuna Indian discourse, *Working Papers in Sociolinguistics,* 83.

Silverstein, M. (1981) The limits of awareness. *Working Papers in Sociolinguistics,* 84.

Stein, N.L.; C.G. Glenn (1979) An analysis of story comprehension in elementary school children. In Freedle (1979).

Introduction to Chapter 2

Wolfson's chapter is concerned with the rules of speech and how they lead to insight into the norms and values of a speech community. Her study is not the study of the surface forms of language or even of individual speech acts. Rather, it is an investigation of how certain speech acts, their surface form, and the values of the speech community interact. This interaction also involves the statuses and realtionships of speakers as they negotiate their relative positions and roles. Wolfson has integrated these various components into a theory that is then able to explain certain apparently contradictory phenomena.

What aspects of language does Wolfson examine and why? Information is presented about compliments, apologies, thanks, invitations, greetings, and partings. These speech acts are the focus since they bring together considerations of surface form, the values of the speech community, and the relationships among speakers. Compliments and apologies, in particular, give evidence for the norms of a speech community. They signal, on the one hand, the values that are highly regarded and, on the other hand, what constitutes an offense to another member of the community. For these two kinds of speech acts, and for others, the relationship that exists between the speakers influences the speech act that is appropriate (who does one owe an apology to) and the surface form of the speech act (for example, how explicit or strong should the apology be). However, the relationship between speakers is not static but is negotiated. In fact the very use of speech acts as compliments and apologies displays the quality of the relationship which the speaker understands to exist and thus allows the second speaker to develop or negotiate the relationship from that starting point. Language is constantly doing this: simultaneously displaying, constituting, and negotiating the relationships between speakers (see Halliday, 1985a and Berger & Luckmann, 1966 for the development of some of these concepts). The specific linguistic factors that Wolfson examines are particularly clear in displaying the interaction of language, social norms, speech acts, and speakers and can be taken as examples of the complex interaction of factors that must underlie language in all its uses.

The choice of linguistic devices that are studied (compliments, apologies, and so on) and the overall theory of how language is put to work in social contexts necessarily points to the study of discourse. Given Wolfson's approach, the analyst cannot look at the structure of single sentences even if viewed as speech acts. The use and meaning of linguistic surface forms, rather, derives from their relationship to other stretches of language and the identity of the speakers.

Speech act analysis made some of the connections among speakers, situation, and language explicit. The work of Austin (1961), Searle (1969), and Grice (1975) started by noticing and outlining specific conditions on utterances; for example, what does it take (in terms of speakers, hearers, their intentions, the circumstances of the utterances) to properly make a promise, give an assurance, or name a ship. It was shown that acts in language could be accomplished in many different ways. For example, the act simply expressed in "Pass the salt" can also be accomplished by numerous other forms of language ("Salt!", "This soup tastes flat", and so on). On the other hand, a single expression, "What time is it?", can accomplish a range of acts including requesting information, suggesting that people leave, insulting someone who is late for an appointment. Given, then, that there are many-to-one and one-to-many relations between expressions and the acts they accomplish, the task is to understand how the mapping takes place (see Searle, 1979).

Once speech acts such as apologies, requests, and directions are examined, not only are mappings between expressions and acts important, but the conditions of the use of various expressions involve the careful examination of social roles in specific social contexts. For example Kirsh (1983) examined directives among nursery school children in terms of the status of the speaker issuing the directive (boy or girl, popular or less popular) the interlocutor and the kind of directive used (imperatives: Close the door; embedded imperative: Could you please close the door; need statements: I need a glass of water; and so on). As expected, there are series of interactions among the factors studied. In Wolfson's terms, not only do we learn the interrelationships of different forms for directives and variables that help create status, but we learn about the social structure of the nursery classroom. The language and the social structure mutually define and constitute each other. To Kirsh's and similar studies of who uses different speech acts under what conditions it will be necessary to add studies that investigate the social strategies of speakers. The question then becomes: What did speaker A mean to accomplish socially by speaking to B in such a way? Intentions of the speaker and reactions of the hearer must be studied to understand the social interaction and explain the choices of linguistic forms within the interaction.

This general framework sets up a series of issues to be examined in second language discourse; namely, which factors of language and social setting are interrelated in which specific ways. Further, the question of why it is these factors and these relationships must be posed. Heuristically, it must be supposed that the relationships among social factors, speakers, and discourse structure is not accidental but motivated by considerations of communication and social interaction. Some such considerations will be invariant across languages and cultures (loud vocalizations are more easily heard than quiet ones) while other considerations (when to be polite and how to appear so) will vary widely. Both theoretical descriptions of second language discourse and practical teaching, assessment and the construction of materials need the details of communication and social interaction. The search for these details is suggested by the theory. Variation in any of the components of social structure, the context of the language being used, and the actual utterance demands investigation of the remaining components. However, this beginning in correlational studies must be followed up by (a) experimental studies of the causal connections among the components and (b) theories of why the connections are the way they are. That is, ultimately, a functional account should be constructed (see Halliday, 1985b). From a practical point of view, the functional account will specify what language features should be taught in what social contexts and for different communicative purposes.

Wolfson's chapter provides some of the detailed statements of the connections of language and social situation suggested in the introductory chapter. Units of analysis such as the speech acts of compliments and apologies are carefully tied to who uses them and when. The approach enables one to see the interactions involved. Pica and Doughty, in their chapter, experimentally vary some social factors to see the effect on negotiation in a second language classroom. They find that the presence or absence of a teacher and the degree of cooperation needed to complete a task influence the kind of language interaction that is produced. In particular, they find that it is socially and interactionally relevant language variables that are adjusted by speakers in different situations. That is, the study provides more of the detail suggested by Wolfson's framework, but in a specifically second language context.

References

Austin, J. (1961). How to do things with words. Oxford: Oxford University Press.

Benson, J.D. & W.S. Greaves (1985) ed., Systemic perspectives on discourse, volume 1: Selected theoretical papers from the 9th international systemic workshop. Norwood, N.J.: Ablex.

Berger, P.L. & T. Luckmann (1966). The social construction of reality: treatise in the sociology of knowledge. London: Allen Lane.

Cole, P. & J. Morgan (1975) ed., Syntax and semantics, Vol. 3, New York: Academic.

Fine, J. & R. Freedle (1983). ed. Developmental issues in discourse. Norwood, N.J.: Ablex.

Grice, P. (1975). Logic and conversation, in Cole and Morgan (1975).

Halliday, M.A.K. (1985a). Systemic background, in Benson and Greaves (1985).

Halliday, M.A.K. (1985b). An introduction to functional grammar. London: Arnold.

Kirsh, B. (1983). The use of directives as indication of status among preschool chil-
dren, in Fine and Freedle (1983).
Searle, J. (1969). Speech acts. Cambridge: Cambridge University Press.
Searle, J. (1979). Expression and meaning. Cambridge: Cambridge University Press.

CHAPTER 2

The Bulge:
A Theory of Speech Behavior
and Social Distance

Nessa Wolfson

University of Pennsylvania

Introduction

The purpose of this paper is threefold.[1] First, I want to outline the major ways in which the study of rules of speaking can provide insights into the norms and values of a speech community. Secondly, I will discuss ways in which the same material can provide information about the interaction process and the situations in which interlocutors negotiate their realtionships with one another. Lastly, I will put forth a theory concerning patterns of interaction within a general middle class American speech community.

The choice of looking at speech behavior in the researcher's own speech community should be understood to be purposeful and critical to the analysis. As Schneider (1968:vi) points out in the preface to his book on American kinship, the insights one has into one's native language and into the behavior within one's own speech community permits a level of analysis which is far deeper than that which can be reached in other field sites:

> There is another reason why the study of kinship in America is especially important to Americans and that is that as Americans, this is a society and a culture which we know well. We speak the language fluently, we know the customs, and we have observed the natives in their daily lives. Indeed, we *are* the natives. Hence we are in an especially good position to keep the facts and the theory in their most productive relationship. We can monitor the interplay between fact and theory where American kinship is concerned in ways that are simply impossible in the ordinary course of anthropological work. When we read about kinship in some society foreign to our own we have only the facts

---

[1] My special gratitude to Susan Failer for editing and helping me to revise this paper.

which the author chooses to present to us, and we usually have no independent source of knowledge against which we can check his facts....

By the same token of course we are able to achieve a degree of control over a large body of data which many anthropological fieldworkers hardly approach, even after one or two years in the field. Hence the quality of the data we control is considerably greater, and the grounds for evaluating the fit between fact and theory is correspondingly greater.

The issue of evaluation by other researchers who are themselves members of the speech community under analysis is of great importance here. Much of what the researcher brings to light about the speech behavior of the community in question and what it reflects about the value system and the social structure of that community may be new in the sense that it has not been noticed or subjected to critical analysis from the perspective of the social scientist. Nevertheless, once an analysis of one's own group has been made, it is open to the evaluation of other social scientists who may also be members of the same community and who therefore have the means of examining and evaluating what has been analyzed through their own observations and intuitions.

One further issue concerning the choice of studying the behavior of middle-class speakers of American English needs to be examined here. This is that the unit of analysis which I refer to as "middle-class speakers of American English" is necessarily circular. In my opinion, the most useful definition of speech community is that given by Hymes (1972, p. 54):

Tentatively, a speech community is defined as a community sharing rules for the conduct and interpretation of speech, and rules for the interpretation of at least one linguistic variety. Both conditions are necessary.

A major point here is that not all speakers of a language do share the same rules of speaking, and therefore, not all may be said to belong to the same speech community. In defining and using the analytical unit which we call a speech community, we need to recognize that speakers of a single language often constitute many different speech communities, each with its own norms and rules of speaking. Where speech community may be said to correspond to geographical area, this fact is relatively easy to deal with. The English-speaking world, for example, is made up of a large number of speech communities, composed of both native and non-native speakers. Even where boundaries may be said to coincide with territory which is politically or geographically or even socially defined, the situation is terribly complex. Nevertheless, it is possible to say, without doing too much violence to the facts or to the feelings of those being spoken of, that the British and the Australians differ sharply from the Americans in many aspects of linguistic usage although all three nations have English as their dominant language. Further, people who have lived in more than one English-speaking country, or who have interacted extensively with people from one of the other English-speaking nations, know that pronunciation, grammar, and lexicon are not the only features that differentiate one set of speakers from another. Norms and values differ and so too do rules of speaking. But within political and geographic boundaries, we have a great variety of smaller social groupings, and these are much less easy to define. For this reason, it is impossible to speak of investigating the rules of speaking for English, or indeed, any other language. Depending on the group studied, the rules are likely to vary. This, of course, leads to some extremely difficult questions. If a speech community is to be defined by shared rules, and if these rules are largely unanalyzed and also, very importantly, unavailable to the conscious knowledge of native speakers, where do we begin? Even where we notice patterns of usage, how can we tell how far they extend? The most straight-forward answer is to focus on groups which have some sort of pre-existing definition apart from speech usage. A group which shares a particular terri-torial space and whose members interact frequently has been called a pri-mary network. It may reasonably be expected that rules of speaking will be shared within such a group (see Milroy, 1980, for example) since interaction is maximal, and people often function in many different roles vis-à-vis one another (on the job, at church, in the neighborhood, and so on). If, how-ever, our concern is to describe the speech behavior or rules of speaking which obtain across such subgroups and which have a wide enough frame of reference to be useful to such applications as language teaching and learn-ing, then we are faced with an inescapable circularity in the definition of our object of study. That is, a speech community is defined as a group which shares rules for the use and interpretation of speech, but there may be no predefined feature external to speech which can be used as a criterion of membership. Furthermore, when the language under consideration is, like English, that of a number of complex, highly industrialized societies, each composed of a great number of subgroups, the notion of speech community must be used at a level of abstraction which ignores many subtle distinctions.

Thus, in speaking here of American middle-class speakers, I am forced, if I wish to make any generalizations, to treat them as a speech community and to investigate what the various subgroups in this category have in com-mon. This does not mean that I wish to ignore differences in norms and values and speech behavior which stem from, for example, regional or eth-nic identities, but rather that I will take such distinctions into account as factors in the analysis. In this respect, I follow Goffman who, in the preface to his book, *Relations in Public* (1971, p. xv), says:

> So the problem is not merely that of having to make statements about groups and communities without sufficient data, but that of not knowing very much about the identity and boundaries of the groupings about which

there are insufficient data. I employ the term 'our' but do so knowing that in regard to small behaviors the 'our' cannot be conventionally or conveniently specified. I can with least lack of confidence make assertions about my 'own' cultural group, the one with which I have had the most first-hand experience, but I do not know what to call this grouping, what its full span or distribution is, how far back it goes in time, nor how these dimensions might have to be changed, according to the particular bit of familiar behavior under question.

In spite of the above disclaimers, with which I agree completely, it is nevertheless the purpose of this paper to attempt to cast some light on the speech behavior of the present-day American urban middle class, and what this behavior reflects about the structure of this society. I do this in full recognition that the unit of analysis is messy at best. Still, as Hymes (1974, p. 75) says:

> The most novel and difficult contribution of sociolinguistic description must be to identify the rules, patterns, purposes, and consequences of language use, and to account for their interrelations. In doing so it will not only discover structural relations among sociolinguistic components, but disclose new relationships among features of the linguistic code itself.

This paper, then, is intended as an attempt to contribute to sociolinguistics.

Speech Behavior as a Reflection of Cultural Values

To begin with, a speech act or act sequence, whether it be apologizing, thanking, scolding, complimenting, inviting, greeting or parting, or even the telling of a performed story, has important cultural information embedded in it. At the most superficial level, sociolinguistic data collected systematically and analyzed objectively can yield information as to what specific formulas and routines are in use in a particular speech community, as well their patterns of frequency and appropriateness in different speech situations. This is, in itself, not a trivial matter. As Ferguson (1976) has so aptly written:

> All human speech communities have such formulas, although their character and the incidence of their use may vary enormously from one society to another. What formulas are in existence and in which situations they are used must be discovered empirically for no two communities are exactly alike.

An example of the sort of information to be gained by an examination of the surface structure of a speech act is the work on compliments in American English (Wolfson and Manes 1980, Manes and Wolfson 1981, Wolfson 1981, Wolfson 1984). In analyzing data collected from a wide range of spontaneous interactions, it was discovered that compliments are characteristically formulaic both in terms of semantics and of syntax.

While the number of words which could be chosen to evaluate positively, or compliment, is almost infinite, the fact is that the great majority of speakers actually used a restricted set of adjectives and verbs in their compliments. Two-thirds of all compliments that make use of adjectives to carry the positive semantic load do so by means of only five adjectives: *nice, good, beautiful, pretty,* and *great.* Because *nice* and *good* lack specificity they are usable with almost any subject. In present-day American English, *beautiful* is rapidly approaching the same status. The fact that *pretty* is used more than *great,* which is the more general adjective, reflects the greater than equal number of compliments directed at women in this society.

In the 25% of compliments which make use of a verb rather than an adjective to carry the positive load, 90% make use of just two verbs: *like* and *love.*

At the syntactic level, 50% of all compliments are characterized by the following formula:

NP {is/looks} (really) ADJ

Two other syntactic patterns:

I really {like/love} NP

and:

PRO is (really)(a) ADJ NP

account for 29% of the data. What this means is that only three patterns are needed to represent approximately 80% of all the compliments given and received by middle-class speakers of American English. Furthermore, only nine syntactic patterns account for 95% of the well over 1200 examples of compliments that make up the data.

The compliment formulas found in this analysis look very familiar and indeed, intuitively obvious to native speakers. What was not obvious until the data was analyzed is that the way in which we give verbal expression to our approval and appreciation of one another's appearance and accomplishments is largely prepatterned. However, the tendency among middle-class Americans interviewed was to regard compliments as sincere or insincere based on whether or not they were given using recognizable formulas. Thus, most people felt that if the speaker was sincere, the compliment would somehow be original, rather than precoded. The easiest way to demonstrate to native speakers that sincerity has very little to do with the form or wording of the compliment is to ask them to give compliments to one another, paying close attention to what they say. In just such an experiment, my colleague Virginia Hymes asked members of her class in linguistics to write down a compliment to the student sitting next to them in the classroom at the moment. All of the 22 student responses fell into the categories of formulas analyzed and discussed in Wolfson and Manes (1980) and in Manes and Wolfson (1981). The following examples are typical:

1. "Your necklace is very pretty."
2. "I like your shirt."
3. "You are looking radiant this morning."

In a similar experiment, I asked members of one of my own graduate seminars in sociolinguistics to give each other verbal compliments. The setting was extremely informal since there were only six students in the group and we were enjoying the last day of summer class by sitting around a swimming pool. The following represent all of the compliments given by members of this group:

4. Rosemarie to Myra: "I love your hat."
5. Myra to Maralyn: "I love your new watch."
6. Maralyn to Lucille: "That's a cute dress."
7. Lucille to Irene: "Your glasses are very attractive."
8. Irene to Midori: "The colors in your sweater are pretty."
9. Midori to Myra: "I like your swimsuit."
10. Myra to Rosemarie: "I love the way you smile."
11. Rosemarie to Nessa: "I love what you've done to your garden."

In addition to the precoded nature of these compliments, it is worth noticing that I (the professor) was the only addressee who received a compliment on something other than appearance. This fits together with findings concerning the ways in which gender and social status interact to condition speech behavior that will be discussed below.

Looking a bit beneath the surface structures, we can, through systematic field work, learn a good deal about the rights and obligations that members of a community have toward one another, information which is culture specific and not necessarily available to the intuitions of the native speaker.

When we examine the kinds of apologies which occur in a specific speech community, for example, we see evidence not only of the linguistic forms in use, but also of the content and the context of what Goffman (1971) has called remedial interchanges. In analyzing the events which elicit apologies in everyday interaction, the researcher can come to some reasonable conclusions about what people feel they have the right to expect from one another. For example, it is commonly believed that middle-class Americans regard their time as a valuable commodity. The notion that members of this group consider themselves under obligation to be prompt and/or to avoid keeping another person waiting is, in fact, evidenced by the large number of apologies that refer to just this situation. When, for example, one party to a previously planned lunch meeting arrived to find that the others were all waiting, she said:

12. "Hi, have you been waiting long? I'm really sorry."

If lateness is something to apologize for, not turning up at all for a social commitment appears, from the data, to be an even greater offense. The following apology, given on the telephone, will exemplify the way vocabulary is used to elaborate the expression of apology. The choice of the lexical item *mortified* as opposed to use of one of the apology formulas such as *"I'm sorry"* demonstrates a type of elaboration which reflects the speaker's recognition that the offense had been great and her strong desire to make the repairs necessary to support the relationship. The speaker had accidentally missed a lunch date with her female colleague who had waited for more than half an hour and then called to find out why she had been stood up:

13. A: "Joan? I'm mortified, I really am. I can't figure out how it happened—I had you in my calendar for tomorrow!"
     B: "Mortified? Is that all? (laughter)"

Obviously, the social obligation not to be late and, more important, not to forget an appointment, are far from the most serious rules one could imagine. They are, however, very typical of the sort of apologies one hears in conversation. As Goffman (1971), in his discussion of apologies as remedial interchanges has pointed out, apologies are an implicit self-judgment that speakers make against themselves, a recognition that they have broken a social norm and are responsible for whatever harm this has caused.

The work of Cohen and Olshtain (1981), Olshtain (1983) and Olshtain and Cohen (1983) has focused on apologies, examining the pragmatic and formal aspects of apologies as used by native speakers and by language learners. Through the use of discourse completion tests which require subjects to write down what they think they would say if they were in a given situation, the researchers attempted to discover the set of formulas that speakers believe they use to make apologies. Olshtain and Cohen hypothesized that the choice of apology form would be related to the severity of the offense and to the social identity of the interlocutors. Finally, using the same data collection technique, they compared data elicited from speakers of English vs. Hebrew with respect to both the formal aspects of apologies and the social situations that elicit them.

While the data collection procedure used does not demonstrate the range of behavior which is found in spontaneous interaction, Olshtain and Cohen (1983) were nevertheless able to ascertain that the conditioning factors leading to apologies were rather different for Israelis than for the Americans in their sample. That is, what were seen as offenses by one group, did not necessarily count as such by the other. Furthermore, the groups differed with respect to the weight each offense carried.

In a much larger, international study, the Cross-Cultural Speech Act Realization Project, Olshtain, Blum-Kulka, and several other researchers around the world[2] carried out a very similar project on apologies and directives, using a variation of the original discourse completion test. As my own contribution to the study, I, along with two other American sociolinguists, Tom Marmor and Steve Jones (1984, 1985 & forthcoming), carried out an observational study of apology behavior in addition to making use of the group questionnaire. In the observational work we looked not only at the pragmatic and formal aspects of apologies, but at the notion of offence itself and what it could be seen to embody for middle-class speakers of American English. We did this with the expectation that the situations which elicited apologies in our own society might not do so in others; that these rules are culture specific.

As an example of what may be seen from the analysis of data from spontaneous speech, let us take the findings on the obligation to respect the property of others. For example, a woman walks into her friend's house, holding the door for the cat to go out. Then, seeing her friend's expression, says:

14.   A: "Isn't the cat allowed out?"
      B: "No, we keep him inside."
      C: "Oh, I'm sorry—I'm so used to letting our cat out, I didn't even think. Shall I try and get him?"

The obligation not to cause damage or discomfort to others. For example:

15.   A: (stopping suddenly while driving so that passengers lurch forward) "Shit. Sorry. Excuse me."

Examples 13 through 15 illustrate major apology categories. More subtle and less commonly found categories are also useful in mirroring the norms

---

[2] The list members of CCSARP are: Shoshana Blum-Kulka, Elite Olshtain, Claus Faerch, Gabriele Kasper, Jenny Thomas, Eija Ventola, Helmut Vollmer, Juliane House-Edmondson, Elda Weizman, and Ellen Rintel.

and values of speakers in the community. A case in point is the obligation not to make others responsible for one's welfare (Wolfson & Jones 1984). For example, after complaining about personal problems the day before, a woman said to a close friend:

16. "I'm sorry I was in such a bad mood yesterday. I shouldn't have bothered you with my troubles."

Apparently she felt that even a long-standing friendship did not entitle her to unlimited attention.

Speakers also shared an obligation not to appear to expect another person to be available at all times. The following example of an apology given for disturbing another person will show the way in which this obligation operates.

17. A woman customer walks into a place of business.
    A: "Hi, Sam, I hope this is a good time for you."
    B: "Well, actually, I'm supposed to be at a meeting upstairs right this minute."
    C: "Oh. I'm sorry. I know I should have called first."

Thus, by observing what people apologize for, we learn what the cultural expectations are with respect to what people owe one another. In contrast, the study of expressions of gratitude yields information about what participants do not take for granted—what they regard as going beyond duty or obligation and therefore in the realm of favors or kindness not necessarily expected but nevertheless appreciated.

To say that the systematic observation of apologies on the one hand and thanks on the other can yield important cultural information is not to suggest that each case in which a speaker is observed to say *I'm sorry* or *Thank you* will constitute an example of the same category of social obligations at work. Indeed, the work of the sociolinguist would be infinitely easier if there were such a straightforward correlation between speech behavior and social reality. Speech behavior is, however, not so simple. In the case of both apologies and thanks, the formulas which are most often associated with the speech act may also be used in ways which are, in fact, not instances of such an act and may, indeed, have a very different meaning in the particular context. Clark and French (1981), for example, demonstrate this point in their description of telephone exchanges which end, not with the standard form *goodbye* or any of its variants, but rather with *thank you*. Further evidence for this pattern emerged from research undertaken by Josephine Rabinowitz who studied the ways in which leave-taking was accomplished in service encounters. Rabinowitz (1983) reports that she found that *thank you* was used very frequently to mark partings but that there were "no *goodbyes* in 89% of the face-to-face encounters" she studied.

In investigating the distribution of the forms *excuse me* and *I'm sorry,* Borkin and Reinhart (1978) found that *I'm sorry,* although usually referred to as an expression of apology in English, is not necessarily used to apologize at all. Rather, it is an expression of regret or dismay "about a state of affairs viewed or portrayed as unfortunate." For this reason it is perfectly appropriate for English speakers to say *I'm sorry* even when no injury or potential injury has been done. Thus, *I'm sorry* is used to express regret when refusing an invitation even though no social norm has been violated.

It is important to point out in this connection that although the intuitions of native speakers are very useful in interpreting the meaning of an interaction, they are not sufficient in the sense of giving us conscious access to patterns of speech behavior. This problem is commented upon by Borkin and Reinhart (1978) who discuss the fact that non-native speakers frequently misuse the forms *excuse me* and *I'm sorry,* and that native-speaking English teachers are themselves unable to explain what the rules are:

> Being native speakers of English is not enough to equip teachers with the kind of conscious knowledge of sociolinguistic rules that is necessary to help students use these formulae in routine, but important, social interactions with native speakers of English.

Perhaps the richest insights into cultural values are gained by analysis of the judgments people express. If we look at the compliments speakers give, we discover what values are made explicit through the expression of admiration and approval. For example, when we see that again and again in the data collected by observing middle-class native speakers of standard American English, compliments are given on objects that are new, and even on appearance that has changed, we can say with some evidence from actual speech behavior, that Americans seem to value newness. When we see, in one compliment after another, that speakers of American English compliment one another on looking thin or on losing weight, it is not difficult to come to the conclusion that Americans, unlike many other cultural groups, regard thinness as a positive attribute. If we look at a large range of compliments collected from naturally occurring speech we see that what is common to all is that in one form or another compliments are directed towards achievement. In many cases, the manifestation of achievement resides in the ability or the good taste or the wherewithal to effect positive change in one's appearance or to purchase new items. In other cases, it may have to do with the kind of family or friends one has or with a particular act well done. We could go on and on listing the cultural assumptions implicit in the compliments which have been collected from the spontaneous speech of native speakers of American English and, indeed, Manes (1983) has given a detailed account of just this means by which values are reflected. The point here is that by looking at what is complimented, we can come to some reasonable conclusions as to what is valued in the society in question. What is important for the purposes of this argument is that all this information is embedded in the speech acts themselves.

Speech Behavior and Negotiation of Rules

Another way in which sociocultural insights may be gained through the study of rules of speaking is to focus on the way the social indentities of interlocutors vis-a-vis one another conditions what is said. Here it is useful to take two different, though overlapping perspectives. On the one hand, by looking to see who has the right or the obligation to invite, compliment, or scold, and who has the obligation to greet, thank, or apologize, we can learn a great deal about how the society is structured.

On the other hand, if we examine the relationship of speech act form, or degree of elaboration used, to the identity of the interlocutors, we can often get at something much more subtle and difficult to characterize—the social strategies people in a given speech community use to accomplish their purposes—to gain cooperation, to form friendships, and to keep their world running smoothly.

When we look first at the way what is said reflects cultural values, it is immediately apparent that not all speech acts are equally informative. The most useful in this regard are, like compliments, thanks, and apologies, of a type that involve a specific topic and that make an implicit or explicit judgment. Speakers compliment one another on belongings or appearance or performance; they thank or apologize for an action. The topics of these speech acts are not necessarily stated explicitly, but they must at least be understood so that they can be inferred from the context. At the other end of the speech act spectrum, we have greetings and partings, which are spoken specifically to mark beginnings and ends, openings and closings of encounters, and which do not necessarily contain evidence of cultural values in themselves. Between the two, we have invitations, which, like greetings, focus on social interaction in and of itself. Because they have to do with planning and commitment to specific activities, invitations do often give us information about the kinds of social events that different groups within the community are likely to participate in, and even about which kinds of activities are planned as opposed to spontaneous or taken for granted.

In some speech communities, for example, it is normal practice for friends, family, and neighbors (who may, in fact, be the same people) to visit or even to turn up for a meal or a weekend or several weeks stay without any announcement at all and certainly with no explicit invitation. That is, in such communities, it is part of the obligations of people in certain role relationships to extend hospitality to one another for any length of time and under virtually any circumstances (Ayorinde Dada, personal communication). In other speech communities, specifically large complex urban communities, even a short visit to the home of another member of the family or to a close friend requires an invitation, or, at the minimum, a telephoned self-invitation. Clearly, the kinds of invitations which the researcher might collect in two such different speech communities would be very different in kind and in distribution.

Using this same body of data and focusing on the social identities of participants, rather different insights are likely to emerge. In this respect, speech acts of all types appear to be equally informative. Thus, if we are interested in analyzing what the rights, obligations, and privileges of speakers are vis-a-vis one another, or of who engages in which speech act with whom and in which situations, we can probably learn as much from studying greetings, partings, and invitations as we can from analyzing thanks, apologies, and compliments. And most interesting of all, if we look at the forms people use spontaneously with different interlocutors, we frequently find that the degree of elaboration corresponds not only to speaker's roles and expectations, but also to the manipulation of roles and the formation or reaffirmation of relationships.

A customer in a busy department store, for example, may, in order to gain the attention and service of a saleswoman, step out of her role as customer and engage in a friendly chat, signaling solidarity of age and sex, and the difficulties they share as working mothers.

THE BULGE: A Theory of Social Interaction:

A case in point is a consistent finding of mine that there is a qualitative difference between the speech behavior which middle-class Americans use to intimates, status unequals, and strangers on the one hand, and to nonintimates, status-equal friends, coworkers, and acquaintances on the other. I call this theory the Bulge, because of the way the frequencies of certain types of speech behavior plot out on a diagram with the two extremes showing very similar patterns as opposed to the middle section which displays a characteristic bulge. That is, when we examine the ways in which different speech acts are realized in actual everyday speech, and when we compare these behaviors in terms of the social relationships of the interlocutors, we find again and again that the two extremes of social distance—minimum and maximum—seem to call forth very similar behavior, while relationships which are more toward the center show marked differences.

On the face of it, this may seem very strange and even counterintuitive. What do intimates, status unequals, and strangers have in common that nonintimates, status unequal friends, coworkers, and acquaintances do not share, and what do the best mentioned group have in common that the first do not share? Very simply, it is the relative certainty of the first relationships in contrast with the instability of the second. Put in other terms, the more status and social distance are seen as fixed, the easier it is for speakers to know what to expect of one another. In a complex urban society in which speakers may belong to a variety of nonoverlapping networks, relationships among speakers are often uncertain. On the other hand, these relationships are dynamic, and open to negotiation. There is freedom here but not security. The emergent and relatively uncertain nature of such relationships is reflected in the care people take to signal solidarity (Brown & Gilman, 1960) and to avoid confrontation.

For example, although compliments are exchanged between intimates and between total strangers, the great majority (the Bulge) occur in interactions between speakers who are neither. This is a question of frequencies and not of absolutes. Compliments do, of course, occur in interactions between interlocutors who are intimates, status unequals, or even strangers. In fact, compliments on performance are often very important in the relationship of boss to employee or teacher to student (see Wolfson, 1983). Where the compliment has to do with appearance, sex is the major variable, overriding status in virtually all cases. This in itself is an interesting finding since it relates directly to the position of women in American society and touches on sociocultural expectations of a very different sort (Wolfson, 1984). For the purposes of this discussion, the important point is that of all compliments, no matter what their topic, the great majority occur between status equals among whom the potential for lessening of social distance exists.

The data on invitations is even more striking in this regard. With respect to this speech act, we have found that the data collected from spontaneous interactions fell into two categories (Wolfson, 1981; Wolfson, D'Amico-Reisner, Huber 1983). The first consisted of unambiguous, complete invitations giving time, place, or activity and a request for response. These unambiguous invitations occurred most frequently between intimates and between status unequals—the two sets of interlocutors whose relationships with the speaker were at the extremes of social distance. The second category of invitations consisted of ambiguous or incomplete references to the possibility of future social commitments. Once a large body of data had been collected, it was possible to recognize these so-called invitations as "leads." Utterances such as "We really must get together sometime" or "Let's have lunch together soon" are typical examples. But in order for a social commitment to result from a "lead," it was nearly always the case that both parties to the interaction took part in negotiating the arrangement. And what was particularly interesting about these "leads" was that they occurred between status-equal nonintimates—that is, between speakers whose relationships are most open to redefinition. As I described it, then (Wolfson, 1981), the data showed that inequality of status favors unambiguous invitations and disfavors attempts at negotiation, and that the same is true of intimacy. What inequality of status and intimacy have in common is that in both situations, interlocutors know exactly where they stand with one another. In contrast, speakers whose relationship is more ambiguous tend to avoid direct invitations with their inherent risk of rejection, and instead negotiate with one another in a mutual back and forth progression which, if successful, will lead to a social commitment. To illustrate the difference between the two types of interactions, we have the following examples:

1. The unambiguous invitation:
   A: Do you want to have lunch tomorrow?
   B: Okay, as long as I'm back by 1:30.
2. The negotiated social arrangement:
   A: You doing anything exciting this weekend?
   B: No, I'll be around the pool here.
   A: Ok, I'll see you.
   B: Maybe we'll barbeque one night.
   A: Ok, that's a nice idea. I'm tied up Sunday night.
   B: All right. We'll keep it loose.

A begins to walk away and then turns and walks back, saying:

   A: We're supposed to do something with Helen tomorrow night. Want to do something with us?
   B: Ok. Let us know.

At the time, I speculated that the fact that Americans seemed, from my observations, so hesitant to put themselves in a position to be refused and so often prefer to arrive at a social arrangement through the mutual effort of a negotiation, this may well say something interesting about Americans.

Since the publication of this work on invitations, studies of other speech acts have uncovered similar patterns. Thus, the findings of work on partings done by Pam Kipers, Jessica Williams, Josephine Rabinowitz, Marsha Kaplan, and myself in 1983 provided, in some respects, even stronger evidence that speakers behave in markedly different ways with those who occupy fixed positions in their social world, and those with whom their relationships are less settled. As Kipers (1983) put it, "Where there is no framework of social contact in place to assure casual friends and acquaintances that a future meeting will take place, partings reflect concern over the survival of the relationship. Mean number of turns in these partings was the highest of any group in this study. Individual utterances were notably longer too...the lengthy negotiations over future meeting time reassure both participants that even though they may not designate a definite time when they will see one another again, they both value the relationship enough to want it to continue." While all partings share certain basic features, our analysis indicates that shared knowledge of social distance and mutual certainty of future meeting are the important conditioning factors. As Williams (1983) says, "Where one or another or both of these factors is shared by the participants, interactions will exhibit certain predictable characteristics. Prepartings will be absent as will lengthy negotiations as to when the parties will meet again. Parting signals and "goodbye" and its variants will occur in only a minority of cases. Conversely, when knowledge of both social distance and time of future meeting are absent, partings diverge from this pattern."

In her work on the speech act of refusals as they are performed by native speakers of American English, Beebe (1985) compared the findings from written questionnaire data with those from data collected from spontaneous speech. While the form of the questionnaire made it difficult for lengthy refusals to be elicited, the ethnographic findings are similar to my own. As Beebe says: "This leads us to discuss the Discourse Completion Test in terms of what Wolfson calls her 'extremes follow similar pattern theory,' or her 'bulge theory.' Wolfson (1981) argued that both inequality of status and intimacy disfavor negotiation. Wolfson (personal communication, 1984, 1985) has claimed that intimates and strangers pattern similarly in all of her work on speech acts in native English. Our ethnographically collected data appears to follow Wolfson's hypothesis. Strangers are brief. If they want to say 'no,' they do so. Real intimates are also brief. It is friends and other acquaintances who are most likely to get involved in long negotiations with multiple repetitions, extensive elaborations, and a wide variety of semantic formulas." (Beebe, 1985, p. 4).

Similarly, D'Amico-Reisner (1983, 1985) in her study of expressions of disapproval, found that among native speakers of American English direct disapproval was expressed almost exclusively to intimates or to strangers in service encounters. When disapproval was expressed to non-intimates, only very indirect forms were used. As D'Amico-Reisner (1985) puts it: "When exchange types are considered with respect to social distance, the data reveal generally low non-intimate participation in disapproval exchanges." Put differently, one could say that interlocutors who are in the Bulge almost never voice their disapproval of one another overtly. Thus we see that a systematic analysis of constraints on the social identity of participants in disapproval exchanges yields additional support for the theory of social interaction that I have put forth."

If the expression of disapproval is relatively rare among speakers within the social category which I have labeled the Bulge, the same cannot be said for expressions of gratitude. Indeed, as researchers into first language acquisition (e.g., Grief & Gleason, 1980) have pointed out, thanking routines are among the earliest which young English-speaking children are explicitly taught. Given the nature of this routine and the importance placed on it, it is very interesting to note that Eisenstein and Bodman (1986) in their description of expressions of gratitude used by native speakers of American English, comment that they found the language patterns used in interactions between status unequals to be the same as those used between status equals. However, they point out, "What was different in the formal setting was that there were few uses of expressing surprise and complimenting. . . . in expressing gratitude, it may be that formality is conveyed by what is not said as well as through specially marked lexical items." That is, they found that the thanks were restrained, or unelaborated in situations where the interlocutors were of unequal status while expressions of gratitude among friends contained not only the formulaic thanks but also considerable elaboration. As they state in their conclusion, "Shorter thanking episodes sometimes reflected greater social distance between interlocutors."

Conclusion

There is, then, evidence for the bulge pattern I have described here, not only in my own analyses but also in a number of studies by other scholars. The fact that this convergence has been found in analyses of investigators who were unaware of the existence of the Bulge theory is, I think, very striking. It follows from this that previous research must be examined to see if there is evidence of the Bulge in the work of earlier scholars.

The fact that urban middle-class Americans live in a complex and open society means that individuals are members not of a single network in which their own place is well defined, but rather belong to a number of networks, both overlapping and nonoverlapping, in which they must continually negotiate their roles and relationships with one another. The importance of the Bulge theory lies in what it tells us about how the very openness and potential for mobility of American middle-class society is reflected in our everyday speech behavior.

References

Blum-Kulka, Shoshana, and Elite Olshtain. (1984). Pragmatics and second language learning. *Applied Linguistics* 5(3):195–213.

Borkin, Ann, and Susan Reinhart. (1978). Excuse me and I'm sorry. *TESOL Quarterly* 12(1):57–76.

Brown, Roger W., and Albert Gilman. (1960). The pronouns of power and solidarity. In Thomas A. Sebeok (ed.), *Style in Language*. Cambridge, Mass.: MIT Press. [Reprinted in J.A. Fishman (ed.), *Readings in the Sociology of Language*. The Hague: Mouton, 1968. Also reprinted in P. Giglioli (ed.), *Language and Social Context*. New York: Penguin Books, 1972.]

Clark, Herbert H., and J. Wade French. (1981). Telephone goodbyes. *Language in Society* 10(1):1-19.

Cohen, Andrew D., and Elite Olshtain. (1981). Developing a measure of sociocultural competence: The case of apology. *Language Learning* 31(1):113-134.

D'Amico-Reisner, Lynne. (1983) An analysis of the surface structure of disapproval exchanges. In Nessa Wolfson and Elliot Judd (eds.), *Sociolinguistics and Language Acquisition*. Rowley, Mass.: Newbury House.

D'Amico-Reisner, Lynne. (1985). *An Ethnolinguistic Study of Disapproval Exchanges*. Dissertation, University of Pennsylvania.

D'Amico-Reisner, Lynne. *An Ethnolinguistic Study of Disapproval Exchanges*. To appear in the series Topics in Sociolinguistics, edited by Marinel Gerritsen and Nessa Wolfson. Dordrecht, The Netherlands: FORIS Publications.

Eisenstein, Miriam, and Jean. W. Bodman. (1986). 'I very appreciate': Expressions of gratitude by native and non-native speakers of American English. *Applied Linguistics* 7(2):167-185.

Ferguson, Charles A. (1976). The structure and use of politeness formulas. *Language in Society* 5(2):137-151.

Goffman, E. (1971). *Relations in Public*. New York: Harper Colophon Books.

Grief, Esther Blank, and Jean Berko Gleason. (1980). Hi, thanks and goodbye: More routine information. *Language in Society* 9(2):156-166.

Hymes, Dell. (1972). Models of the interactions of language and social life. In J.J. Gumperz and D. Hymes (eds.), *Directions in Sociolinguistics*. New York: Holt, Rinehart & Winston.

Hymes, Dell. (1974). *Foundations in Sociolinguistics: An Ethnographic Approach*. Philadelphia: University of Pennsylvania Press.

Kaplan, Marsha A. (1986). The social implications of saying goodbye. Paper for seminar in sociolinguistics.

Kipers, Pamela. (1983). Partings: A sociolinguistic perspective. Paper for seminar in sociolinguistics.

Manes, Joan. (1983). Compliments: A mirror of cultural values. In Nessa Wolfson and Elliot Judd (eds.), *Sociolinguistics and Language Acquisition*. Rowley, Mass.: Newbury House.

Manes, Joan, and Nessa Wolfson. (1981). The compliment formula. In Florian Coulmas (ed.), *Conversational Routine*. (Janua linguarum 96: Rasmus Rask studies in pragmatic linguistics). The Hague: Mouton.

Milroy, Lesley. (1980). *Language and Social Networks*. (Language in Society 2). Baltimore, Md.: University Park Press.

Olshtain, Elite. (1983). Sociocultural competence and language transfer: The case of apology. In S. Gass and L. Selinker (eds.), *Language Transfer in Language Learning*. Rowley, Mass.: Newbury House.

Olshtain, Elite, and Andrew D. Cohen. (1983). Apology: A speech-act set. In Nessa Wolfson and Elliot Judd (eds.), *Sociolinguistics and Language Acquisition*. Rowley, Mass.: Newbury House.

Rabinowitz, Josephine F. (1983). Parting talk in short face-to-face service encounters. Paper for independent study in sociolinguistics.

Schneider, David M. (1968). *American Kinship: A Cultural Account*. Englewood, N.J.: Prentice-Hall.

Williams, Jessica. (1983). Partings: Elicited vs. spontaneous. Paper for seminar in sociolinguistics.

Wolfson, Nessa. (1979). Let's have lunch together sometime: Perceptions of insecurity. Paper presented at the 13th Annual TESOL Convention, Boston, Mass.

Wolfson, Nessa. (1981). Invitations, compliments, and the competence of the native speaker. *International Journal of Psycholinguistics* 24(4):7–22.

Wolfson, Nessa. (1983). An empirically based analysis of complimenting in American English. In Nessa Wolfson and Elliot Judd (eds.), *Sociolinguistics and Language Acquisition*. Rowley, Mass.: Newbury House.

Wolfson, Nessa. (1984). Pretty is as pretty does: A speech act view of sex roles. *Applied Linguistics* 5(3):236–244.

Wolfson, Nessa. (1985). Research methodology and the question of validity. Paper presented to the TESOL Research Interest Group, 18th Annual TESOL Convention, New York, April 1985.

Wolfson, Nessa, and Elliot Judd (eds.). (1983). *Sociolinguistics and Language Acquisition*. (Issues in Second Language Research). Rowley, Mass.: Newbury House.

Wolfson, Nessa, and Joan Manes. (1980). The compliment as a social strategy. *Papers in Linguistics* 13(3):391–410.

Wolfson, Nessa, and Steve Jones. (1984). Problems in the comparison of speech acts across cultures. Paper presented to the AILA Convention, Brussels.

Wolfson, Nessa, Lynne D'Amico-Reisner, and Lisa Huber. (1983). How to arrange for social commitments in American English: The invitation. In Nessa Wolfson and Elliot Judd (eds.), *Sociolinguistics and Language Acquisition*. Rowley, Mass.: Newbury House.

Wolfson, Nessa, Thomas Marmor, and Steve Jones. (1985). Problems in the comparison of speech acts across cultures. Paper presented at the 18th Annual TESOL Convention, New York, April 1985.

Wolfson, Nessa, Thomas Marmor, and Steve Jones. (forthcoming). Problems in the comparison of speech acts across cultures. In Shoshana Blum-Kulka, Juliane House-Edmondson, and Gabriele Kasper (eds.) *Cross-Cultural Pragmatics: Requests and Apologies*. Norwood, N.J.: Ablex Publishing Corp.

Introduction to Chapter 3

In the following chapter Pica and Doughty pose the question: What helps second languge acquisition in classroom settings? Their method is experimental with a focus on conversational interaction. First and second languages are mainly used in interactive situations and the first language is acquired in such situations. Thus, there is an important role of interaction in the building of languge. The authors see specific elements of conversational interaction contributing to the learning of a second language.

Working from second language acquisition theory, Pica and Doughty focus on the importance of conversational modification in classroom interaction. Second language learners who are concerned with the effectiveness of their interaction will want to seek clarification of what other speakers mean and will want to confirm that their own utterances have been understood properly. By such close monitoring of the interaction, discovering what does and does not work as effective communication, the second language learner will develop efficient use of language. Earlier investigations of the theory led to perplexing results. It seemed that there was little modification of conversation in the second language classroom. If there was little such adjustment to the communicative needs of the speakers and hearers, how could the interaction contribute to the learning of the communicatively effective language patterns in the second language (and conversely, the learning of what should not be said)? The answer of Pica and Doughty is that previous studies were missing an essential aspect of the social situation: the necessity of exchanging information among the participants. The authors therefore introduce an "information gap" in the current study to force their subjects to be certain that information is exchanged accurately. This change in the social situation has the clear effect of increasing conversational modification in the second language classroom.

For the experimental study, Pica and Doughty identify two elements of the social setting of language use and examine the effects of these elements on language. One element is the manipulation of the task by either requiring or making optional the exchange of information. The other element of situation is the participant pattern of the interaction: is a teacher present or not. The two elements of situation were found to effect language differentially. The presence of a teacher increases the quantity of speech in the second language classrooms studied but there was little modification of speech. On the other hand, requiring the exchange of information did increase the rate of speech modifications. Furthermore, there is more modification of speech when the teacher is not involved in the interactions. Thus we have clear, if not simple, effects of the social factors on the linguistic variables.

The social factors of the study and the linguistic variables are not just distributionally related but are functionally related. The particular conversational modifications and how they change indicate the functions of these linguistic patterns with respect to improving the exchange of information. The implications for the second language classroom then follow from the theoretical position that indicates that more conversational modification heard and used by second language learners will facilitate their learning.

The methodology of the Pica and Doughty work parallels the experimental approaches of Walters and Wolf and Canale. In theoretical perspective it resembles the approaches of Fine and Wolfson in seeking the functional connections between language and situation. It also provides some of the detailed analysis of language variation that Fanselow's evaluation program can specifically chart for individual second language learners.

CHAPTER 3

Variations in Classroom Interaction as a Function of Participation Pattern and Task

Teresa Pica
Catherine Doughty

University of Pennsylvania
Graduate School of Education

Introduction

In keeping with the currently popular, though highly controversial use of an "eclectic" approach to language teaching, many second language classrooms feature a wide variety of instructional activities and student-to-teacher interactional patterns.[1] Classroom assignments are regularly devoted to the practice of rules for grammatical accuracy as well as to tasks which foster the use of the second language in problem-solving and decision-making situations. In addition, class time is often apportioned between traditional teacher-fronted lessons in which teachers assume control in directing classroom interaction and small group work in which two to four students carry out assignments, with varying degrees of supervision from their teachers.

These and other organizational changes taking place, in the English as a Second Language classroom in particular, have been examined in an ongoing series of studies (Doughty & Pica 1986; Pica & Doughty 1985a, 1985b; Pica, Doughty, & Young, 1986a, 1986b). These studies have aimed at determining whether newer classroom practices such as use of problem-solving and decision-making tasks and arrangement of students into small groups foster conditions favorable to second language acquisition. One of these conditions—learners' participation in conversational interaction, which

---

[1] A version of this paper was presented at the Colloquium on Classroom Centered Research, VII AILA Congress, Brussels.

may allow them to comprehend words and structures beyond their current linguistic repertoire—has been of major concern in our research.

For the past several years, researchers (particularly Hatch 1983; Krashen 1980, 1982; and Long, 1980, 1981, 1983a, b, 1985), in emphasizing the importance of comprehensible input to second language acquisition, have speculated on the role played by interaction in making input comprehensible. Long, in particular, has claimed that modifications in the interactional structure of conversations between native speakers and non-native speakers (NSs and NNSs), triggered by the native speaker's reaction to or anticipation of the non-native speaker's lack of comprehension, are what allow the non-native speaker to understand unfamiliar linguistic items which they could not otherwise handle (Long 1981, 1983a, 1985). For Long, conversational modifications occur when native speakers, engaged in social interaction with non-native speakers, alter, adjust, or restructure their conversations in any of the following ways:

(1) By seeking clarification or confirmation of the non-native speaker's production, that is, through use of (a) *confirmation checks* of (b) *clarification requests* as underlined):

    (a) NNS: I need a pen.   NS: *a pen?*
         NNS: I've lived here for five
               years.   NS: *did you say five years?*
    (b) NNS: I need a pen.   NS: *could you please say that again?*
         NNS: I've lived here for five
               years.   NS: *how long did you say?*

(2) By verifying the non-native speaker's comprehension of the (native speaker's) input, that is, through use of comprehension checks:

    NS: you need to fill out this form. *do you understand?*
    NS: first you take Bus No. 42, then you have to change to No. 3. *do you follow me so far?*

(3) By repeating, expanding, or paraphrasing the (native speaker's) input or the non-native speaker's production, that is, through use of (a) self- or (b) other-repetitions:

    (a) NS: you need to bring a jacket, remember, *a jacket.*
        NS: that's a difficult decision. *it's not easy.*
    (b) NNS: I have three children.   NS; *you have three children.*
        NNS: that's a lot of money.   NS: yes, it's too *expensive*

Although these kinds of modifications can be observed when native speakers converse with each other, they have been found to be statistically more numerous when native speakers engage in conversation with non-native speakers (Long, 1980). Additional examples of these conversational modifications, together with operationalized definitions, are shown in Table 1 (see Analysis section below).

Based on theoretical claims about the role of such conversational modifications in achieving the input comprehensibility necessary for second language acquisition, the present research sought to identify their presence in the second language classroom, specifically in decision-making and problem-solving activities and in small group work. Attention was given not only to conversational modifications produced when the native speakers (the teachers) sought clarification or confirmation of student productions or checked student comprehension of their own utterances, but also on these modifications as produced by the non-native speakers (the students) in interaction with teachers, as well as with each other.

In the first study in the series (Pica & Doughty, 1985), teacher-fronted and small group interactional patterns were compared during decision-making tasks adapted from ESL textbook exercises. In the teacher-fronted activity, teachers and students, working together, had to solve a problem involving social issues. Each class was given biographical data on five families living in the 21st century and then was asked to elect the family most eligible to adopt a child. In the group activity, four students, working together, had to reach a consensus as to which one of six potential recipients would benefit most from a heart transplant.

Comparisons of the teacher-fronted and group interactional patterns revealed a greater proportion of conversational modifications (confirmation and comprehension checks and clarification requests) during teacher-directed interaction than within group work. However, these proportions comprised only 11 percent of the total number of utterances in the teacher-fronted situation and six percent of the total number of utterances among the groups. Thus, they were extremely low in number in both situations. In view of the importance attached to conversational modifications in achieving comprehensible input, the results of this initial study presented discouraging implications for classroom language learning. It appeared that neither format, teacher-fronted or group, gave students opportunities to hear language modified for their communication needs as second language learners.

Since these results were counter-intuitive to what had been predicted in the study, an explanation was sought. Review of this research design indicated that the results may have been due to the nature of the tasks in which participants had been asked to engage. Re-examination of the decision-making tasks used in the study revealed that such tasks at times encouraged interaction; however, they did not require it. Each participant's contribution to the decision, primarily in the form of arguments and opinions, may have been of assistance in the class or group solutions, but was not absolutely necessary for reaching a final solution. This was because the activities lacked an information gap component, that is, they contained no built-in requirement for information exchange.

Davies (1982) and Long (1980, 1981, 1983a, 1983b) have stressed the importance of using information-gap activities as a means of promoting conversational modifications among classroom participants. In such activities, each participant has information which is unknown to fellow participants but is required by them in order to execute a task successfully. It has been claimed by Long (1981, 1983b) that such materials promote optimal conditions for students to adjust their input to each other's levels of comprehension and thereby facilitate their second language acquisition.

Completion of the decision-making tasks of the initial study did not oblige individual participants to share with others information known only to themselves. As a result, the teacher and a few class members monopolized the conversational interaction in the teacher-fronted lesson, and the more fluent students did likewise within their individual groups. Typically, the less linguistically proficient students participated at a very minimal level, if at all. Thus, the more expressive participants supplied most of the input in either situation. This input was apparently beyond the processing capacity of most of the students, and therefore, totally incomprehensible to them; or the input was at the students' processing level, hence readily understood. As a result, most of the students had little impetus to seek confirmation or clarification of what they heard or to check others' comprehension of their own productions.

In order to examine further teacher-fronted vs. group participation patterns on tasks which were theoretically more conducive to modified conversational interaction, additional research was undertaken. In a follow-up study, to be reported below, participants engaged in information gap tasks. It was believed that more conversational modifications would be generated in both teacher-fronted and group activities on these tasks than had been the case with the decision-making activities of the initial study. It was suspected, furthermore, that the group situation would be particularly sensitive to this change of task. Thus, it was believed that more conversational modifications would arise within the group format than under the teacher-fronted conditions.

The Task

Information gap tasks, requiring a two-way exchange of information, were specially developed for this second study. These tasks were carried out in teacher-fronted and small group activities. Figure 1 provides an abstract representation of the materials used for this task.

For the teacher-directed activity, each participant, including the teacher, was given a felt board and a number of loose felt flowers, each flower having a distinctive color, shape, and pattern. The boards represented gardens

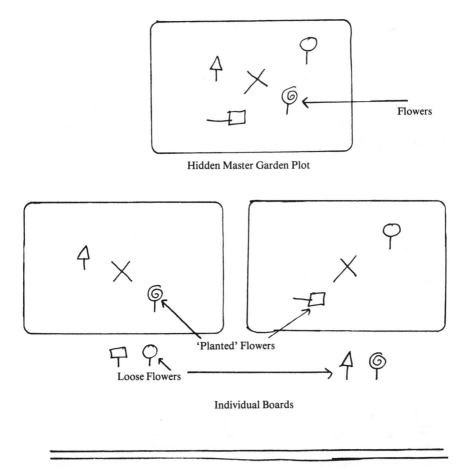

Figure 1. The Garden-Planting Task (shown in a reduced version, using abstract figures to represent the flowers used in the task).

which had to be "planted" by individual participants, using the loose flowers distributed among them. The object of the task was for each student to recreate the master plot on his/her own board. The master plot was to be revealed only after completion of the task. A tree, glued down in the center of each board, and also displayed on the master plot, served as a point of reference. Individual boards displayed two flowers, corresponding to two identical flowers on the master plot. Every participant's board displayed a different pair of flowers. If all individual felt boards could have been superimposed upon each other, the master plot would have been formed.

Each participant was required to exchange with other participants information concerning the color, size, shape, and location of the two flowers on his/her board. All work had to be carried out behind the boards, out of sight of other participants.

For the small group task, the teacher was asked to choose, at random, a group of four students. This time the task involved arranging a new set of flowers of different shapes and colors into a different configuration, under conditions identical to those described above; that is, each student had to share information regarding his/her own flowers in order to enable everyone to replicate the master plot on the individual boards.

It was believed that the information exchange requirement of these garden-planting tasks would prevent students from withdrawing from the activity and, furthermore, would insure opportunities for modified conversational interaction among them. Each student was obliged to participate because no other student possessed information regarding the location of specific flowers on the individual boards. In addition, all participants were compelled to understand each other's directions for selecting and planting the flowers because the task could not be completed successfully unless individual participants had *All* the information required to arrange the flowers on their boards identically with those on the master plot board.

Data Collection

For both the initial and follow-up studies, data were collected through audiotaping procedures. The researchers were not present during the tapings so that data could be collected as unobtrusively as possible. Activities were conducted first in teacher-fronted, then in group, interaction.

To insure that differences obtained between the two participation patterns were not due to a practice effect, two precautions were taken: (a) The teacher conducted a demonstration lesson with the class during which directions for planting the garden were given, the various materials to be used were introduced and described, and frequent checks of students' comprehension were made; (b) The teacher-fronted lesson, although always conducted before group work, was carried out in two parts. After 15 minutes of activity, the teacher stopped the task and conducted a question and answer period and class discussion. The 10-minute sample used for research purposes was taken from the final third of this phase.

In both cases, the activity had been in progress for at least 20 minutes before the 10-minute sample for transcription was selected. It was believed that, by that time, students would be familiar with all materials and procedures, so that they would not find one format easier to understand than another, a condition which, otherwise, might have biased their need to modify conversational interaction in making themselves understood.

Subjects

All participants were adult students and teachers from intermediate English as a Second Language classes. The students came from a variety of first language backgrounds. The teachers were native speakers of English, all with many years of teaching experience. Six classrooms were represented altogether, three in the initial study and then three in the follow-up study which were carefully matched to the first set (see Results section below).

Analyses

Features of modified conversational interaction used in analyzing the data of both the decision-making and garden-planting tasks are defined and, along with examples, are shown in Table 1. These include: percentage (in t-units and fragments) of clarification requests, confirmation and comprehension checks (as defined by Long, 1980), as well as self- and other- repetitions. In the repetition category, it was necessary to distinguish between classroom-related moves and conversational modifications claimed to be necessary for second language acquisition. Thus, the only repetitions considered were those which occurred during actual or perceived communication breakdowns among classroom participants or when both interlocutors took an active role in establishing or developing topics. Eliminated from analysis were those classroom repetitions used for such purposes as initiating topics during structuring moves, insuring topic adherence or attention to the task, or offering feedback on appropriateness of response.

Hypotheses

The second study addressed a subset of questions which had been raised in the earlier research. The primary aim, again, was to compare teacher-fronted with student-to-student classroom interaction. Attention was focused on variations in conversational interaction as a function of classroom participation pattern and task type.

Since earlier research had shown that the optional exchange (decision-making tasks) generated so few conversational modifications, it was predicted that the required two-way exchange activities in the present study would generate many more. Furthermore, it was believed that in the teacher-fronted activity, the teacher's presence and large group interlocutor would reduce the amount of conversational modification. It was predicted that the teacher, more experienced in deciphering interlanguage productions, would

Table 1. Analyses Used in the Study

(1) Percentage of Clarification Requests in T-units and Fragments.*

As defined by Long, 1980, these comprised all expressions designed to elicit clarification of the preceding utterance(s), and consisted of Wh-, yes-no, uninverted intonation, and tag questions, as well as statements such as *I don't know* and *try again.*

Examples of *clarification requests* from the present data:

(a)	S1:	she is on welfare.	S2:	*what do you mean by welfare?*
(b)	S:	this is very bad...I think she never estay home.	T:	*you're opposed to that? you think that's not a good idea?*

(2) Percentage of Confirmation Checks in T-units and Fragments.

These consisted of elicitations immediately following the previous speaker's utterance to confirm that the utterance was understood or heard correctly (Long, 1980). They were characterized by repetition, with rising intonation of all or part of the speaker's preceding utterance.

Examples of *confirmation checks* from the present data:

S:	the homemaker woman.	T:	*the homemaker?*
S:	Mexican food have a lot of ulcers.	T:	*Mexicans have a lot of ulcers? Because of the food?*

(3) Percentage of Comprehension Checks in T-units and Fragments.

These were defined according to Long (1980) as expressions designed to establish whether the speaker's own preceding utterance has been understood by the addressee. They are usually in the form of tag questions, repetitions with rising intonation of all or part of the utterance, or by questions such as *do you understand?*

Examples of *comprehension checks* from the present data:

(a): there is no man present, *right?*
(b): *do you know what I mean?*

(4) Percentage of Self-Repetitions in T-units and Fragments.

These were realized in the following two forms:

1. Speaker's exact or partial repetition of the same lexical item(s) from own preceding utterance, incorporated into a new utterance, within five speaking turns. Repetitions of functors were not included.

2. Speaker's semantic repetition (by synonym substitution, paraphrase, morphological expansion, or word order change) of the content of own preceding utterance, within five speaking turns.

Examples of *exact repetition* from the present data:

(a) do you agree with that? *do you agree with that?*
(b) I think Carlos Whannon is very young, *is very, very young.*
(c) the health is very bad...*the health* of both the male and female *is very bad.*

Examples of *semantic repetition* from the data:

(a) do you share his feelings? *does anyone agree with Gustavo?*
(b) he is more young. *he has a lot of life.*
(c) maybe there's a cure, *something that can improve his sight.*

(continued)

Table 1.   (Continued)

(5) Percentage of Other-Repetitions in T-units and Fragments.

These were also divided into two groups:

1.   Exact or partial repetition of lexical items, within five speaking turns, of the previous speaker's preceding utterance, without the rising intonation characteristic of a confirmation check.

2.   Semantic repetition (by synonym substitution, paraphrase, morphological expansion, or word order change) of the content of the previous speaker's preceding utterance, without the rising intonation characteristic of a confirmation check.

Examples of *exact other-repetitions* from the present data:

(a)   S1:   I think she has three children   S2:   this is the thing. *she has three children.*

(b)   S1:   I think the fourth family.   S2:   you *think the fourth family.*

Examples of *semantic other-repetition* from the present data:

(a)   T: he doesn't do anything   S: *he no work.*

(b)   S: he has a job for many time.   T: yeah, *he's had a job for a long time he's stable.*

(c)   S: is no normal relation.   T: yes, *it's not normal for two women to raise a child.*

---

*   *T-Unit:* an independent clause and related subordinate clauses and non-clausal structures embedded in it (Hunt, 1965).

Examples:

(a)   *you're opposed to that* (1 T-unit consisting of 1 independent clause)

(b)   *you think that she's lost?* (1 T-unit consisting of 1 independent clause (*you think)*) and 1 related structure attached to it (*that she's lost*)

(c)   *the people who work hardest should have the child* (1 T-unit consisting of 1 independent clause (*the people should have the child*) and 1 structure embedded in it (*who work the hardest*).

Fragment: non-clausal items such as single word or phrasal utterances used as initiations or responses as well as false starts and self-repetitions.

Examples:

(a)   *the housewife* (Noun phrase not attached to or embedded in an independent clause)

(b)   *later* (Single word not attached to or embedded in an independent clause)

Interjection: single lexical responses: *yes, no,* and *ok*; and their non-lexical counterparts, i.e., *um, hmmn,* and *ah,* which were not incorporated into T-units, phrases, or fragments (e.g., frames were not included in this category).

Inter-rater reliability checks for exact self-repetition obtained a coefficient of .88. Inter-rater reliability checks for all other measure in the above analysis obtained coefficients .93 or better.

be less likely to seek clarification or confirmation of the students' utterances, and that, furthermore, the more proficient students, shown to be more active participants in earlier research, would be confident about the accuracy of their English and hence unlikely to check on their comprehensibility to listeners. Less linguistically proficient students, on the other hand, might feel reluctant or embarassed to indicate their lack of comprehension in front of their teacher or an entire ensemble of their classmates.

Thus, it was anticipated that the presence of the teacher and the dynamics of a large group interlocutor would reduce the amount of modified conversational interaction in the teacher-fronted activities. In group work, on the other hand, participants, sitting in closer, face-to-face view of each other, might be more likely to notice confusion on the parts of fellow interactants, and consequently, would check on their comprehension. In addition, it was believed that the face-threatening nature of the task would diminish in proportion to the number of participants. Thus, opportunities for interactional modification would be more pronounced in the group situation where participants interacted only with each other.

These reasonings generated the hypotheses of the study:

H1: Activities which required a two-way information exchange for their completion would generate substantially more conversational modification of message meaning than those in which such exchange was optional. Thus, there would be more comprehension and confirmation checks, more clarification requests, and more self- and other- repetitions in the former than in the latter activity.

H2: Although conversational interaction would be generated by both required information exchange tasks, more modification would occur in the group situation than teacher-fronted situation.

Results

Similar patterns and trends obtained throughout the results of the study. However, the following discussion is presented with a certain amount of caution due to the relatively small sample size of three classrooms in each of the two studies. In making comparisions between the results of earlier and present studies, it is important to note that the two sets of data were collected from different sets of subjects. To offset this factor, however, all classrooms were carefully matched on the variables of proficiency level, age, size, and teacher experience.

The aims of this discussion are: (a) to compare the amount of modified conversational interaction generated in teacher-fronted activity during optional vs. required information exchange tasks, and to make similar comparisons for group work, and (b) to compare the amount of modified conversational interaction generated during teacher-fronted vs. group interaction on the required information exhange task alone. Therefore, the presentation of the results is divided into two categories: Task Manipulation and Participation Pattern Manipulation.

Task Manipulation

The findings for Task Manipulation are summarized in Table 2. Comparisons of the amount of conversational modification obtained during optional

Table 2.   Comparison of Modified Conversational Interaction Generated by Optional vs. Required Information Exchange Tasks on Teacher-Fronted and Group Participation Patterns: Conversational Modifications as Percentage T-units and Fragments Combined.

| Task | Participation Pattern | | | |
| | Teacher-Fronted | | Group | |
	n	%	n	%
Optional Information Exchange	347	49	145	40
Required Information Exchange	385	45	400	66

Hypothesis 1:   Activities which require a two-way exchange of information for their completion will generate significantly more modified conversational interaction than those in which such exchange is optional. Thus, there will be more comprehension and confirmation checks, more clarification requests, and more self- and other-repetitions in the former than in the latter activity.

Results: Optional vs. Required Information Exchange Task
Teacher-fronted: $X^2 = .02$, $p < .900$ n.s.
Group: $X^2 = 67.78$, $p < .001$
Hypothesis 1: Supported by data for group participation pattern only.

Hypothesis 2:   On a task requiring information exchange, more modified conversational interaction will occur in the group than teacher-fronted participation pattern.

Results: Teacher-fronted vs. Group: $X^2 = 66.62$, $p < .001$
Hypothesis 2: Supported by data.

and required information exchange tasks indicated significantly more modifications during the latter task type for the group participation pattern only. ($\chi^2 = 67.78$, $p < .001$). Thus it was found that, regardless of task, in the teacher's presence, confirmation and comprehension checks, clarification requests, and self- and other repetitions remained within four percentage points of each other in the total production. However, in the teacher's absence, (i.e., during group interaction), a task requiring a two-way information exchange promoted a 26 percentage point rise in such modification among students.[2]

Manipulation of the task from an optional to required exchange pattern also resulted in a considerable change in the proportions of an important subset of interaction features, particularly in the group environment. As noted above, confirmation and comprehension checks and clarification requests, even when taken together, were extremely few in number in both the teacher-fronted and group situations. They accounted for only 11% of the total T-units and fragments in the teacher-fronted interaction and only 6%

---

[2] Regarding the design of the study, it is important to note that, although the group activity always occurred after the teacher-fronted task, either (a) there was no practice effect, or (b) if there was an effect for practice, it did not appear to inhibit motivations to convey message meaning. Specifically, the groups of students actually generated more conversational modifications during their interaction without the teacher. This, of course, is contrary to what would have been expected from a practice effect, i.e., if participants had become more familiar with the task and task-related materials as the activity progressed.

among the groups. On the other hand, during the required information exchange tasks of this present study, these conversational adjustments accounted for 15% of the teacher-fronted T-units and fragments and 24% of these utterances among groups. Particularly noteworthy is the finding of a quadrupling of modifications among the groups of students as a result of changing their task. Table 3 summarizes this analysis.

Participation Pattern Manipulation

The results of varying the interactional pattern, while holding the task constant (i.e., on the required information exchange task) are also given in Table 3. There was a 21% difference in the proportions of conversational modifications during the teacher-fronted situation compared with the group format. Thus, as the number of interlocutors decreased, the proportion of conversational modifications increased significantly, going from 45 percent of the total production during the teacher-fronted activity to 66 percent of the total production of the groups ($\chi^2 = 62.62$, $p < .001$).

In further, more informal analysis of the data, additional effects for the manipulation of task type and participation pattern were examined.[3] One area of interest was the total amount of speech produced because, at first glance, it appeared that much more speech was produced in the teacher-led activity during both task types. However, while there was more speech in the teacher-fronted situation, a dramatic increase was induced by the requirement of information exchange in the group situation (a 5% increase for the teacher-fronted pattern and a 33% increase in the group situation). Thus, the requirement of exchange promoted about half again as much speech as was generated in the optional exchange task.

Upon further analysis, it also became clear that the quality of interaction during the two tasks was a very important parameter to consider. While the amount of total speech increased in both participation patterns when information exchange was required, there were differences in the type of interaction which accounted for the increase. In the teacher-fronted situation, the entire increase in speech was in the area of unmodified interaction (See Table 4). In striking contrast, all of the additional speech generated by the

---

[3] These and the following results are somewhat less formal than those presented thus far. This is due to the fact that two of the data samples for the GROUPS working on decision-making tasks (first study) were five, instead of ten, minutes in duration. Therefore these two samples had to be adjusted for purposes of comparison with all other samples. The adjustment was carried out by doubling the number of modified and unmodified utterances. Percentages were calculated on the basis of the adjusted raw numbers. Only these two raw scores were adjusted; the raw scores from the other ten participation pattern/task combinations were used in their original form.

Table 3.   Comparison of the Amount of Comprehension and Confirmation Checks and Clarification Requests in Optional vs. Required Information Exchange Tasks: Comprehension Checks + Confirmation Checks + Clarification Requests as a Percentage of T-Units and Fragments Combined.

| Task | Participation Pattern | | | |
| | Teacher-fronted | | Group | |
	n	%	n	%
Optional Information Exchange	79	11	23	6
Required Information Exchange	127	15	145	24
	36% increase		400% increase	
	or		or	
	an increase of		an increase of	
	4 percentage points		18 percentage points	

Table 4.   Comparison of Change in Modified and Unmodified Utterances as a Function of Change of Task: As Percentage of T-Units and Fragments Combined.

	Modified Utterances	Unmodified Utterances	Total
Teacher-Directed Optional vs. Required Information Exchange	5% decrease	13% increase	5% increase
Group Optional vs. Required Information Exchange	55% increase	13% decrease	33% increase

requirement for information exchange was in the form of modified interaction. In fact, there was a real decrease in the amount of conversational interaction which was unmodified and this portion of the total speech was, in a sense, "replaced" by the more desirable modified interaction (Again, see Table 4).

Of considerable note, as well, was the finding that the optional exchange group activity engendered the least amount of total production and the smallest proportion of modified utterances of all four situations studied. Thus, if left on their own, without their teacher to guide, alter, or compel their participation, and without a task to require their interaction, students did not have as much to say to each other or much motivation to make their message meanings understood.

Conclusions

Results of this study provide support, on a conditional basis only, of current practices in English as a Second Language instruction which encourage group work in the classroom. The teacher-fronted activities, whether requiring or leaving optional the exchange of information among participants, generated a good deal of linguistic production; however, more than half of this was in the form of unmodified utterances and represented primarily the output of the teacher and more proficient class members. Group work, on the other hand, engendered less total production; however, on a task requiring information exchange, group productions were characterized by more conversational modification than those of teacher-to-student activity.

Task appeared to be a particularly critical factor in group work as the decision-making, optional information exchange task, when pursued during group interaction, generated the least amount of linguistic production and the smallest number, by far, of conversational modifications of any situation studied. This finding is especially important because decision-making tasks of the kind used in the present research are becoming very popular in many classrooms, particularly those which are designed around a more communicative approach to language teaching. However potentially interactive such tasks may appear to be, they are essentially divorced from pressures on participants to work toward a single outcome; hence, in the present research, they triggered relatively few conversational modifications on students' parts.

Current second language acquisition theory holds that modifications in the interactional structure of conversation are important to second language comprehension and, in turn, to the acquisition process itself. The combined results of the studies reported in this paper have revealed that certain tasks and participation patterns are more conducive than others to modified conversational interaction in the classroom. Reinforcing current practices in classroom organization, results of the present research have shown that group work can be an effective classroom arrangement for stimulating student interaction. However, group work alone does not appear to be an effective aid to classroom learning. Rather, what seems essential is the combination of group interaction and a task requiring the exchange of information among group participants.

References

Davies, N. Training fluency: an essential factor in language acquisition and use. *RELC Journal,* 1982, 13, 1 1–13.

Doughty, C. and T. Pica. "Information gap tasks:" an aid to second language acquisition? *TESOL Quarterly,* 1986, 20, 2, 305–25.

Hatch, E. *Psycholinguistics: a Second Language Perspective,* Rowley, Mass.: Newbury House, 1983.

Hunt, K. Grammar structures written at three grade levels. *Research Report 3.* Urbana, Ill.: NCTE, 1965.

Krashen, S. The input hypothesis. In J. Alatis (Ed.), *Current Issues in Bilingual Education.* Washington, D.C.: Georgetown University Press, 1980.

_____. *Principles and Practices of Second Language Acquisition.* Oxford: Pergamon Press, 1982.

Long, M. Input and interaction in second language acquisition. Unpublished doctoral dissertation. University of California at Los Angeles, 1980.

_____. Input, interaction and second language acquisition. In H. Winitz (Ed.), *Native Language and Foreign Language Acquisition. Annals of the New York Academy of Sciences,* 1981, 379, 259–78.

_____. Linguistic and conversational adjustments to non-native speakers. *Studies in Second Language Acquisition,* 1983a, 5, 2, 177–93.

_____. Native speaker/non-native speaker conversation in the second language classroom. In M. Clarke and J. Handscombe (Eds.), *Pacific Perspectives on Language Learning and Teaching.* Washington, D.C.: TESOL, 1983b.

_____. Input and second language acquisition theory. In S. Gass and C. Madden (Eds.), *Input and Second Language Acquisition.* Rowley, Mass.: Newbury House, 1985.

Pica, T. and C. Doughty. Input and interaction in the communicative language classroom: a comparison of teacher-fronted and group activities. In S. Gass and C. Madden (Eds.), *Input and Second Language Acquisition.* Rowley, Mass.: Newbury House, 1985a.

_____. The role of group work in classroom second language acquisition. In C. Faerch and G. Kasper (Eds.), *Foreign Language Learning in a Classroom Setting.* Special issue of *Studies in Second Language Acquisition,* 1985b, 7, 233–48.

_____. and R. Young. The impact of interaction on input comprehension. Paper presented at the 20th Annual TESOL Convention, Anaheim, March, 1986a, 72, 1–25.

_____. and R. Young. Making input comprehensible: do conversational modifications help? *ITL Review of Applied Linguistics,* 1986b.

Introduction to Chapter 4

Fanselow introduces a practical model for varying the language in a second language classroom and for discussing the language produced. It is a model that emphasizes description of characteristics of communication that can have an effect on language. The characteristics of communication that Fanselow identifies are: source (largely teacher or student in the classroom situation), purpose of communication, medium, the uses of the medium, and the content. The author does not propose that the learning of his set of labels for language activity will provide insight into second language classroom activity, but rather that the model provides a tool for discovering language and behavioral variation and for inducing such variation.

Although the emphasis in this chapter is on practical classroom interaction, experimental studies (of the kind done by Pica and Doughty) can follow from the framework. Starting from informal observation by teachers, the framework can be used to examine the functional value of discourse features; that is, what functional change is created and through what specific discourse features. The work of Slaughter (Chapter 5) complements that of Fanselow by providing a comprehensive technique of measuring proficiency that can be induced by Fanselow's methods.

CHAPTER 4

What Kind of a Flower is That?
An Alternative Model for Discussing Lessons

John F. Fanselow

TESOL Program
Teachers College
Columbia University

Introduction

As a botanist uses specific, non-judgmental descriptions that are part of a conceptual framework to help see different varieties and characteristics of plants and other parts of the plant kingdom, so we teachers can see more clearly what we do if we describe what we do rather than judge what we do. The purpose of this chapter is to make a plea, and provide a rationale and a means so we can initiate and engage in the process of examining our own teaching on our own, without the benefit of supervisors or other outside experts.

One is as likely to hear "a rose" as "beautiful" in response to "What kind of a flower is that?" But in my experience, when we substitute *lesson* for *flower* in the question, one is more likely to hear "beautiful" or some other judgment rather than a name or description, especially if the person responding is a supervisor. Teachers, too, it seems are more likely to judge their lessons than describe them.

Since judgments are so widespread as a model of discussing lessons I think we need an alternate model for discussing lessons, one that emphasizes description. Not only are judgments widespread, but they also obscure what actually happens because they are based on preconceived notions of what is good and bad. Judgments are also likely to inhibit change because as soon as we say what we have done is good or effective we are likely to become invested in it. And as soon as we say something is bad we are likely to avoid it. While a botanist may like some plants more than others, in the work of learning about the plant kingdom, discussions are governed by a

59

conceptual framework and a set of operationally defined terms rather than by judgments based on preconceived notions. By using a framework and set of terms in the discussions of lessons, we will be able to be as precise about what we do as the botanist is about many aspects of the plant kingdom and we will be free to explore, uninhibited by preconceived notions.

The purpose of using a framework to discuss lessons is to discover the rules teachers follow, not to improve lessons. The idea that rules—unconscious conventions—control much of what teachers do is one reason it is vital to concentrate on description rather than judgment. We may be amused by elaborate mating rituals animals perform, but when we recall that we tend to say "Now" each time we shift a topic in class and we glance towards the direction a bus is coming from when waiting for a bus, as if glancing will make the bus come faster, we realize that invisible, unconscious rules govern much of what we do. And we further realize that until we see the rules we cannot substitute others for them. (Eibl-Eifesfeldt, 1974).

Before I describe the system I and others have found useful in describing lessons, let me say that though the system can be used by anyone, my dream is that teachers will use it on their own to discuss their own teaching, without the benefit of supervisors or other outsiders. While supervisors that describe rather than judge may be a refreshing change from supervisors that judge, a supervisor is still a supervisor. Until teachers tape record, transcribe, and describe their own lessons, discover the rules they follow, and generate alternatives on their own—all the time suspending judgments—they cannot be free (Cogan, 1973, Gallwey, 1974).

Classroom Observation System

Given a brief background describing the need for description, attention will now be turned to some characteristics of the observation system for describing lessons. Along with this are examples of a few ways the system has been used in discussions of lessons.

Though emphasizing that the system is useful for discussing lessons, the system has been developed so that it can be used to observe and describe communications both in teaching and nonteaching settings. After all, we read, listen, speak, and write in all settings, not just in classes. To compare the way we read outside of class—usually with a drink in hand, in an easy chair, and with background music—with the way we read inside of class—sitting upright in a hard chair in absolute silence—is vital if we are to learn the rules we follow. We can learn through the contrasts. Though teachers may make extensive use of the observation system, it can also be used for systematic and sustained research for very detailed analyses of communications.

Source and Target of Communication

Since the instrument is designed to meet so many goals it is multidimensional. It contains categories for five separate characteristics of communications. The first characteristic—the obvious one that almost all systems describe—is the source of communication: Who or what is communicating to whom? Often *teacher* and *students* are considered as sources of communications. The category *Other* accounts for books, noises, and other sources of communications: an alarm on a clock, for example.

Since the system is designed for use both in and out of teaching settings, the word *teacher* does not refer only to a person who is paid to teach but to anyone who is in charge or who takes control. When asking for directions from a hotel clerk, the clerk assumes the role of teacher. If we are just talking to the clerk about the weather, then we are communicating as peers and both speakers would be coded as *student*. That is, *student* means peer as well as a person in the role of a student.

Unit of Analysis

The second category coded along with the source and target of communications is the purpose of the communication. The four purposes are: *structuring, soliciting, responding,* and *reacting* (Bellack, 1966). These four move types determine the unit of analysis as well. Whenever the purpose of a communication changes, another unit starts. *Structuring* and *soliciting,* as the words suggest, are initiatory moves and *responding* and *reacting* are reflexive moves. Communications that set the stage for subsequent communications or review what has occurred but do not require any responses are *structuring* moves. Examples of structuring moves are the captain's announcements on a plane and the introductory notes in a concert program or playbill.

Asking questions, giving commands or requesting either actions or any other types of responses constitute *soliciting.* They are different form *structuring* moves because solicits require responses. Providing answers to questions, complying with requests or commands are all considered *responses.* Any communications that do not fit in any of these three categories and comment on what has happened are considered *reacting* moves.

Appendix A, *Green Cakes,* is an example of the coding of source, target, and move type.

Though this dialogue took place outside of a classroom, there are elements in it that are parallel to the usual pattern in some classrooms. One person is assuming the role of teacher, asking questions and providing feedback. The other is being treated as a student. Just as any setting can become a teaching setting, as Appendix A illustrates, so all settings in classrooms are not necessarily teaching settings as Appendix B, *Before Class* illustrates.

Just looking at the source and target of communication and the move types can aid in discovering some rules and generating some alternative sequences of moves. For example, one obvious alternative that *Green Cakes* (Appendix A) illustrates is that students can serve in the role of teachers. At a very early age students solicit and react. But though they can communicate with these purposes, the language being studied obviously presents new challenges. Such teaching does force the use of a great many solicits and reactions. These two types of communications are rare for students in their roles as students because the most frequent moves of students is, of course, responding.

Before Class (Appendix B) suggests that if structuring is communicated by the presence of the nuts (the source category *other*), a series of peer-to-peer reactions is likely to follow. After a concert—another structuring move that would be coded *other*—one often hears a series of reactions too. As more and more similar patterns or sequences are noted it is possible to make generalizations about the likelihood of certain sequences. These generalizations are descriptions of rules.

Mediums

Though the move is the basic unit of analysis, it is not the only unit. Another unit is the message. A move can have one or more messages. The number of messages in a move is determined by three other characteristics of communications; the mediums used to communicate, the way the mediums are used, and the content the mediums communicate. Each medium used in more than one way or that communicates more than one area of content signals a separate message.

It might seem strange to describe the mediums in an observation system designed in the first instance for language classes. But in fact mediums other than language are central to communication even in language class. Remember, the nuts in Appendix B set the stage for the students' comments. And without the green cake in Appendix A, Rodney would not have had anything to talk about.

There are three categories of mediums. One is *linguistic*—the print in front of you, words you hear others say. Another is *non-linguistic,* like a picture or a nut or noise or music. Gestures and tone of voice constitute the third one, called *para-linguistic*. Another medium is the absence of the others: *silence*. The categories of mediums, together with the source and target of communication and move types are shown in Table 1 in the form of a substitution table.

The coding instrument shows both what mediums are used in a particular series of communications as well as those that are not used: paradigmatic

Table 1.   Three Characteristics of Communication

1. Who/What communicates with whom?*	2. What is the pedagogical purpose of the communication?	3. What mediums are used to communicate content?**
Source and Target	Move type	Medium

	to structure	
teacher		linguistic
	to solicit	
		non-linguistic
student (sgc)†		
	to respond	
		para-linguistic
	to react	
other		
		silence

* See Appendix D for subcategories of source and target.
** See Appendix E for subcategories of mediums.
† (s = individual student; g = group of students; c = class)

alternatives are built into the system. If a teacher consistently reacts by say-ing, for example, "very good," one can simply point to *linguistic* in Column 3 and say, "You have been reacting with this type of medium each day. Tomorrow, communicate your reactions with a *para-linguistic* medium instead." As the two mediums are contrasted, the teacher can both begin to deliberately alter them in class and begin to see what consequences seem to follow from each alternative. Over time, the teacher can substitute *non-lin-guistic* mediums such as pointing to a green sheet of paper after correct responses and a red sheet of paper after incorrect responses. Finally, the teacher can react by doing nothing, *silence*. As the major categories of mediums are distinguished, the subcategories of course can be used. As the note on Table 1 indicates, the subcategories of the mediums, with examples, are shown in Appendix E.

The most central step in changing teaching perhaps is for those involved to notice what occurs. Noting the mediums in general terms at first and then in detail does, in fact, over time provide teachers with a means to see the relative values of different mediums for different needs. And they have to be used in a great range of ways. Ultimately, the teaching act is performed in a series of split second decisions. Most of these are normally quite unconscious. By deliberate manipulation of the mediums, and the other characteristics of communications as well, it is possible to gain more and more conscious control over many of the split second decisions during the act of teaching because deliberate use of alternatives prevents us from acting in our normal ways and thus allows us to first see and later break out of some of the invisible rules that control much of what we do.

Uses of Mediums

The next thing to look at is how the mediums are used, the fourth characteristic. The first major distinction between different uses of mediums is simply noting whether the mediums are received or produced. In silent reading, tasting, touching, smelling, and looking at pictures the mediums are simply attended to, not produced. When we engage in these receptive activities we are *attending*. By classifying the taking in of all mediums as one category, we highlight the fact that some of the predictions needed when *attending* to a linguistic medium such as print might be similar in some ways to the predictions when looking at pictures, listening to music, or reading the expressions on people's faces. Obviously, seeing the word *smoke,* looking at smoke, and smelling smoke require some different mental processes. We can recognize smoke, yet not be able to read the word in a language we do not know, for example. But equally obvious is the fact that each activity requires taking something in. What makes the difference is which medium we, in fact, receive.

There are six ways mediums can be used (see Table 2). The categories are arranged alphabetically, not hierarchically: *attend, characterize, present, relate, reproduce,* and *set.*

For the productive activities, I make use of Searle (1969), though the categories were developed independently. First Searle has a category of talk; for instance, saying "This is a piece of chalk." I call this *presenting* content. Then you can *characterize* talk; you can say "*Chalk* is a noun," for example, or "*Is* is a copulative verb." I call this *characterizing* content. Then you

Table 2. Four Characteristics of Communication

1. Who/What communicates with whom?*	2. What is the pedagogical purpose of the communication*	3. What Mediums are used to communicate content?	4. How are the Mediums used to communicate content*?
Source and Target	Move type	Medium	Use
teacher	structure	linguistic	attend
			characterize
	solicit	non-linguistic	present
student (sgc)	respond		relate
		para-linguistic	reproduce
	react		
other		silence	set

* The subcategories of the uses are listed in Appendix F.

can also *explain* talk; that is, make a generalization or a rule about talk; for example, "All copulative verbs have certain characteristics and one of them is that they have more than two forms." That is a rule about copulative verbs. I call this *relating* content. *Relating* essentially requires a combination of *characterize* and *present*. One looks at many characteristics of things and many things and then one is ready to make a generalization about the examples and their characteristics.

The other way we produce communications in language classes, shop classes, and subject matter classes, as well as outside of classes is by *reproducing*. Searle does not speak of this use of mediums. One example of *reproducing* is copying. Another one is repeating what another has said or done, or imitating what another has done. You can *reproduce* speech, with gestures or actions or any other medium. To cite one example of the results of lack of attention to *reproducing* with gestures, I will share my experience of Americans who learn Japanese. I can often tell whether a person's teacher was a man or a woman by the way the person bows. Japanese women bow with their hands crossed in front of them while men bow with their hands at their sides. Many non-Japanese imitate not only their teachers' speech but also their gestures, even though the teacher may not ask them to imitate their gestures. When I see American men bow like Japanese women I usually find after talking with them that indeed they did have female teachers.

One can even *reproduce* silence. In fact, one alternative to telling a class in a loud voice to be quiet is to stand totally still, say nothing, and just wait. Some students imitate the silence they meet in these settings in the same way that those who go to a concert imitate the silence they find in members of the audience who were there earlier.

Finally, mediums can be used to *set* content. In a solicit such as "Repeat this: I'm hungry as a lion" the sentence referred to by *this*, is setting content. Setting content is communicating models or other items that are referred to by words such as *this, that, it* and *one*. In some conversations, referents are never named. In the following examples, the underlined words all refer to items I'd say were setting content: "*This* sure didn't fit well; Did you fix *'em* up?; Wonder how old *they* were?"

By simply looking at the use, as well as the *medium, source* or *purpose,* one is provided with alternatives. And, with the same categories, one can describe communications outside a classroom or teaching setting that on the surface may seem quite different but with the categories become simply a rearrangement of the same basic elements.

Looking at the *mediums* in Column 3 and the *uses* in Column 4 in different moves cannot only point out characteristics of communications, but also can show relationships between communications that on the surface seem to have nothing to do with each other. In classrooms, one reaction to a student response is to repeat what the student says with rising intonation. For example, if a student says "I am go home" a teacher is likely to say "I am go home?" with rising intonation. The words—a linguistic medium— are used to *reproduce* one message. When I order ice cream, the person behind the counter often repeats my order with rising intonation much as a teacher repeats a student response, both when it is correct and incorrect. The exchange might go like this:

Customer: *Two vanilla, one chocolate.*

Clerk: *Two vanilla, one chocolate?*

Customer: *Hum.*

When the wrong number of cones or the wrong flavors are handed over, the customer sees what he was asked about earlier. Often, no difference is heard between the words used in the order and in the repetition of the order. But when the cones come—in a *non-linguistic* medium—then the difference is discovered.

Following is another common communication that can be described using the *mediums* and *uses* in combination in a way that is likely to make teachers see more clearly what they are doing. When saying a pair of words, phrases, or another unit, one normal pattern is to use rising intonation after the first sample and falling after the second. For example, it is likely that most people say "Are these the same or different—beach (rising intonation) beach (falling intonation)?" Well, to the student who listens well, they are different in intonation and the same in pronunciation and spelling. The communications are analyzed this way:

teacher to student	solicit	linguistic aural	set	beach
		linguistic aural	set	beach
		paralinguistic aural	set	rising intonation
		*paralinguistic aural	set	falling intonation

The rising and falling intonation communicates a separate message in this case. The asterisk next to the second *paralinguistic aural* indicates that the message is in contrast to the previous one.

Realizing that we use many mediums as well as words to communicate is a truism. The *mediums* and *uses* can be used to translate this truism into precise descriptive language. To say two words or phrases with falling intonation takes deliberate effort since it is necessary to break the normal rule we follow in presenting contrasting pairs of anything. Specific attention to the *mediums* and *uses* can both help reveal rules we follow and can also be used to provide alternatives to anyone interested in substituting different *mediums* and using them in different ways.

The mediums and uses can be used to vary the messages in any type of move and communicated by any source. If students are consistently responding only with speech and if they are using speech only to *present* content, one alternative is to have them *characterize* in their responses. Rather than giving answers to questions such as "Use *plumber* in a sentence," they can be asked a series of questions that require nothing but a *yes* or *no* about a vocabulary item being taught. For example, the teacher, or another student, can state a fact such as "These people work with water." The students are required to respond with either a *yes* or a *no*. Such a response requires no knowledge of grammar because one does not have to form a sentence.

Responses such as "He work the water" are thus avoided as are tangents in which such errors of grammar are treated to such a degree that the lexical information about the word in question is forgotten. If a series of questions are asked—"these people use planes, these people repair sinks, these people repair phones"—students can begin to see characteristics of plumbers and at the same time receive practice in classifying information, an activity that many believe is crucial in understanding anything (Smith, 1978, Vygotsky, 1962). But aside from the argument that such a series of tasks may help people make predictions, the more important point is simply that if 90% of student responses require the use *present,* one obvious alternative is to require more responses that require the use *characterize.* In the same way, if all responses require speech—a *linguistic aural* medium, one obvious alternative is print—a *linguistic visual* medium. Another is *non-linguistic* visual: pictures, objects, or graphs. Obviously asking a student to draw a plumber or act the way a plumber would with a broken pipe are not original suggestions. What is slightly original is to show how these different tasks can on one level be considered simply different combinations of four mediums and six uses.

Content Communicated

The last characteristic to be coded is the content communicated by the mediums used in different ways. To keep matters simple, only three major categories of content are used: *life, procedure,* and *study.* Formulas of greeting and other types of ritual language, personal feeling, or information and general knowledge are classified as *life,* and matters of administration, law, bureaucracy, and directions as *procedure.* Communicating a topic of instruction, whether language, other academic subjects, hobbies, or skills is classified as *study. Life* and *study* can be likened to Dewey's *experience* and *education* or Barnes' *world knowledge* and *school knowledge* (Dewey, 1938, Barnes, 1976).

Dickens' description of a class in Gradgrind's school in *Hard Times* illustrates both the separate categories and the tension between them in any teaching setting. A sample coding of the content of the messages is shown in Appendix C, *Facts.*

Further Considerations

There are times, either when doing research or when critiquing lessons as part of a program of teacher preparation, when two communications are obviously different in some way, yet the major categories in Table 3 do not reveal any differences and the differences are beyond those obvious ones

Table 3.   Five Characteristics of Communication

1. Who/What communicates with whom?*	2. What is the pedagogical purpose of the communication*	3. What Mediums are used to communicate content?	4. How are the Mediums used to communicate content*?	5. What areas of content are communicated†
Source and Target	Move type	Medium	Use	Content

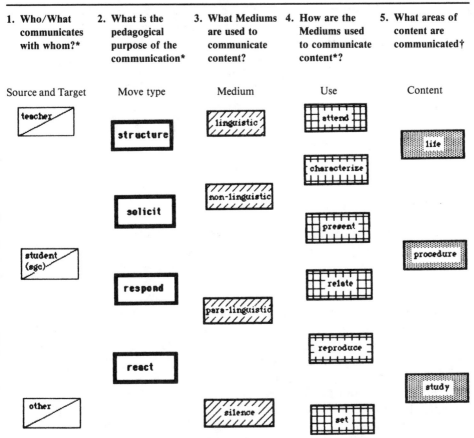

* To describe communications at a larger level, a zero column can be added to the left of Column 1. This could be used, say, to code the functions or sequences of moves. We might say the first group of six moves is depersonalized, for example. And the set of the next twenty moves is simply to give information. The next 15 moves might have the function of establishing control over the class. So we are not limited to the five columns. Sinclair and Coultard (1975) have developed similar units but their interest is in discourse analysis rather than applying the units in teacher preparation.

We can add features of communications to further distinguish items that are obviously different but coded the same way. The features can be added to a sixth column, to the right of Column 5. In addition to showing that some messages are in the target language and some in the native language, communications that are incorrect can be noted. Those that seem to be jokes can too, as can other features that distinguish messages that are obviously different from each other.

† See Appendix H for subcategories of Content.

such as target language or native language and other differences noted as features of the communications. In these cases, the subcategories in Appendixes E, F, G, and H can be used. When the subcategories are used, of course, people begin to say the system is complex. The major method for developing and using subcategories is simply to say "Are these two communications the same or different in a particular way?" The advantage of a multidimensional coding system, rather than a unidimensional one (e.g. Flanders, 1963), is that more differences can be described and generated.

Some Applications

Tallying

With Table 3, we can describe from one to five characteristics of any communication. Without a tape or transcript, it is not possible to describe all five characteristics. But it is possible to code one or two characteristics in an actual classroom. For example, if you want to see what content students are communicating in responses and reactions, you simply need to make two columns, one headed *response* and the other *reaction*. Under each, write an *l* for *life,* a *p* for *procedure* and an *s* for *study* each time a student responds or reacts. Tallying these three characteristics live provides a quick index or what areas of content are most frequent in reflexive student communications. Are the frequencies similar across all levels taught by the same teacher? Do reading classes contain more *life*? Are the proportions different according to the level of the classes? What differences are there between classes set up with different aims that use different books and syllabuses? These are just a few of the questions that a tally of content could help answer.

Of course, a tally is just the first step. And again, a high frequency in one category is not better than a high frequency in another. For example, if you bring drinks to a classroom with older people, they'll most likely communicate *life* a great deal, especially if the teacher sits in the back of the class. As you code, you will begin to see that some communications are hard to fit in either category because they contain attributes of more than one category. You will begin to see that areas of content are sometimes integrated, and then see the types of activities that produced the communications of this type. Activities that produced responses and reactions that at the same time communicated genuine information and contained patterns of language that were being introduced can be noted. Thus, tallying categories can lead to the generation of alternatives in still another way—through the substitution of activities that consistently produce communication that contain either different proportions of say areas of content or contain the integration of two areas of content.

Manipulating Messages

While tallying is possible for noting some characteristics of communication, transcribing communications or re-listening to them on tapes may be necessary for noting all five characteristics. Once communications are transcribed and coded the categories can be used to manipulate the original communication just as words in substitution tables can be used to manipulate a basic sentence. Let's say that you were interested in structuring moves, for example. One pattern you might find is this: teacher structures with a *linguistic aural* medium used to *present procedure.* An example of this could be "Today, we're going to have a test." Now, by definition, one apsect of structuring is to give directions since structuring moves prepare for subsequent behavior. Knowing this, it is hard to imagine that, say *life,* or *study* could be substituted for *procedure.* But another alternative to substitution is addition. Stating what the test was to be about would add *study* as in "Today, we're going to have a test on films." One way to add *life* as well would be to add still another statement: "Today, we're going to have a test on films—I know how much you hate test and like films; I prefer films to tests too." If the structuring moves that were transcribed already contained a great number of messages, similar to the one just presented with all three categories of content in it, then, the obvious alternative would be to subtract messages rather than to add them. But whether you add, subtract, substitute, or integrate and combine categories, the major purpose in the first instance is simply to describe what is. The description makes the pattern being followed explicit, and therefore open to change.

Observing Outside the Classroom

If coding the five characteristics of communications in teaching settings does not suggest variations, or if one grows tired of tallying and manipulating communications only in teaching settings, another avenue is to collect and code communications—structuring moves for example—in nonteaching settings. Masters of ceremonies on game shows on television, at concerts and at many other public performances structure. Noting the characteristics of these moves will suggest alternatives for teaching settings. And at the same time, clearer, more precise differences and similarities between teaching and nonteaching settings will emerge. The usual practice of describing communications only in classrooms ignores the usefulness of contrast in all learning.

Conclusion

I'd like to conclude with an example of the coding system that shows it can aid in revealing relationships between communications in different settings that a surface description may not reveal. The example is from the area of feedback. If you were to drop a student in a parachute almost anyplace and the person pulled a door that needed to be pushed, nine times out of ten another person would either say "push" or would push the door for the stranger. What happens in the classroom? Teachers follow a similar rule. When a student makes a mistake, teachers usually give the answer. We sometimes indicate "no" which is less necessary in the case of an unopening door since the lack of movement is a kind of "no." So both inside and outside of the classroom, a *set* communicated by the teacher is very likely after an error. To tell teachers in a critique to do something else when in fact the treatment of some errors in a particular way seems to be a pattern both inside and outside classrooms is unlikely to have any lasting effect. This rule, like many, is probably very deeply ingrained. Even some who think they have a different philosophy and believe that giving an answer is not good, often do, because feedback, like most of teaching, is not always conscious and deliberate. By coding communications and deliberately substituting alternatives we are more likely to become conscious of what we do and so better able to alter and control what we do.

One might ask "Why is the extra step needed to translate comments into this language?" Or, one might ask "Why not just look at communications precisely?" "Why ask teachers to use the terms in Table 3 rather than their own terms?" The terms in the table provide a conceptualization which can help reveal relationships that may otherwise remain obscure. In placing communications in categories, one becomes so involved in the process of classifying that it becomes difficult to make judgments at the same time. Furthermore, if suggestions are not placed in a framework they are likely to be forgotten. Most critical is the belief that deliberate control and added variety, and thus real change, can come only when teachers themselves describe their own and other's communications in a range of settings precisely and nonjudgmentally and substitute alternative communications that at once break the usual patterns and reveal what they really are.

Said another way, this chapter suggests a process similar to one that has made responses possible to the question in the title, "What kind of a flower is that?" Just as a botanist uses a framework to classify flowers, I am presenting a framework to classify communications. In classifying flowers, precise, nonjudgmental descriptions of multiple characteristics are required just as such descriptions are useful in critiquing. Botanical taxonamies put flowers that on the surface seem different together—strawberries and roses in the same family, for example. This framework does the same thing with communications. Finally, new varieties of flowers come about by understanding the characteristics of the flowers and the rules they follow in their life cycles. Control of flowers—keeping weeds under control or making sure some flowers produce desired crops—is possible only after the rules they follow are discovered.

The disadvantage of the question "What kind of a flower is that?" is that it implies that the main aim is to come up with a name or label. Because of the emphasis on the categories or labels both in much classroom observation work and in botany, the ability to learn names and labels and apply them is all too often considered the central aim. But both in critiques and in botanical work the central aim is the process of classification and the use we put the results of our classification to. The process of discovery, not the discovery itself, is the central aim. Paradoxically, the learning of the terms has to be emphasized in order for the relationships they show, the rules they imply, and the alternatives they suggest, to be revealed. But when the importance of the process rather than the mastery of the labels and names is not emphasized, too many get bogged down in naming, even for its own sake.

References

Barnes, Douglas. 1976. *From Communication to Curriculum.* Harmondsworth, England: Penguin.

Bellack et al. 1966. *The Language of the Classroom.* New York: Teachers College Press.

Cogan, Morris L. 1973. *Clinical Supervision.* Boston: Houghton Mifflin.

Dewey, John. 1963. *Experience and Education.* New York: Collier-Macmillan. (Originally published in 1938)

Eibl-Eibesfeldt, Irenaus. 1974. *Love and Hate—the Natural History of Behavior Patterns.* New York: Shocken Books.

Gallwey, Timothy W. 1974. *The Inner Game of Tennis.* New York: Random House.

Flanders, N.E. 1963. "Intent, Action and Feedback: A Preparation for Teaching" in *Interaction Analysis: Theory, Research and Application.* New York: Holt, Rinehart and Winston.

Searle, John. 1969. *Speech Acts.* Cambridge: Cambridge University Press.

Sinclair, J. McH., and R.M. Coulthard. 1975. *Towards an Analysis of Discourse: The English Used by Teachers and Pupils.* London: Oxford University Press.

Smith, Frank. 1978. *Understanding Reading: A Psycholinguistic Analysis of Reading and Learning to Read.* 2nd ed. New York: Holt, Rinehart and Winston.

Vygotsky, Lev S. 1962. *Thought and Language.* Cambridge: The MIT Press.

Material containing further information on the observation system and its application.

Fanselow, John F. 1977. "Beyond *Rashomon*—Conceptualizing and Describing the Teaching Act. *TESOL Quarterly,* Vol. XI, March.

Contains the rationale for an observation system and provides definitions and examples of the categories.

Fanselow, John F. 1978. "Breaking the Rules of the Classroom Game Through Self-Analysis" in *Teaching English as a Second Language: Themes, Practices, Viewpoints.* New York: New York State English to Speakers of Other Languages Bilingual Educator's Association. ERIC ED 145 720

Provides practice in learning the purposes of communication—structuring, soliciting, responding and reacting and contains suggestions for altering the source and target of each move types so that the usual pattern of teacher structure, solicit and react can be altered and new rules followed.

Fanselow, John F. 1980. "It's Too Damn Tight." *TESOL Quarterly,* Vol. XIV, June.

Shows how the mediums in the observation system you just read about can be used to highlight differences between language communicated in teaching and non-teaching settings. The aim of the article is to discuss some aspects of English for specific purposed, and to reach this aim, the importance of different mediums is highlighted.

Fanselow, John F. 1987. *Breaking Rules: Generating and Exploring Alternatives in Language Teaching.* New York: Longman.

A methods book based on FOCUS which provides suggestions for altering behavior, and exercises for coding for those that are busy, and observation guides and suggestions for generating alternatives for those with loads of time. Transcripts of communications from both teaching and non-teaching settings are used to illustrate categories of the observation system and rules that we follow unconsciously.

Appendix A
Green Cakes

Setting: The living room of an apartment. Two four-year-old boys are sitting on the floor next to a tea table on which they have just been playing a game. After the game the following exchange takes place.

			SOURCE	TARGET	MOVE
1.	Joseph:	What you do at Janie's party?	teacher	student	solicit
2.	Rodney:	(tugging at the edge of his short pants as he speaks)			
		She had a big cake.	student	teacher	respond
3.	Joseph:	What kind?	teacher	student	solicit
4.	Rodney:	(spreading his arms widely)			
		A big one.	student	teacher	respond
5.	Joseph:	What kind of a big one?	teacher	student	solicit
6.	Rodney:	A *real* big one.			
		(said emphatically)	student	teacher	respond
7.	Joseph:	What color were it?	teacher	student	solicit
8.	Rodney:	(touching his lips with wandering fingertips)	student$_1$	student$_1$	react
9.		What color were it?	student	teacher	react
10.		Green	student	teacher	respond
11.	Joseph:	(waving his hand disdainfully)	teacher	student	react
12.		Aw, you dumb.	teacher	student	react
13.		They ain't no green cakes.	teacher	student	react

Appendix B
Before Class

Setting: A language classroom before the teacher arrives. One student brought some nuts which he and another student are beginning to eat.

		SOURCE	TARGET	MOVE
1. (nuts are in a bag on a desk and students take the nuts)		other &	students	structure
2. Carlos:	These are great.	student₁	student₂	react
3. Yoko:	Yeah. But are they oily.	student₂	student₁	react
4. Carlos:	They're fattening too. I'm already overweight and really don't need them.	student₁	student₂	react
5. Yoko:	I like these as well as two-legged nuts! I like them both.	student₂	student₁	react
6. Carlos:	I like peanuts better than these.	student₁	student₂	react
7. Yoko:	My father likes them better too. They go better with beer.	student₂	student₁	react

Appendix C
Facts

Setting: A large, stone-walled classroom with desks in rows and a very high ceiling. Mr. Gradgrind, the master teacher, is present along with another teacher. Sissy Jupe, the student being asked about horses, has been described earlier. She lives in a room with wallpaper decorated with horses. Her father raises horses, or trains them at least, and so she rides them frequently, feeds them, and cleans up after them. She has had extensive experience with horses!

			Content
1. Now, what I want is, facts. Facts alone are wanted in life.	t to students	str	_____
2. Girl number twenty—who is that girl!	t to students	sol	_____
3. Sissy Jupe, sir.	s to teacher	res	_____
4. Sissy is not a name.	t to student	rea	_____
5. It's father as calls me Sissy, sir.	s to teacher	rea	_____
6. Then he has no business to do it.	t to student	rea	_____
7. What is your father?	t to student	sol	_____
8. He belongs to the horse riding, if you please sir.	s to teacher	res	_____
9. We don't want to know anything about that here.	t to student	rea	_____
10. ...Give me your definition of a horse.	t to student	sol	_____
11. (Sissy Jupe thrown into the greatest alarm by this demand.)	s to teacher	rea	_____
12. Girl number twenty unable to define a horse. Girl number twenty possessed of no facts in reference to one of the commonest of animals!	t to student	rea	_____
13. Some boy's definition of a horse?	t to students	sol	_____
14. Quadraped. Graminivorous. Forty teeth, namely twenty-four grinders, four eye-teeth, and twelve incisive. Sheds coat in the spring; in marshy countries, sheds hoofs, too. Hoofs hard, but requiring to be shod with iron. Age known by marks in mouth.	s to teacher	res	_____
15. Now, girl number twenty, you know what a horse is.	t to student	rea	_____

Key: 1. *p*rocedure; 2. *p*rocedure; 3. *p*rocedure; 4. *s*tudy; 5. *l*ife; 6. *p*rocedure; 7. *l*ife; 8. *l*ife; 9. *p*rocedure; 10. *s*tudy; 11. *l*ife; 12. *p*rocedure; 13. *s*tudy; 14. *s*tudy; 15. *p*rocedure.

Table 4 *Five characteristics of communication* contains the major categories of each of the five characteristics I describe.

Appendix D
Subcategories of Source and Target

teacher   —person in charge of a class
—person who assumes the role of teacher by taking over
—an informant used by a teacher to aid instruction
—a visitor used by the teacher to aid instruction
—paid aide in a class

student   —individual student clearly identified because of being in a class
—person in any setting who is trying to learn something or do some-thing and is being helped by another who is not a peer
—any person treating another as a peer in any way

group of students   —a part of any class, either formed by common interests or assigned to act in a group by the person in charge
—the number of players on the field that are only part of a larger team
—a part of a band or any other organization that at times acts independently of the entire organization

entire class   —all the individuals acting or being treated as part of one organization

other   —texts
—roads, sidewalks and other structures that provide frameworks for us to communicate in
—tools, typewriters, and other objects we use that communicate any kind of content with one of the four purposes
—a fire alarm, blinking lights, or any other signals that structure, solicit, respond, or react and communicate content
—pictures, printed messages such as EXIT that communicate content and perform one of the four purposes
—tests, examinations

Note: The teacher, student or groups or classes can be male, female, or mixed; the communications can be transmitted by the sources not only in many mediums but electronically, through an amplification system or just with natural means; alternative means for delivering the moves can be noted if you have an interest in comparing consequences and seeing whether rules change when such features of the sources change.

Appendix E
Mediums and Subcategories

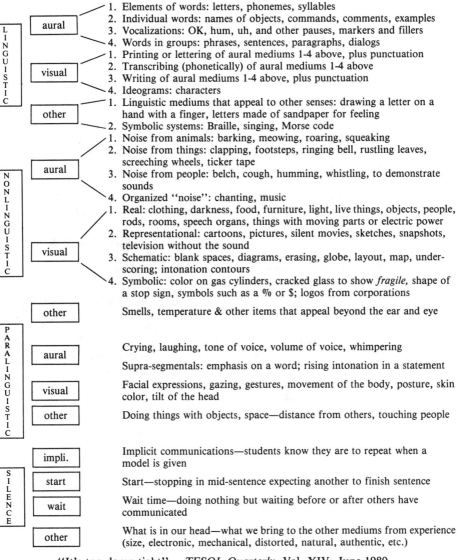

LINGUISTIC

aural
1. Elements of words: letters, phonemes, syllables
2. Individual words: names of objects, commands, comments, examples
3. Vocalizations: OK, hum, uh, and other pauses, markers and fillers
4. Words in groups: phrases, sentences, paragraphs, dialogs

visual
1. Printing or lettering of aural mediums 1-4 above, plus punctuation
2. Transcribing (phonetically) of aural mediums 1-4 above
3. Writing of aural mediums 1-4 above, plus punctuation
4. Ideograms: characters

other
1. Linguistic mediums that appeal to other senses: drawing a letter on a hand with a finger, letters made of sandpaper for feeling
2. Symbolic systems: Braille, singing, Morse code

NONLINGUISTIC

aural
1. Noise from animals: barking, meowing, roaring, squeaking
2. Noise from things: clapping, footsteps, ringing bell, rustling leaves, screeching wheels, ticker tape
3. Noise from people: belch, cough, humming, whistling, to demonstrate sounds
4. Organized "noise": chanting, music

visual
1. Real: clothing, darkness, food, furniture, light, live things, objects, people, rods, rooms, speech organs, things with moving parts or electric power
2. Representational: cartoons, pictures, silent movies, sketches, snapshots, television without the sound
3. Schematic: blank spaces, diagrams, erasing, globe, layout, map, underscoring; intonation contours
4. Symbolic: color on gas cylinders, cracked glass to show *fragile,* shape of a stop sign, symbols such as a % or $; logos from corporations

other
Smells, temperature & other items that appeal beyond the ear and eye

PARALINGUISTIC

aural
Crying, laughing, tone of voice, volume of voice, whimpering

Supra-segmentals: emphasis on a word; rising intonation in a statement

visual
Facial expressions, gazing, gestures, movement of the body, posture, skin color, tilt of the head

other
Doing things with objects, space—distance from others, touching people

SILENCE

impli.
Implicit communications—students know they are to repeat when a model is given

start
Start—stopping in mid-sentence expecting another to finish sentence

wait
Wait time—doing nothing but waiting before or after others have communicated

other
What is in our head—what we bring to the other mediums from experience (size, electronic, mechanical, distorted, natural, authentic, etc.)

"It's too damn tight" —*TESOL Quarterly,* Vol. XIV, June 1980.

Appendix F
Mediums: Uses and Subcategories

attend   *taking in communications made in any medium*
—listening
—silent reading
—smelling
—tasting
—touching
—viewing

characterize   *communicating about content or things to distinguish them or set criteria or limit choices*
—differentiate: indicating that communications are the same or different
—evaluate: prescribing or indicating that communications are true or false, correct or incorrect; responding to yes/no or either/or questions
—examine: counting or locating parts of words; emphasizing; diagramming sentences
—illustrate: giving attributes of items; making judgments that are not explicitly good or bad
—label: naming parts of speech or assigning category names to any groups

present   *communicating content itself directly*
—elicit: communicating questions, commands or requests in order to practice content being taught or in order to see whether others know the responses the person soliciting already knows
—query: communicating questions one does not know the answers to or commanding or requesting in order to seek unanticipated responses
—state: communicating declarative sentences, responding to questions with words or phrases or giving answers in any way that does not fit in the other categories.

relate   *communicating in such a way that higher level mental processes are required*
—explain: giving long definitions of words or concepts, making generalizations or developing and stating rules
—interpret: making inferences, synthesizing

reproduce   *communicating what another has in the same medium, with or without changes*
—in a different medium
  —changing mediums by reading orally, doing dictations naming objects or in any other way changing one medium into another
—in the same medium
  —combining: putting two small units given by another together
  —editing: making technical changes in material
  —expanding: adding words, phrases or other units to phrases or sentences provided by another
  —imitating: copying, repeating or in any way re-presenting what another has presented with no changes
  —paraphrasing: restating or rewriting what another has communicated in one's own words but keeping the meaning as close to the original as possible
  —substituting with or without change: changing words, letters, or any other units whether the change requires altering the original pattern or not
  —transforming: changing the order of letters, words or larger units

set   *communicating models, examples, texts or anything that is referred to by words such as "that," "this," "one," "it," or "those"*

Appendix G
Content and Subcategories

life f
ff formula   Good morning. So long. Hello. Please.
fg general knowledge   Truman took long walks. Huck Finn was really cleaver.
                            Rent control is bad. (factual or fictional—issues or
                            information)
fp personal   I'm sick. I'm a dentist and have two sisters. I hate rice.
                            (factual or fictional—feelings or information—about life
                            or work)

procedure p
pa administration   Answer the roll. We're going to have a test. Rules for
                            games.
pg assign roles   Pretend you are angry. You are the customer and you're
                            the clerk.
pc check   Do you understand? I don't follow. It's not clear. Rising
                            intonation.

class behavior:
pl language   Say it louder. I can't see the board.
po social   You are making too much noise. Don't throw paper on
                            the floor!
pd difficulty factor   This is easy. The next exercises are really difficult.
pn nuturing   You can do it. You're coming along fine.
ps salute   Ali...Maria...(Calling the names of students or groups.)
pu teaching direction   Repeat. Take the dictation. Tell me what this is. Define it.
pr teaching rationale   We are doing this exercise because it will lead to clarification.
pe time/space me   (Waiting for an answer, a train or a question.) Finish
                            quickly. Come here and other comments about measures
                            of space and time.
pt transition   OK, Now...umm...
pw work   The parts of one's job that require routine and procedural
                            matters.

study s
1 language

See Appendix H for subcategories of the study of language

other
    academic areas   School subjects other than language such as biology, history.
    special areas   Art, crafts, hobbies, music, sports, and other things that
                            require language.

teaching	Studying actual transcripts or tapes of teaching, not only advice.
unspecified	When the area of content is difficult for many observers to agree on.
use	When one of the uses on Column 4 is the content as when giving examples or when re-presenting uses other than sets.

Appendix H
Content and Subcategories

language 1

lc	context	The setting communications occur in; in reading, the title or cover; topic.
ld	dialects	In Florida, they say "Stand in line" and in New York "Stand on line."
lo	discourse	The analysis of conversations: turn taking, use of power, sequencing; pauses, markers and fillers.
la	format	The artistic or graphic design and layout of material; speed and loudness of speech, amount of background noise.
lf	functions	Use of mediums to interact, seek knowledge, pray, demand, request, etc.
lj	genres	Characteristics of poems, short stories, essays; literary criticism.
lx	grammar:form	Appearances of words that signal ways languages work.
lxf	function words	*The, at, through, did* and other words we can list that serve as glue.
lxi	inflections	Suffixes, internal changes in words for agreement, tense signals: ed.
lxw	word order	"Fire help" to mean get rid of workers or seek aid due to flames, depending on position each word occupies.
lz	grammar:meaning	Tense, parts of speech, singular, plural, etc.
ll	lexis:literal	Naming: "That's a book." Factual meaning: "Plants have leaves."
ln	lexis:non-literal	Figurative, historical, humorous, idiomatic, ironic, meanings, etc.
lm	mechanics	Spelling, formation of letters, holding of a pen or pencil.
lq	punctuation	Use of question marks, capital and lower case letters, indentation.
lr	register	Usage of different social groups and classes.
le	rhetoric	Organization of passages, logic, sequence, details & main idea, etc.
ls	sound	Pronunciation.
lsb	blending	Reductions: *he's* for *he is; gonna go* for *going to go*
lsg	segmental	Consonants, consonant clusters, syllabification, vowel sounds, etc.
lsl	sound/letter	Correspondence between sound and spelling; phonics.
lsp	supra-segmantal	Intonation, stress, and rhythm and tone.

lh	speech production	Your tongue should be up. The voice box vibrates. Look at my lips.
lk	style & usage	That's florid. Use that word in polite places only. Slang, etc. shifts from formal to informal to intimate, etc.
lt	ties:cohesion	Connections between paragraphs and sentences— noting what *it* refers to.
lv	ties:collocation	Ties between words: A desert can be arid but not your throat.
lw	ways of life	Patterns of thinking, feeling, living, etc. of different groups.
lwa	actual	What people from different age, sex, ethnic, language groups actually do.
lwi	interpretive	Novels, soap operas, satires, magazines, plays, artistic productions and other products that contain a point of view and attempt to interpret the patterns of life of different groups.
lu	unspecified	When the area of language cannot be determined or when more than three subcategories are contained in the same communication.
		When two or three subcategories are contained in the same communication the major category *study of language* is used to code the communications:sl.

Introduction to Chapter 5

Slaughter presents a method of bilingual language assessment that is detailed enough to be applied and is rooted in sociolinguistic and ethnomethodological analyses. She regards language as negotiated continually in social contexts and therefore requiring methods of analysis and assessment tied to social contexts. The entire framework is a statement of what is necessary for an assessment of language proficiency from a discourse perspective.

In the negotiation of language interaction four kinds of context must be taken into account: the physical circumstances, social and linguistic contexts, and the shared assumptions of speakers. Proficiency in a second language entails the proper reading of each of these factors. The measurement of proficiency, therefore, requires language samples that enable the display of proficiency in these different kinds of contexts. Slaughter's assessment system sets up such different contexts. The next problem, however, is that once language samples are obtained, how are they to be analysed or scored?

Consistent with a negotiated and functional view of language, a variety of levels of analysis are needed to account for the different kinds of interaction. Slaughter's specific measures include grammatical relationships, verb tenses, use of context, and conversational control. That is, each of the measures can be interpreted in terms of its communicative effect in the particular circumstances. Slaughter's paradigm is outlined in detail so that it can be applied and tested. Given variety in schools, language learning, and teachers, aspects of the paradigm may need to be modified. However, the scope of the paradigm indicates where the modifications will have to be made and the systematic connections between proficiency in specific instances and the linguistic features necessary to assess that proficiency.

CHAPTER 5

A Sociolinguistic Paradigm for Bilingual Language Proficiency Assessment

Helen B. Slaughter

Associate Professor
College of Education
Dept. of Curriculum and Instruction
University of Hawaii at Manoa

This paper describes a sociolinguistic discourse analysis model for oral language proficiency assessment that was used to develop the *Language Proficiency Measure* (LPM), a language proficiency assessment instrument designed to measure the language proficiency of Spanish-English bilingual and other linguistic minority students in a large school district in the southwestern United States. A sociolinguistic-discourse model is especially appropriate for oral language assessment in that it recognizes that speaking and listening occur in a context of human interaction, involves units of language that are often greater than isolated words or statements, and has social meaning to the participants.

A sociolinguistic-discourse model is a radical alternative to conventional approaches to testing and evaluating language in the importance placed upon the assertion that language as one aspect of communication must be evaluated within the context of its occurrence. Every communication act, whether it is described as academic or social, formal (where the interactants may or may not be strangers), or informal where the interactants may be familiars, written or oral, occurs in a sociocultural context. Hymes (1972) has shown that social contexts are governed by norms of interaction developing over time. These norms, called sociolinguistic rules by Hymes, influence such things as when and how an individual speaks, what and how much he or she says, to whom messages may be addressed, and how one gets a turn in the conversation. Social contexts are not, however, preset but are continually created and negotiated by the participants. Oral language discourse, as an ongoing fluid process, has a contingent, open-ended quality that is less apparent than that of written texts (Gumperz & Hymes, 1972; Mehan, 1979; Erickson, 1982). This notion of collaborative and dynamic transactions among participants in constructing a communicative context, especially when extended to adult-child discourse, has important implications for the way language proficiency assessment should be conducted.

All communication can be analyzed in terms of the intentions of the persons involved (called interactants in the sociolinguistic research) and the social context, as well as the language used. Conversely, language being a distinctly human phenomena where intent and meaning are paramount, cannot be analyzed adequately out of context. Therefore, we prefer the term communicative competence to that of language proficiency, for describing the domain being assessed. This is especially appropriate in situations like those of bilingual or English as a second language assessment where the persons conducting the assessment, and those being assessed, may differ widely from each other in age, status, cultural, and linguistic background.

When developing criteria for judging the adequacy of speaking and listening, it is important that criteria appropriate for examining oral language is distinguished from criteria more appropriate to the evaluation of written language. A number of sociolinguists have noted that on the surface, adults, and this may be especially true of teachers, tend to presume higher levels of proficiency for language which is similar in form to that used in decontextualized written texts and evaluate as a lower order proficiency, language of a more personal and/or contextualized nature, that is, language as found in oral language interaction (Bennett & Slaughter, 1983; Akinnaso, 1981; Hymes, 1982; Scollon & Scollon, 1984; Stubbs, 1980). Furthermore, in school contexts teachers are more familiar with evaluating student's written language, both reading and writing, rather than with systematic attempts to analyze and objectively evaluate oral discourse. Schools have been seen as places where students should learn to read and write and have less often been viewed as places where new forms of oral discourse are systematically taught and learned. Yet, recent sociolinguistic research in classroom discourse has documented the process whereby teachers impose rigid constraints upon teacher-student discourse during instruction (Peterson, Wilkerson, Spinelli, & Swing, 1983; Mehan, 1979; DeStefano, Pepinsky and Sanders, 1982; Cazden, 1986). Reading and writing assessment has long been formalized while the oral language of "normal" students has been assessed informally.

Stubbs (1980) has discussed the ambivalence and confusion among theorists regarding whether oral or written language has primacy in modern society. Stubbs showed that while oral language historically and chronologically predates written language, the advent of written language has had an impact on how people speak, as when spelling influences pronunciation, as well as how we think about language and evaluate the quality of oral discourse. Certain registers of oral language may be regarded as a higher level if they conform more closely to standards of certain kinds of written texts then to oral traditions. For instance, children's oral stories that are similar in organization and form to written stories may be evaluated as more comprehensible than children's stories organized through dialogue or associational patterns of the oral traditions of minority cultures (Labov, 1972; Bennett, 1983; Michaels & Cazden, 1986).

An understanding of how oral discourse functions both on its own terms as an irreducible channel of communication and in relationship to written texts is fundamental to oral language proficiency assessment. It may be necessary for the literate adult, especially the teacher, to reconceptualize his or her framework for analyzing discourse when assessing oral rather than written language. For instance, in the analysis of oral discourse we use the term clause, not sentence, to describe a basic meaning unit. A clause is the expression of a single predicate with its accompanying complement of nouns or noun phrases. Proficient speakers do not necessarily speak in "complete sentences," rather they speak appropriately within a communicative context. Often spoken responses of one or two words to others are sufficient and appropriate within a given context: a longer response resembling a complete sentence in some instances could be seen variously as a "put down," too formal, an expression of irritation, or a signal of one's higher status, depending upon the situation and constituency of the participant group.

The issues of oral language versus written language contexts and the interrelationships between the two are controversial and complex (see Canale, this volume); aspects of this issue will be touched upon herein only at points where it is especially pertinent to this study. However, the ensuing development of a sociolinguistic paradigm for language proficiency assessment may more fully elucidate some aspects of the issue.

The Role of Context in Assessing Communicative Competence

There are any number of ways to define the contexts of communicative participation. Four of these are especially pertinent to language proficiency assessment. They are (a) the physical situation, (b) the linguistic context, (c) the social context and (d) the invisible context.

First, the *physical situation* or context in which communication occurs is important. As will be discussed later in the section on the elicitation of discourse, a decision needs to be made about how and where to collect samples of student discourse. For purposes of economy, efficiency, and practicality, language proficiency assessment usually involves using a deliberate elicitation procedure, with an adult examiner and a single student in a small area or room removed from ordinary classroom events. Even when the assessment is audio-taped (as it was in our study), the process of removing the student from the classroom and the informal rapport building conversation to and from the testing room is not recorded. While it may be feasible to conduct the assessment in a quiet undisturbed place, far from distraction, and even this is not always the case, the relatively sterile environment and unfamiliar situation may have an effect on the outcome.

Other situational contexts also have their limitations. For instance, some individuals are more reserved in group contexts than they are in face-to-face dyadic interaction. Researchers have shown that classroom discourse is dominated by the teacher and a few higher achievers, (Cazden, 1986). In several instances in our study, students who refused to speak in the classroom were found to be proficient during individual interviews. More proficient or aggressive students may dominate group discussions. In an English language assessment study in Israel, researchers found that students preferred other contexts over student group discussions when their own English language proficiency was being evaluated (Nevo & Shohamy, 1984).

The physical setting also effects language performance in more subtle ways. We found that when students were asked to tell a story from a wordless book, it made a difference in the kind of narrative produced if the adult could see the pictures or not. Students produced less background information and tended to exhibit more pointing behaviors, using demonstratives like "here", "there", "this" and "that", and younger students, especially, more often used pronouns without making the nouns to which they referred to explicit, when they sat on the same side of the table with the examiner than when they sat across the table from the adult and refrained from showing the pictures during story telling.

The *linguistic context* refers to the way something that is said relates to what was said previously, by the speaker or others, or relates to what will be said later. The meaningfulness of what is said at any one point during conversational discourse often relies heavily upon the ongoing conversation, or past conversations, for interpretation. The analysis of conversational discourse, therefore, requires attention to the total linguistic context, not merely abstracting isolated statements made by the students in the analysis. Drawing attention to the linguistic context, does not of course deny the importance of paralinguistic factors, such as body language, to interpretation.

The *social context* refers to the social meaning of the communicative situation for the participants and in the larger sense, that of the society. Status relationships among speakers, especially, influence adult-student discourse in assessment settings. Adult examiners are perceived as, and usually create, a discourse structure in which they enact a role as an authority figure with command over topic selection and turn taking. Then, too, larger cultural patterns of how adults and children "ought to" interact, and more specifically, how teachers and students interact influence the situation. As Bateson (Lipset, 1980) showed, cultural differences in children's background results in children from some cultural backgrounds perceiving semiformal adult-child discourse exchanges as demanding that they, the children, exhibit their verbal skills, whereas the opposite is true for other cultural groups where it is the adult, rather than the child, who is expected to display verbal fluency.

Equally important, but unfortunately very often overlooked in assessment, is what I have come to call the "invisible" context. The *invisible context* refers to assumptions, shared or unshared among participants, regarding background information or what is known or implicitly understood about a topic under discussion, and what is not shared information but must be articulated by a speaker if a listener is to comprehend the significance, or point, of what is being said. Researchers have discussed this issue in a multiplicity of contraditory and confusing ways in the "topic-comment" literature, using different and sometimes overlapping terminology such as new information-old information, figure-ground, comment-topic, focus-theme, emphasis-theme, and so on (Bates & MacWhinney, 1979, p. 176). According to Bates and MacWhinney (1979, pp. 175–176), "The pragmatic writings of information, foreground and background, are analogous to the lights and shadows applied to the sketch, drawing the viewer's attention to some elements and away from others." Speakers select from a wide variety of surface devices, for providing background information or highlighting new information such as:

- aspects of lexical selection (e.g., definite and indefinite articles, adverbials, adjectives)
- sentence embedding (e.g., relative clauses and clefting)
- various word orders (e.g., the passive versus the active)
- ellipses versus pronominatization versus nominal reference (along a continuum of reference specifications)
- intonation contours (e.g., contrastive stress). (Bates & MacWhinney, 1979, pp. 176–177)

Key issues arising in the assessment of communicative competency relate to maturational, that is, developmental, age-related differences among "student" speakers in considering listener needs. For instance, younger students tend to omit adequate background information prior to point making more often than do older students. Cultural and experiential differences between adult examiners and students also create difficulties in establishing conversational topics of mutual interest. Indeed, adult teacher examiners sometimes assume that students know more, as seen in indirect requests for information, than they actually do.

Direct Measurement of Speaking and Listening in a Naturalistic Context: The Development of the Language Proficiency Measure

In developing the Language Proficiency Measure we have taken the position that in order to be valid, oral language assessment must take place in a meaningful communication context where normal communicative cues are provided and that the resulting interactional variables can be systematically analyzed and integrated into evaluations of student communicative competencies. An attempt was made to simulate, as nearly as possible, an assessment situation in which the student's communicative competencies could be evaluated on the basis of the way speaking and listening function in ordinary social contexts. Discourse was elicited from students in an oral language interview during which an adult examiner engaged the student in conversation and encouraged him/her to talk freely upon several topics mutually arrived at during the course of the conversation. Conversational elicitation was followed by asking the student to tell a story from a wordless picture book after the student had been given the chance to look through the book to discover the story sequence. The elicitation procedure, conversation, and story-telling task was first attempted in the minority and/or home language, that is, Spanish, followed by an elicitation in English. Different but similar wordless picture books (Mayer & Mayer, 1975; Mayer, 1974), were used in the Spanish and English elicitations.

The elicitation procedures were developed with these criteria in mind: (a) use of topic or activity of interest to students, (b) use of culturally appropriate topics or activities, (c) feasibility in terms of adult-student interaction carried on outside of the classroom within 30-minutes, and (d) use of procedures that elicit a range of language competencies related to instruction. All sessions were audiotaped. Each session was about 15 to 25 minutes long, including discourse in both Spanish and English. To this date, examiners have not deliberately attempted to elicit conversational codeswitching, although there has been some discussion of the possibility of doing this in future research.

These procedures, by placing the student into an interactive speaker-listener role, constitute a *direct measure* of communicative proficiencies or competencies where the multifaceted, synchronous aspects of oral communication (i.e., semantic, syntatic, lexical, prosodic, and pragmatic) can be exhibited and analyzed. Wallat and Green (1980), describing the sociolinguistic constructs underlying the study of communicative competence, state that the various aspects of communication *cannot be understood* in isolation from one another because "these features are not separate cues to meaning; rather, they occur in varying combinations and provide a degree of redundancy for message interpretation."

A student's ability to interpret and provide various communicative cues co-occurring within a context created during a conversational interview is a broader view of competency or proficiency than found in other, more indirect approaches to language assessment. Indirect measures of language out of context, such as sentence repetition tasks or multiple choice tests of grammatical correctness, may produce results that falsely suggest a student knows how and when to use a form he or she cannot use in any other context than the test context. Conversely, failure may falsely imply that the student cannot produce a structure that would be produced in more meaningful social contexts.

The research base for understanding how children learn and use language in natural contexts is also limited. Language acquisition researchers have often tested the acquisition of complex structures under experimental conditions that have placed children into an artificial situation where the normal contextual and paralinguistic cues accompanying speech have been removed. This has lead some researchers to question the generalizability of knowledge of language acquisition based upon this so-called scientific research tradition (Karmiloff-Smith, 1979). Furthermore, indirect measures of language competency often assume a single standard "language" rather than recognizing functionally proficient dialectal variations. More importantly, they may assume a shared, but unspoken, background understanding of the demands of the assessment task that may not be valid in testing linguistic minority students. Comparative psychologists (Cole & Means, 1981) have shown there are marked cultural differences in subjects' perceptions of psychological tasks but that performance differences seem to disappear when supporting contexts are provided.

Recent work by cognitive and developmental psychologists in nonminority populations has yielded remarkable performance differences on tests of cognitive development when directions are modified to clarify the intent and contexts of the required task rather than omitting contextual cues from the discourse (Donaldson, 1978; Keating, 1981).

The elicitation of conversation and narrative discourse can be viewed as midway between an ethnographic-sociolinguistic study of spontaneous speech produced in a variety of interactional situations and more highly structured and indirect measures of specific linguistic abilities. Spontaneous speech in natural social contexts has often been used to study language proficiences and/or more broadly conceived communicative competencies of a small sample of children over a long period of time. While some measurement specialists in education consider spontaneous speech samples to be "the most suitable method for evaluating which morphological and syntactic rules and structures the child has learned readily in his language," (Wiig & Semel, 1980, p. 97), they view the *disadvantages* of this language method of basing judgments about students' language proficiencies to be overwhelming because of the size of language samples needed, the difficulty of collecting data, and the complexity and time required for analysis. The use of an elicitation strategy to obtain audiotaped data upon which to directly base judgments of language proficiency was mentioned by Rosansky (1980) in her suggestion that modifications of the Foreign Service Institute Oral Language Interview Test for determining language proficiency might be useful in school district assessment programs. There is also a growing recognition among test developers that speaking and listening skills should be tested directly under performance conditions requiring students to demonstrate their skills (NWREL, 1980).

The question then of whether and how well this situation can be said to represent a naturalistic context for assessing communicative competency must be addressed. The analysis of conversational data from this study has suggested that several different types of "contexts" may result from the interaction of an adult and a student during an oral language interview. These different contexts, that is, examination, interview, or conversation appear to have a marked influence upon the level and quality of discourse elicited from students, especially that of younger and/or less proficient students. A conversational context where the student is encouraged to engage in mutually established topics of conversation with the adult, and where the adult builds upon the students responses appears optimal for eliciting discourse. Conversely, an examination sequence, one version of which was described by Mehan (1979) as a repetitive initiation, response, evaluation pattern, tended to result in more sparse discourse production, especially in the younger age range, for example, five to seven years old.

An adult-child interrogation pattern was also found to result in sparse child discourse samples by Sulzby (1981) in a study of kindergarten students from highly literate home backgrounds. In the LPM study, some students, especially older students, elaborated upon topics after single or "first" questions, which indicated that an interview pattern of initial open-ended questions and follow-up question would suffice to elicit an adequate discourse sample in these cases. A few students, perhaps perceiving that the purpose of the situation was for them to talk in an elaborated way, responded with extended discourse to questions that would have been given yes/no answers by other students. In other words, some students needed little in the way of background decontextualization from the examiner in order to elaborate upon topics while others only gave elaborated responses or even clause level responses after the examiner had interacted conversationally with them over a number of turns on one or several topics. In the latter cases, the examiner must use questions and other utterances such as comments on the topic, that are *situated* in the ongoing conversational discourse (Cook-Gumperz, 1977). One indicator of the "naturalness" of the assessment context is the use of *situated* elicitations similar to natural conversation rather than a standard set of interview questions in an assessment process.

The question of the relevance of an individual adult-child interview context outside of the classroom to within classroom and other socially valued contexts is an important one. Some classroom communicative competencies, such as getting a turn, are not measured in this one-to-one context while others, such as holding the floor and knowing what and how much to say to whom, are interpreted differently in a one-to-one adult/child conversational context than in a classroom context. However, we suspect future research would show that the student's ability to actively participate in and sustain a conversation with an adult teacher-examiner would be directly related to his or her ability to communicate with teachers in classroom discourse. Also, the ability to use discourse strategies to build a narrative text appears to be an important aspect of proficiency in language use as it is encountered in schools in developing literacy skills. Communicative competencies that can be observed in the analysis of audiotaped data of adult-student interviews are shown in Table 1.

In their discussion of communicative competence in the classroom, Wallat and Green (1980) stated, "We still have not decided...whether we can realistically continue to assume that an ideal instructional situation and ideal

Table 1. Communicative Competencies Observable in Conversational Discourse Elicited on the Language Proficiency Measure

Interactional/Conversational Management Strategies	Topic Development Strategies
Negotiating the conversational context	Responding to topics broached by another
Negotiating a misunderstanding	Changing topics
Exhibiting poise/comfort in the situation	Initiating a topic
Keeping the floor when interrupted while heeding listener clues to redirect or terminate talk	Talking about a variety of topics
Terminating a topic/conversational exchange	Disagreeing with way a topic's stated, stating own view
Varying register as appropriate to context, e.g., conversation, interview, test-like questions, narrative, personal	Building on another's discourse within a topic
Varying prosodic clues to enhance meaning	Engaging in extended discourse on a topic
Eliciting listener responses, e.g., clarifications, evaluation	Providing adequate listener background, information, e.g., identifies who she/he is talking about, provides context relating an old topic
Varying register to improve communication, e.g., checking listener's understanding, commenting	Producing narratives a) of personal experience b) to elicitations, e.g., TV movies
Eliciting information, e.g., vocabulary	
Adequate response to questions, e.g., how to, why questions	

speech situation exists." Certainly, there are few opportunities for students to demonstrate productive communicative competencies in many classrooms (Cazden, in press). Mace-Matluck, Hoover & Dominguez (1981) found that bilingual students' language in the classroom was sparse when compared to that of their playground and home interactions. The authors concluded that the students had few opportunities to engage in extended discourse within the bilingual classroom. Therefore, an individual assessment situation may provide a much greater opportunity for students to display an optimal level of competency than does the typical classroom setting.

A more important issue is whether children are required to talk about topics such as helping at home or how to play a game in naturally occurring speech in contexts other than the assessment situation. What are the topics that are familiar to students and which they would be likely to initiate in naturally occurring conversations with adults, both within and outside of classroom contexts? More research is needed in this area.

Scope of the Study

The research procedure involved listening to a wide range of data samples from Hispanic linguistic minority students in Spanish and English, by two or more members of the research team (Slaughter, Bennett, Arrietta, Santa Ana-A, Garcia & Prather, 1982). During the preliminary stages of selecting samples for the study, the researchers reconstructed the interactional and linguistic context of the assessment, compared interpretations of various aspects of the child language sample, and developed criteria for analysis and evaluation. Procedures for completing a preliminary analysis of taped data of kindergarten students without use of a transcript were developed and used to train the linguistic analysts and a bilingual research assistant in methods of analysis. (These forms are included in Appendix A.)

After tapes were selected for inclusion in the research study, they were transcribed and typed. The Spanish transcripts were then translated into English by persons familiar with Tucson Spanish, reflecting as much as possible what was said. Written reports were prepared for the analysis of the discourse samples.

This preliminary work and transcripts of entire samples served as the basis for the data analysis performed for the study. Transcripts were checked out by replaying the tapes as necessary throughout since written transcripts can sometimes be misleading. As the methods of analysis were refined and extended, data analyzed earlier in the study were reanalyzed. Several atypical transcripts were also included in the report for purposes of showing how the proficiency of students that the school district discourse analysis committee found problematic, might be evaluated.

Procedure

The initial focus of the research study was upon discourse elicited from children at the earliest grade levels, especially kindergarten students. During the first part of the study a relatively large number of kindergarten tapes (64) in Spanish and English were listened to, discussed by the research team and consultants, analyzed using a variety of procedures, transcribed (15) and summarized in written form. This intensive analysis of kindergarten data served to facilitate a developmental approach to describing the range of proficiencies and suggested factors that might be influencing students' performance on the Language Proficiency Measure. The need for a method of describing and evaluating discourse was also greatest at the earliest grade levels, as approximately 50.8% of linguistic minority students assessed in the school district were in Kindergarten and 15% were in Grade 1. After the Kindergarten and Grade 1 samples were completed, the remaining samples for each level, 2 through 5, were selected to provide a representative sample from high to low proficiency in each language, for the conversational elicitation separately from the narrative elicitation. Samples were also selected that illustrated common abilities or variations in the way the tasks were performed.

Sample

The resulting sample upon which the sociolinguistic discourse analysis methods were based consisted of the audiotaped discourse of 47 students in Kindergarten through Grade 5. Samples were drawn separately for Spanish and English discourse reflecting a range of proficiency from high to low in each language. As the study progressed it became apparent that the two tasks, the global topics task and the wordless book task, elicited different registers of language; samples were further refined to reflect a range of proficiency in Spanish and in English for each task at each grade level. Students who were proficient (a) talked at length, (b) talked in coherent and semantically complex discourse, (c) could talk on a range of topics, (d) might be creative and imaginative in language use, and (e) showed an ability to contribute actively to and influence the course of the development of an interactional situation (Slaughter et al., 1982). The first four of the above are similar to aspects of fluency as defined by Fillmore (1979). Accordingly, the focus of our sampling design was upon language proficiency in each language, Spanish or English, considered separately and not upon individual bilingual proficiencies. Discourse from an individual child might be included from both languages and both tasks or only for one; conversely, an individual's audiotaped discourse in one language or task might be included with the remainder not selected. While many children in the sample were bilingual, some were monolingual.

Since the main goal of the study was to make recommendations regarding the analysis and interpretation of discourse for purposes of determining language proficiency, selection of a sample that approximated the range of proficiency, within the limitations of the study, would best illustrate the methods of analysis. To have, instead, selected a sample from categories of students with various degrees of both proficiency and bilingualism would have been overly complex and would have required a much larger sample. Even if this had been done, the data would still have had to have been organized to describe a range of proficiency within and between grade levels and for both languages studied. Our purpose here was not to describe a population, but rather to suggest a method or framework for analyzing and evaluating samples of elicited discourse. These *methods* then can be used in other studies as a basis for assessing an individual's proficiency or to describe the range of proficiency within a specific population. Modifications in criteria could be made as needed on the basis of new data.

Students whose tapes were included within the sample were of Hispanic background and were assessed because their parents had indicated some exposure to Spanish in their home background. Most students were the correct age for their grade placement level. The data was obtained from individual testing sessions on the LPM administered by a trained bilingual resource or classroom teacher.

Proficiency Levels

The school district used four major language proficiency categories to describe a range of communicative competence from limited to fully proficient. These categories were (a) limited, (b) functional, (c) moderately proficient, and (d) proficient. Briefly, a limited speaker is one who can only speak in single words or phrases and cannot understand or respond to all requests. A functional speaker is one who understands most requests and responds in relatively simple language, but whose language is not developed to the level expected of his or her age group. A functional speaker of the language can "make do" in many ordinary situations but appears to be less fluent or to comprehend less easily than native speakers of the language. A moderately proficient speaker is one whose speaking and listening proficiency is equivalent to that of a native-speaking monolingual or bilingual student. A moderately proficient speaker may appear to perform less well in academic or formal situations than in informal situations. He or she may have a restricted sociolinguistic repertoire. A fully proficient student is one whose range of sociolinguistic skills is equivalent to that of a native speaker in a variety of formal and informal contexts. The term native speaker is intended to include varieties of, and/or dialectal regional differences in the language acceptable in the home and school speech community for this age student. For a more detailed description of language proficiency levels see Appendix B.

Discourse Analysis

Discourse analysis of elicited samples was undertaken at different levels. First, descriptive accounts were written of selected samples of student discourse reflecting a range of proficiency from low to high for students at various grade levels. From these analyses, specific categories or criteria were derived that appeared important in specifying how and why certain samples exemplified proficiency while others did not. We (Slaughter & Bennett, 1982), applied concepts from face-to-face interaction (Gumperz & Gumperz, 1976; Erickson & Schultz, 1981) developmental pragmatics, (Ochs & Schlefflin, 1979), and Latino discourse (Duran, 1982) in the analysis. Then members of the school district discourse analysis team selected those variables that appeared to distinguish between students rated fully proficient, moderately proficient, functional, or limited. In the discussion below, language proficiency criteria that emerged from the research are given first, followed by school district descriptors used in scoring the LPM (when applicable). There was not always full agreement between the researchers and the district discourse analysis team on the specific features that should be scored in assigning proficiency levels, partly because researchers are interested in comprehensiveness and implications that spin-offs of the assessment might have for instruction, while school personnel needed to be concerned with ease and efficiency of scoring as well as validity. Therefore, some interactional aspects of discourse were not scored in the district assessment process; however, the items that were scored are based upon extensive analysis of student discourse and are keyed to examples of discourse elicited on the LPM for various age groups. The procedure used is similar to that used in the Foreign Service Institute of the United States Department of State Oral Interview Test in that the ratings examiners assign are based upon careful interpretations of the amplified definitions of ratings and not merely on the checklist to record their judgements (Wilds, 1975; Clark, 1975).

Interactional Proficiencies

There were a number of interactional proficiencies exhibited by students during the conversation and narrative elicitation that contributed to the development, maintenance, and direction of the interactional situation and information conveyed. These included elements of appropriate backchannel feedback to the speaker and the prosodic patterning of responses as well as conversational clarification strategies. Particular attention was given to the *conversational context being negotiated between* student and adult interlocutor rather than focusing only upon the student *responses to* the examiner. A theoretical discussion of a socially active notion of context is found in Cook-Gumperz (1975) and Gumperz (1975). In order to focus upon the context mutually developed between examiner and student, it was necessary to consider relatively large segments of discourse in making judgments about proficiency. In other words, the focus must be upon discourse level units of analysis containing a number of turns between examiner and student rather than focusing upon clausal level units or a single examiner/student response interval.

The list of interactional proficiencies given in Table 2 were those, derived from the data, that appeared to contribute to the comprehensibility of the conversation and that indicated a student's growing awareness of his/her role as a conversational partner. Many of these interactional proficiencies are context-bound in that they can only be expected to appear in some contexts and not others. For instance, an important skill is the detection and negotiated repair of misunderstandings occurring during the course of a conversation since such misunderstandings are not uncommon in naturally occurring speech and, if undetected, tend to break down communication. However, in some conversations, including many in our sample, misunderstandings did not occur and therefore the skill of negotiating a misunderstanding could not be observed. Also if misunderstandings occurred constantly this might be a sign of lack of proficiency. We feel that in evaluation it is important to distinguish between interactional behaviors sustaining or improving communication and those impairing communication. Also we hypothesize that clusters containing more instances and varieties of interactional proficiencies will be more descriptive of proficient students than of limited or less proficient students. In other words, a particular behavior may not occur but some cluster of interactional skills will be observed in more proficient students. In our data we observed a trend of more instances and varieties of interactional proficiencies in older students.

Because of the nature of the LPM, that is, the relatively short time period for the interview and the semiformal nature of the assessment session, interactional proficiencies were perhaps less likely to appear than in more natural contexts. Then too, other criteria for judging proficiency described below seemed more parsimonious for scoring the LPM than the interactional proficiencies. Except at the earlier grade levels, grade one and two, the presence or absence of these features in student discourse samples appeared not to be a determining factor in assigning a proficiency level.

Student language proficiency cannot be evaluated without also evaluating examiner competencies in interacting with students. The adult plays a dom-

Table 2.   Interactional Proficiences Exhibited by Students During the LPM Oral Interview

1. Responses:
    Responses to elicitations were semantically, syntactially and pragmatically appropriate.
2. Prosody:
    Prosodic features, i.e., pitch, rhythm, loudness, were synchronous with ongoing in-
        teractional context, (e.g. pauses between/within utterances were within a range
        expected of competent speaker of the language).
    Used prosody for conveying relationships between different parts of the discourse (e.g.
        linking, contrasting, highlighting).
3. Monitoring:
    Detected and corrected examiner misunderstandings.
    Asked the examiner for clarification of the task.
    Elicited an evaluation from the examiner.
    Asked whether or not the examiner understood what he or she said.
    Commented upon or made asides about what he or she was talking about.
    Qualified or self-corrected information previously given.
    Monitored speech resulting in improved communication by repairing or editing
        utterances.
4. Negotiated/Constructed the Context:
    Successfully shifted the topic of conversation.
    Used strategy of digressing from topic.
    Initiated topic of conversation.
    Ended or closed-down topic of conversation.
    Changed registers, as in switching from a conventional to a narrative style or reducing/
        increasing the formality of the interaction.
    Made conversational intentions explicit, such as relating what was said to knowledge/
        experiences assumed to be shared with listener or in the listener's experience.

inant role in conveying communicative intentions in the assessment session. Linguistic minority students may not always share the same perception of communicative interactions with the examiner, even when they are both from the same ethnic background. For instance, some Hispanic children may assume that standards of respect and politeness call for brief responses to questions while others may assume that more elaboration is expected. We recommend that examiners be trained in strategies for providing more ex- plicit cues regarding the social and linguistic context to students who may be unfamiliar with the "educator" expectations of the assessment context.

Since the influence of the examiner upon language samples elicited from students is of fundamental importance to subsequent evaluations, it is sug- gested that the quality of the examiner's performance be evaluated previous to evaluating a student's language proficiency. Table 3 shows a format that could be used as part of a scoring system for the Language Proficiency Mea- sure. This format could be used when training examiners to administer the LPM. Appendix C includes definitions and examples of discourse from dif- ferent interview contexts.

Table 3.   Validation of Assessment Procedure

Tape No. _____   Analyst _____

Quality of Recording: _____ *easy to hear*   _____ *difficult to hear*

Quality of Examiner's Performance:

1. Generally, the examiner elicited conversation from the student by which method?
   _____ examination _____ interview _____ cooperative conversation
2. Did the examiner allow the student time to respond to the topic(s)?
   _____ often _____ sometimes _____ rarely
3. Did the examiner's responses to the student indicate he or she understood what the student said? _____ often _____ sometimes _____ rarely
4. Did the examiner build on the student's utterances?
   _____ often _____ sometimes _____ rarely
5. Did the examiner abruptly change topics?
   _____ often _____ sometimes _____ rarely
6. Did the examiner elicit a narrative from the wordless book by saying, "Tell me a story..."? _____ yes _____ no

Students Whose Discourse was Difficult to Elicit:

7. If the student tended to respond with "close down" strategies, e.g., "I don't know, that's all," did the examiner repeat or redirect the questions?
   _____ often _____ sometimes _____ rarely _____ not applicable
8. If the student was reluctant to talk, did the examiner attempt to elicit language by providing context or background information to the student?
   _____ often _____ sometimes _____ rarely _____ not applicable
9. In the beginning of the wordless book, did the examiner provide additional probes to clarify the task? _____ yes _____ no _____ not applicable

Discourse Proficiencies

The discourse features listed below are those that were central in judgments of the language proficiency or communicative competency of linguistic minority students. While the interactional context, and thus, the opportunity or probability of these features occurring may be different in the conversational and wordless book tasks, these features were important in the assessment of elicited discourse samples from both tasks. Expected differences in performance due to task and age or acquisitional level will be discussed. The features are:

1. Coherence/Comprehensibility of Utterances
2. Appropriateness and/or Negotiated Context of Utterances
3. Complementarity as a Conversational Partner and Ability to Produce Extended or Elaborated Discourse
4. Effective Use of Prosody

5. Background or Contextual Information
6. Completeness of Information
7. Richness or Complexity
8. Pointmaking and Highlighting
9. Verb Tense in Narrative Discourse
10. Summarizing/Synthesizing
11. Flexibility and Range of Communicative Competencies

While these features may overlap in varying degrees in specific instances, each will be discussed separately.

Coherence/comprehensibility of utterances. The most important feature of a student's language is to determine whether and how much meaning is communicated to the listener. A focus on comprehensibility, especially when assisted in this interpretation by persons familiar both with children's language and with the communication styles of the ethnic minority community, provides a basis for language proficiency assessment where dialectal variations and communicative intent can be considered when making judgments about proficiency. The comprehensibility or sense-making aspect of the student's language is fundamental to further and more detailed descriptions of proficiency. It is the point of departure for discourse analysts. In interpreting the language of young bilingual children especially it is important that analysts be knowledgeable about the characteristics of child language and the cultural background of students.

With repeated listenings to tapes, and acknowledgment of developmental, age-related differences in student speech, we found incomprehensible utterances to be relatively rare. This was true to such an extent that we removed an item referring to comprehensibility from the LPM scoring sheet.

The range of utterances accepted as appropriate will be much broader in a sociolinguistic discourse approach to assessment than those accepted in other types of language assessment, especially that of discrete item tests. This is partly because the student has an opportunity to construct the context as well as respond to the adults utterances during the interaction. We recognize a variety of ways conversations can be meaningful, including explicitly shifting or changing topics of conversation and we recognize that there are a wide range of forms narratives can take.

Appropriateness and/or negotiated context of utterances. Judgments of language proficiency will include judgments about whether or not the students utterances are appropriate in terms of semantic and pragmatic context. Such features as whether the student stays on the same topic as the examiner, selects an appropriate register in terms of a formality dimension and genre, and selects the "right" sort of thing to talk about, will affect judgments of proficiency. Black's (1979) scale for rating young children's communicative competencies in the classroom contained items regarding appropriateness such as the child's ability to vary responses according to conversational topic.

Student's elaborated discourse *matched* examiner elicitations to a remarkable degree both in information content and syntax. This matching was often very subtle. For instance, a student gave more of a summary statement about a TV show rather than a description of events when asked "tell me something about..." rather than the usual "what happens on..." Generally "what," "who," "why," questions elicited short responses while "how," and "can you tell me about" questions elicited longer responses. Also substantive conversational discourse by the examiner in which he or she shared information with the child rather than questioning the student tended to elicit the same type of discourse from the student. This type of elicitation seemed to produce more extended discourse from the students who had appeared less competent in their responses to interview type questions. In this situation the examiner's utterances provided more specific context cues to the student regarding appropriateness or type of conversation desired.

Complementarity as a conversational partner and ability to produce extended or elaborated discourse. The model suggested by this approach to language proficiency assessment is based on the recognition that competence in face-to-face communication is central to issues of language proficiency assessment. In assessing proficiency, data must be obtained indicating that the student can effectively interact as a conversational partner over a number of turns. The ability to talk at length which we have very minimally defined as turns of talk of three or more clauses, is essential to demonstrating proficiency. In examining transcripts, it appeared that it required at least three clauses for a student to be able to explain or describe something about a topic. This arbitrarily established decision rule, that is, that extended discourse would be defined as three or more uninterrupted clauses in length, worked very efficiently with our data set. Indeed, the wordless book task was included in the assessment procedures partly because it provided a device for encouraging extended talk. We recognized that students might have varying skills in producing extended talk due to topic or genre differences. Therefore examiners attempted to elicit elaborated responses about (a) a process of doing or making something, (b) narratives of personal or vicarious experiences, and (c) narratives from a wordless book. Because the linguistic context, that is, the influence of preceding examiner utterances on the content and style of students discourse, is different in interactive and narrative discourse, they are evaluated separately.

In scoring the LPM, (see Appendix D), the extent of connected discourse from one or two words up to elaboration on two or more topics is recorded for the conversation (Item 1). Then the extent of narrative elicited is scored from simple labeling to telling complete narrative (Item 6).

Effective use of prosody. The importance of effective prosodic patterning has already been mentioned in the previous section in terms of the student's proficiency as an interactant. Effective communication involves the ability to manipulate and monitor multiple levels of co-occurring variables in a stream of discourse which has a melodic and rhythmic, as well as a grammatical and lexical organization (Bennett, 1980; Crystal, 1979). Prosodic features are not a separate feature, but involve an intricate interplay with cues from semantic, lexical, and syntactic systems. Misleading, exaggerated, or reduced prosodic cues are possible causes of miscommunication. Prosody is used to establish relations across the discourse, as for example, when rising intonation at the end of a tone group serves to hold the floor and implies that more is going to be said, or when stress placed on certain words serves to highlight certain information or parts of the discourse.

Prosodic analysis was not included in the scoring of the LPM not only because of the analysis of prosody is a highly technical skill requiring extensive linguistic training but also because of the problematic issues of examiner bias in making judgments about second language accent. We felt that it was better to focus upon the meaningfulness and intent of student utterances and deliberately omitted prosody from scoring the LPM.

Background or contextual information. Students vary in the amount of topic specification or use of reference specifying mechanisms, in the amount of background information provided to the listener, and in displaying an awareness of listener's needs during the conversation. Many of the students in our sample appeared to presuppose that the listener, that is, the adult examiner, shared a large amount of information with the speaker and that this shared information could be omitted from discussions about a topic. However the children's use of nonspecific reference and lack of descriptive background information resulted in topic talk that was sometimes not readily comprehensible to his or her adult partner. This false assumption of shared knowledge between conversationalists on the part of young children has been noted in the acquisition literature (Maratsos, 1979) and sometimes attributed to the egocentricity of the child. However, Bates and MacWhinney (1979, p. 179) suggest that it is the child's lack of experience with a variety of different listeners and viewpoints that is responsible for their faulty judgment of shared information. The LPM data would support this hypothesis since the students appeared to be intent on communicating with the examiner as seen through their on-topic responses and prosody, but often seemed unconcerned about providing a great deal of topic specification. If the examiner asked for further specification the children readily supplied the information. In some instances, examiner probes for background information were small instances of the process children might go through in classrooms in learning to supply more topic specification.

Children who appeared less proficient at developing topics used pronominalization while those who appeared more proficient used nominal lexicalization sometimes provided with modifiers such as adjectives or adjective clauses. Bates and MacWhinney (1979) state:

> In all cases, the heuristic for deciding what kind of surface topicalization mechanisms to use is always the speaker's assessment of the listener's ongoing knowledge base. . . . This suggests that acquisition of syntax by children will be related to the child's ability to predict a need for topic-specifying mechanisms (p. 182).

It was not unusual for young children, e.g. students in kindergarten and grade one, to use pronouns in a narrative or description without first specifying their reference. When this happened it was difficult to interpret who the child was referring to without questioning him/her or without direct access to the book itself, as in the following example: "He was going to. . .eat and the dog said if he want him to go he wanted to go with them." Nonspecific reference in narratives from the wordless book gave the stories an unplanned and incoherent quality. This occurred both in conversational discourse where the listener presumably did not share the context and in the wordless book where the child may have assumed that the adult did share the context as the book itself was usually visible to both. King and Rentel (1981) found that children's economy and precision of pronoun reference increased sharply between Grades 1 and 2. We would expect a greater precision in use of reference for older students but in younger students overuse of pronouns with nonspecified referents would not indicate a lack of proficiency. Because the use of reference was so closely related to development or maturation, rather than language proficiency per se, it was omitted from the scoring criteria for the LPM.

In our data there was a tendency for *older* students to provide more specific reference, including the use of adverbial clauses, and background information. Syntactically, intralingual co-reference of the actors being described within a topic appeared to be difficult for many students. In the Grade Two data containing students descriptions of team games we noticed especially the use of the strategy of referring to other players or teams with ambiguous reference to "another one," "the other one," and so on. Perhaps these students were in the process of developing structures for explaining case role relations between actors. Herein lies a dilemma for language proficiency researchers: students who do not attempt lengthy and involved utterances may appear more communicatively proficient than those who attempt to use more complex structures.

It is important to note that even when students were observed elaborating on a topic, the topic was almost always introduced by an examiner elicitation. A student's judgment regarding the degree of topic specification required within the assessment context may also be related to his/her perception of the pragmatics of the situation, such as notions of appropriateness of content and amount of talk desired by the examiner and the formality-informality of the situation. Differences in amount of topic specification and elaboration may be related to ethnic or social-class differences as suggested in other research (Berstein, 1970; Ervin-Tripp, 1973; Parishi & Giannelli, 1974). Bateson observed that American children were expected to "display" their verbal and intellectual abilities for their parents and other adults while English children were expected to be more reserved and instead give the floor to their parents (Lipset, 1980). Many of the children in our sample were members of a lower socioeconomic status group. The Hispanic bilingual resource teachers who were administering the Language Proficiency Measure suggested that some of the students were from homes where children were not encouraged to engage in lengthy interactive discourse with their parents. Wald (1981) found that Hispanic students with a low length of residence in the United States were disinclined to use extended English speech over more than three clauses.

Contextual information was used in scoring the conversation part of the LPM but was eliminated from scoring the narrative. It appeared that because a wordless book was used to elicit the narratives, the production of extensive background information in story telling was less likely to appear than in other story telling contexts when the speaker is more in control of the story context and can modify the story line based upon audience response.

Completeness of information. In elaborating about how to make or do something or telling narratives, one indication of proficiency is that the topic or narrative is adequately described. While there are wide variations in the amount of detail any one speaker might include in talking about a subject, yet at a very minimum a description or story requires depiction of a beginning, middle, and end. Models were developed for analyzing the structure of descriptions about how a game is played and models for analyzing the episodic structures found in the wordless story books used in the study (Slaughter et al., 1982). However use of these models are too time-consuming for scoring purposes. When a child's discourse seemed incoherent, we found it useful to refer to these models to understand how missing pieces of information might be related to lack of coherence. Elements related to richness or complexity, and pointmaking discussed below are also aspects of completeness of information. Moreover, completeness of information can be conceptualized in various ways and for various degrees of specificity. The two that were important in the analysis of the data samples in this study were ennumeration or description and summarizing or synthesis of information. The conversational part of the LPM included an item regarding whether or not a student could give a comprehensible explanation of how to make or do something.

Richness and complexity of interclausal relations. Students who were proficient speakers used discourse that was rich in semantic complexity. This involved selection among alternate words where choices were readily available and the use of a repertoire of various syntactic strategies for relating clauses to show complex relations. Originality was also discussed as adding to the richness and was observed in some of the student narratives. Original means that some aspect of the narrative is unusual, unexpected, surprising, in such a way that this original aspect can be seen to fit with/or be integrated with other parts of the story and thereby appears to be a result of the narrator's intentions rather than accidental. It also means that the narrative is atypical in relationship to the narratives produced by most other students at the age/grade level. The use of the same wordless books across students in the assessment provided an opportunity to notice originality in some of the narratives. However, originality was not used in scoring the Language Proficiency Measure because it would have required too much time and individual judgment on the analysts part to be practical. Also highly original narratives occurred rarely. It was more feasible to score complex semantic relations.

Examples of some complex semantic relations that were scored on the Language Proficiency Measure were cause-effect, event-consequences, motive-actions, and event-human response (Appendix D). The integration of a variety of these semantic relations within discourse on a topic or in constructing a narrative text was observed in the discourse of more highly proficient students. The more proficient students also used a variety of different connectors including in addition to "and" and "and then" subordinating conjunctions to introduce adverbial clauses and make it clear exactly what the relation was between clauses. Adverbial clauses, as well as connectors, were much more apparent in the conversational data than the use of adjectival clauses although some use of adjectival clauses was noted among older students. The students frequent use of subordinate adverbial clauses was compatible with findings in Loban's (1976) language development research but their infrequent use of adjectival clauses may indicate a relatively low level of language development in the research sample. However, this is suggestive only and in need of further research as it is problematic to compare findings from two studies using such widely different research methodologies.

In scoring the LPM, students were given credit for conveying complex meaning, that is, semantic, relationships, and/or using complex grammatical relationships in both the conversational and narrative discourse. In this way the discourse analyst's attention was directed to the meaning of the students' utterances as well as to the form. Of course, the two features of semantic and grammatical complexity were often present in the same discourse segment as in: "the turtle and the dog, as you know, really feel bad because they don't get to go." However, sometimes a student gave complex meaning relations without complex grammar as in the following example from a student in Grade 4: "He jumped out and then he was right there and the lady got scared, and he jumped out."

Complex grammatical relationships were defined, for purposes of scoring the LPM, as using subordinate classes. It was our intention to keep the grammatical analysis of the instrument to a minimal level so that the student's discourse sample could be scored within a reasonable time limit. In order to distinguish between overuse, isolated use of one or two subordinating conjunctions, and a more developed use of complex grammar, a higher score was given to students who used different kinds of connectors (Appendix E).

Verb tenses in narrative discourse. As stated previously, ranges of discourse proficiency are described in terms of multiple co-occurring variables across lexical, semantic, syntactic, and prosodic systems. Structure, for example tense, cannot be evaluated in isolation from its meaning in discourse. This was best seen in variations in strategies students used to produce a narrative text from the wordless books. More highly proficient students distinguished foreground from background information by switching tenses. Less proficient students, while using tenses correctly in terms of semantic meaning at the clause level, did not use verb tenses as consistently or flexibly to enhance the meaning of their narratives. The inconsistent and seemingly haphazard use of verb tense by the less proficient students seemed unrelated to the story line and thus was confusing to the listener.

Further complicating this issue is the fact that one cannot tell the function of a clause from its tense. In analyzing student narratives from the wordless books it became apparent that the function of a clause, for example background orientation or event sequence, could only be discerned from examining the narrative context in which it occurred (discussed at length by Bennett in Bennett & Slaughter, 1983; Slaughter & Bennett, 1982).

In our data we also noted unevenness of performance in the skillfulness with which a child handled similar topics, for example, descriptions of two games. Yet these differences did not appear to be related to changes in the interactional context or examiner elicitations. Our data suggest that children were applying various strategies in attempting to describe complex action sequences and relationships between people and events. Bowerman (1979, p. 304) in quoting Cromer, suggests that while there are individual differences in these premastery phases of the acquisition of complex sentences, these strategies disappear at a later stage when this is achieved.

> The problem, as Cromer points out, is that children seem to apply strategies to sentences that they cannot process fully. Once they can process these sentences, they no longer need the strategies and begin instead to interpret them on the basis of structural knowledge. But how is the necessary knowledge acquired? This is the critical question, and it is one for which we as yet have few answers . . . . Different children appear to use different strategies for the same sentence structures, and some children seem to use no consistent strategies at all. Yet as Cromer notes, they all end up learning the constructions . . . . (Bowerman, 1979, p. 304).

Students were given credit on the LPM if they could vary tenses in a way that improved the meaning of their narrative. A higher score was given if the student varied tenses throughout the narrative in a way that contributed to the coherence of the narrative. In the following, example 1 is given credit because the tense variation contributes to the coherence of the story but example 2 is not since the variety of tenses used does not add to the coherence of the narrative as a whole but rather appears to be a coping device for telling each event as a separate unit:

> *EXAMPLE 1: Kindergarten—Give Credit*
> They were singing a song, and then the frog was dancing. They got louder and louder. And then the man was looking inside the horn, he didn't know what it was, and they all got angry, and then the frog jumped on the man's head.
>
> *EXAMPLE 2: Grade 2 Student—Do not credit*
> She touching that dog/and then she say/bye/there/..then she came(now)....and then see reading there/..and the frog going in the horn/...and the frog came, to his face/..the frog jumped to the...lettuce/...(when) she. when to eat/she saw the frog/...the frog jump. jumped/when she's gonna drink. the -in there is a frog/and...right here a man wasn't want to get the frog/.

Pointmaking and highlighting. More proficient students were more likely to be clear about the point they were making in their talk and provided more highlighting emphasizing important events or factors in their descriptions or narratives. It was often difficult to discern any point or major emphasis in the discourse of less proficient students and they were less likely to make foreground-background relations explicit. In other words, it was more difficult to discern the communicative intent of utterances from less proficient students.

A few students made highly effective use of dialogue in their narratives. In effect, these students told the story through dialogue. In these cases, which were rather exceptional, our method of scoring would not adequately credit the student's discourse skill since dialogue commonly does not require complex syntax. (See Bennett, 1983, for a discussion of the animated dialogue narrative style). Point making, highlighting, and/or use of highly original (and often entertaining) discourse styles were not scored as separate items since they were subsumed under other indicators such as providing contextual information or using complex syntax and semantics, or occurred rarely (animated dialogue).

Summarizing/synthesizing. The ability to summarize or synthesize information at a more abstract level than that of enumeration or description of action sequences was viewed as an important proficiency that appeared in the discourse of some older students. By summarizing, a speaker is able to convey information in a relatively condensed fashion and may be able to ascertain the needs or interests of the listener before going into a more detailed description. Summaries also are economical ways of establishing a shared context before engaging in speech for other purposes, e.g. to give opinions, provide an evaluation or make comments. Summarizing may also be a more appropriate response when the speaker can assume a shared general knowledge background with the listener.

Summarizing was not scored as a separate feature on the LPM because it did not seem to add more precision to the score. This was because summarizing, when it did occur, usually occurred when the student was rated highly proficient on the other indicators anyway. It is mentioned here as a caveat to those who would confuse fluency with proficiency.

Flexibility and range of communicative competencies. More proficient students were able to vary the communicative strategies they used to interact in the conversational situation and also demonstrated command of more different types of strategies, such as making topic shifts explicit, qualifying statements, and so on, than less proficient students. They were also more likely to shift to a narrative style when appropriate.

Applying the Discourse Analysis Criteria when Assigning Language Proficiency Ratings

To obtain a rating of fully proficient, a student need not obtain a "perfect" LPM score but he or she must display more proficiencies, and proficiencies used in various complex combinations, or clusters, than less proficient students. The notion of a cluster of proficiencies or communicative competencies is central to the method used to transpose LPM scores on various items to an overall Language Proficiency Level Rating. For any given grade level, students were required to obtain a certain number of points out of the total possible, but less than a perfect score, when rated as fully proficient or less.

When scoring the LPM, a Discourse Evaluation and Summary form (see Appendix F) is first marked to record the level or frequency of each of the critical discourse variables. Then, the analyst refers to criteria for assigning a proficiency rating for that age and/or grade level student (see Appendix G). If the second listener disagrees with the resulting rating, reasons and documentation is provided for assigning a rating that is lower or higher. Since each tape is numbered and filed for easy retrieval obtaining a second opinion is relatively easy to obtain.

In developing the criteria for each of the proficiency categories, a cross-tabs analysis was used to determine which clusters and indicators were predictive of a specific rating and placement into various language proficiency categories (C. Tompkins, personal communication, Spring 1983). For instance, the indicator, "initiates, shifts, changes topic" appeared to enter into decisions about the proficiency of grades one and two students only and therefore this item is not scored for the other grade levels.

A study (Powers, Johnson, Slaughter, Crowder & Jones, 1985) of the concurrent validity of the LPM, using the Language Assessment Scales (LAS), (De Avila & Duncan, 1981) as the criterion, indicated that the LPM was substantially correlated with the LAS (Spanish LPM with LAS, r = .74; English LPM with LAS, r = .63). This finding of significant correlation is similar to validation studies of other language proficiency measures (National Institute of Education, 1981). Previous studies have also shown that different language proficiency measures classify students quite differently, especially with reference to the "limited English proficient," (LEP), student. In other words, despite consistency among language proficiency measures, there is a great deal of disparity in the actual cut-off criteria used to determine whether or not a student falls within the LEP category. The Powers et al. study shows that the LPM classified 35% of the students LEP, whereas the LAS classified 52% of the same students LEP.

Training Teachers or Paraprofessionals to Administer and Score the Language Proficiency Measure

Examiner training and scoring issues are very large, but we believe not insurmountable, obstacles to the application of a sociolinguistic discourse approach to language proficiency assessment in school districts. Ideally, a school district considering implementing this approach to assessment should be committed to an extensive inservice/retraining program for its teachers based upon current research in sociolinguistics, the ethnography of communication, and bilingual education. The experience of the school district in training bilingual teachers and paraprofessionals in the elicitation procedures used in the Language Proficiency Measure (LPM) has shown that the teacher-examiner's involvement in listening to and analyzing audio-taped data from the LPM is indispensible in training people to conduct valid elicitations. The examiner's discourse style strongly influences the complexity and coherence of the language produced by students. It is important that adults examiners build their responses and elicitations upon the discourse produced by the student in order to provide an optimal context for student performance. Wells, et al. (1981) stated that this discourse style was also used by parents of more proficient preschool children. In summarizing from a number of research studies, Wells reports:

> What distinguished the speech of the mothers of the fast developers was the greater proportion of their utterances that were related to the preceding child utterances in the form of expansions and extensions of the child's contribu-

tions. Similar results have emerged from the Bristol study, with the additional finding that amount of speech is also important. (Wells, et al. 1981, p. 115)

Several issues may be discussed briefly regarding training. First, examiners must be trained to the level where they command "clinical" interactive strategies appropriate to a variety of individual adult-student conversational contexts. Second, the discourse skills learned in conducting a number of LPM elicitations are quite different from the "known answer" examination sequences observed in classroom teacher discourse. On the other hand, teacher training and sensitivity to individual differences suggest a predisposition towards acquiring these skills readily, after appropriate training. Furthermore, we suspect that this increased sensitivity to context by teachers trained in this method would increase their effectiveness in the classroom. Third, examiners had to be trained to *not* interfere with the students narrative story telling once the student began his or her narrative. (The evaluation of narrative discourse in the LPM was predicated on the student's unaided story, not a narrative that was directly elicited by the examiner at critical points).

Next, the assessment context may be improved when examiners are sensitive to cultural and ethnically distinct styles of communication of the linguistic minority group being assessed. Articulation of alternatives in communication styles and selection of topics among the assessment team members enhances the probability of the cultural appropriateness of the assessment procedures. Listening to tapes and discussing various interpretations of the interactional situation and discourse elicited from students as a group is an important part of training examiners. It is also important for examiners to recognize that a student's use of loan words from his or her other language (when it reflects usage in the speech community) and/or codeswitching, that is, changing languages at the phrase or clause level, may be a sign of bilingual proficiency rather than a sign of incomplete mastery of the language of the elicitation (Penalosa, 1981; Valdes, 1981; Poplack, 1981).

Finally, in training people to score the LPM, a degree of interrater reliability must be obtained among those doing the scoring. Training for standardization of scoring methods occurred in small groups where agreement was sought on recording the occurrance and frequency of each of the descriptors for the LPM. Experience in listening to and scoring multiple tapes for students at various stages of language proficiency and for different age groups is necessary. It is also important that a sample of tapes be double-scored for quality control of the assessment procedure, reliability of scoring, and the accuracy of the resulting overall language proficiency rating. In a validation study, Powers (1985) obtained a relatively high degree of interrater reliability for the English discourse portion of the LPM for kindergarten discourse (kappa = .65) and grade two discourse (kappa = .88).

Advantages, Disadvantages, and Remaining Questions

In summary, the advantage of a sociolinguistic approach to language proficiency assessment is that it measures language in the contexts in which it is used, and gives recognition to the cultural, social status, and role dimensions of communicative behavior. As mentioned by Grosjean, (1982) "many a member of a linguistic minority has a tale of mistreatment and hostility." (p. 65) By using the students' home language first in the assessment process, the school symbolically, and in fact, supported the use of the minority language. The oral language interview is an approach that can be used with students at various stages of language acquisition and attempts to provide a setting in which linguistic minority students can display optimal performance. Skills learned by teachers regarding the elicitation and analysis of discourse are potentially relevant to teacher interaction with students in other contexts such as during classroom discussions.

In determining and evaluating the degree to which a person can speak and understand English and any other language it is important to recognize the influence of the broader society upon second language learners. People who do not speak the "official" language of a country may be unwilling to demonstrate the full range of proficiency in either the "home" language or English under certain conditions. It is important to note that for the Hispanic population in the United States the "home" language and/or the language of preference may be either Spanish or English, or a true bilingualism where the speaker choses the language that best fits a particular situation. Grosjean (1982) cites rough estimates that of the 11 million Spanish speakers in the United States in 1976, 49 percent say English is their usual everyday household language and 46 percent say Spanish is their usual everyday language (p. 52).

Just as different countries have different official policies regarding bilingualism (Grosjean, 1982), school districts also vary regarding their recognition and support of bilingualism and bilingual education. These attitudes and differences in values may be reflected in the kind of assessment procedures used for placement into educational programs. We found that in order to be able to adequately evaluate the English language of a linguistic minority student, when the English language sample was judged below the level of a fully proficient student, it was extremely useful to be able to listen to the student interact in his or her home language. Hispanic bilingual resource teachers emphasized the importance of reassuring the student that speaking Spanish was both encouraged and fully acceptable in a school context. The LPM was administered first in Spanish, usually by a person from an ethnic background similar to that of the student. The development of the LPM was aided by translations of Spanish discourse into English (when needed by those of us who were neither Hispanic nor bilingual) and group consensus among researchers and bilingual resource teachers regarding the specific details of applying the discourse proficiency criteria to Spanish discourse. An essential feature of the development process was collaboration with bilingually proficient teachers who were able to articulate age-grade expectations regarding student proficiency in the home language, and who were intimately familiar with expectations of children's spoken Spanish in the community.

First language assessment was crucial in interpreting results when a second language student was rated as less than fully proficient in English. Sometimes the English language sample suggested that the student had a speech problem such as stuttering, or a learning disability stemming from difficulties in processing complex relations—yet the same student would be fully proficient during the Spanish part of the LPM. Assessment in both languages provided a more valid opportunity for school people to distinguish between the second language learning needs and other program needs of linguistic minority students so that fewer minority students would be misdiagnosed and placed in the wrong educational program.

Disadvantages of the approach are that much research remains to be done because it is a new type of measurement; examiners and discourse analysts must be thoroughly trained to a level of "clinical" skills; methods of scoring and providing feedback to classroom teachers need to be established and the method is more time consuming and expensive to use than other testing approaches.

The development and validation of direct measures of speaking and listening may require more time, money, and analytical-research expertise than many school districts are willing to expend. As mentioned previously, there are similarities between the LPM and the Foreign Service Institute's Oral Language Interview Test. Both are labor intensive procedures requiring a high level of examiner and scoring skills. As Clark (1975) said, "An obvious concern is the need to involve expensive humans in both the test administration and scoring process. . . . there appears to be no alternatve to such an approach—" (p. 15). School districts, of course, have much smaller budgets for research and development than the state department—yet the persons whose language is being evaluated, young linguistic minority children, are much more complex research subjects (because of the confounding of language and social development with second language acquisition) than are adult subjects.

We have not discussed in any detail how this approach could be used in practice in making decisions about placement into bilingual program and for developing instructional programs for linguistic minority students. We feel that conceptualizing language proficiency under the broader construct of communicative competency holds promise in the development of more successful programs. We plan to include recommendations about this in future work, some of which, however, require verification through ethnographic observations outside of the assessment context. Briefly, we feel that overall, the language assessment procedures undertaken by the school district and the research team, involving relatively large numbers of teachers, researchers, and teacher-researcher collaborators in the development of more appropriate language proficiency measures is valuable in developing greater awareness about what is involved in being communicatively competent, and also about *contexts* that promote or retard the linguistic minority child's language development. In traditional approaches to language proficiency assessment contextual variables are hidden from view and consequently ignored. Therefore an extremely important variable influencing language performance, that of context, is ignored not only in judgments of language proficiency but also in educational programs designed to meet the needs of linguistic minority students. An important aspect of a sociolinguistic discourse approach to language proficiency assessment is its insistence on paying attention to context. We have found in our work with teachers and nonspecialists that there is little awareness of sociolinguistics and discourse analysis in the field of education. We feel this approach is a potentially valuable and, as yet, untapped source of knowledge for teacher training and development. Further, we feel that future research will indicate a clear relationship between the development of more autonomous oral proficiencies and literacy, a relationship that has recently been seen in the work of King and Rentel (1981) and Sulzby (1981).

Notes

Note 1. This chapter is based upon "Methods of Analyzing Samples of Elicited Discourse in English and Spanish for Determining Student Language Proficiency," H.B. Slaughter and A.T. Bennett, final report to InterAmerican Research Associates and the National Institute of Education, NIE Grant No. 400-79-0042, Assessing the Language Proficiency of Bilingual Persons, 1982. No endorsement of this report by either agency or the Tucson Unified School District where the research was carried out is implied.

Acknowledgments are gratefully given to Adrian Bennett who initially developed the framework for discourse analysis upon which subsequent work was based; to our bilingually proficient linguistics analysts, Olivia Arietta and Otto Santa Ana; and to our bilingual research assistants, Betty Garcia and Margaret Boyce. For so large a project it is not possible to name everyone in the Tucson Unified School District who contributed to the Language Proficiency Measure (LPM). However, special appreciation is given to Christopher Crowder, Assistant Director for Testing, who was in charge of instrument development; Estanislado Paz, Director of Bilingual Education; Maria A. Ortiz, Acting Coordinator for the Lau Project; and Caroline Tompkins, who developed procedures for implementing the various LPM pilot studies. Appreciation is also given to consultants Susan Philips and Ricardo Duran.

Note 2. Excerpts from the Language Proficiency Measure Discourse Evaluation Handbook and from the LPM Manual for Discourse Analysis to use in Documentary Behaviors for the Communicative Competency Inventory, a preliminary and more comprehensive earlier version of later manuals, are reprinted by permission of the authors, Slaughter et al. and the Tucson Unified School District, (c) 1982, 1983.

References

Akinnaso, F.N. (1981). The consequences of literacy in pragmatic and theoretical perspectives. *Anthropology and Education Quarterly, 12* (3), 163-200.

Bates, E. & MacWhinney, B. (1979). A functionalist approach to the acquisition of Grammar. In E. Ochs & B.B. Schieffelin's *Developmental Pragmatics.* New York: Academic Press.

Bennett, A.T. (1980). Rhythmic Analysis of Multiple Levels of Communicative Behavior in Face-To-Face Interaction. In W. Von Raffler-Engel, (Ed.), *Aspects of Nonverbal Communication.* Lippe, Germany: Puetz and Zeitlinger, B.V.

Bennett, A.T. (1983). Discourse of power, the dialectics of understanding, the power of literacy. *Journal of Education, 165*(1), 53-74.

Bennett, A., & Slaughter, H. (1983). A sociolinguistic/discourse approach to the description of the communicative competence of linguistic minority children. In C. Rivera (Ed.), *An ethnographic/sociolinguistic approach to language proficiency assessment.* Clevedon, Avon, England: Multilingual Matters LTD,.

Bernstein, B. (1970). A sociolinguistic approach to socialization: With some reference to educability. In F. Williams, (Ed.) *Language and poverty: Perspectives on a Theme.* Chicago: Marksham Publishing Company.

Black, K. (1979, May). There's More to Language Than Meets the Ear: Implications for Evaluation. *Language Arts. 56,* (5), 526-533.

Bowerman, M. (1979). The acquisition of complex sentences. In P. Fletcher & M. Garman (EDS)., *Language acquisition: Studies in first Language Development.* New York: Cambridge University Press.

Cazden, C.B. (1986). Classroom discourse. In M.C. Wittrock (Ed.), *Handbook of research on teaching* (3rd Ed.). (pp. 1-126). New York: Macmillan.

Clark, L.D. (1975). Theoretical and technical considerations in oral proficiency testing. In R.L. Jones and B. Spolsky (Eds.), *Testing Language Proficiency* (pp. 10-28). Arlington, Virginia: Center for Applied Linguistics.

Cole, M. & Means, B. (1981). *Comparative Studies of How People Think, An Introduction.* Cambridge, Ma.: Harvard University Press.

Cook-Gumperz, J. (1975). The child as practical reasoner. In B. Blount and M. Sanchez (Eds.), *Sociocultural Dimensions of Language Use.* New York: Academic Press.

Cook-Gumprez, J. (1977). Situated instructions: Language Socialization of School Age Children. In C. Mitchell-Kernan & S. Ervin-Tripp, Eds., *Child Discourse.* New York: Academic Press.

Crystal, D. (1979). Prosodic development. In P. Fletcher and M. Garman (Eds.) *Language acquisition: Studies in first language development.* New York: Cambridge University Press.

DeAvila, E.A., & Duncan, S.E. (1981). *Language assessment scales: Spanish/English Level 1, Form A.* San Rafael, CA: Linguametrics.

DeStefano, J.S., Pepinsky, H.B. & Sanders, T.S. (1982). Discourse rules for literacy learning in a classroom. In L.C. Wilkinson (Ed.), *Communicating in the Classroom.* New York: Academic Press.

Donaldson, M. (1978). *Children's minds.* Glasgow, Great Britain: William Collins Sons and Co. Ltd.

Dore, J. (1979). Conversation and preschool language development. In Paul Fletcher and Michael Garman's (Eds.), *Language Acquisition.* New York: Cambridge University Press.

Duran, R. (Ed.). (1981). *Latino Language and Communicative Behavior, Vol. V in Advances in Discourse Processes.* Norwood, N.J.: Ablex.

Erickson, F., & Schultz, J. (1981). When is a Context? Some Issues and Methods in the Analysis of Social Competence. In J. Green & C. Wallat (Eds.), *Ethnography & Language in Educational Settings.* Norwood, N.J.: Ablex.

Erickson, F., & Mohatt, G. (1982). Cultural organization of participation structures in two classrooms of Indian students. In G. Spindler (Ed.) *Doing the Ethnography of Schooling.* New York: Holt, Rinehart and Winston.

Ervin-Tripp, S. (1973). *Language Acquisition and Communicative Choice.* Selected and introduced by Anwar S. Dil, Stanford, Ca: Stanford University Press.

Ervin-Tripp, S. & Mitchell-Kerman, C. (1977). *Child Discourse,* New York: Academic Press.

Ervin-Tripp, S. (1979). Children's verbal turntaking. In E. Ochs and B.B. Schieffelin (Eds.), *Developmental Pragmatics.* New York: Academic Press.

Fillmore, C.J. (1979). On Fluency. In C.J. Fillmore, W. S-Y Wang, & D. Kemper (Eds). *Individual differences in language ability and language behavior.* New York: Academic Press.

Genishi, C. (1982). Codeswitching in chicano six-year-olds. In R.P. Duran (Ed.) *Latino Language and Communicative Behavior, Vol. V in Advances in Discourse Processes.* Norwood, N.J.: Ablex.

Green, J.L., & Smith, D. (1983). Teaching and Learning: A Linguistic Perspective. *The Elementary School Journal, 83* (4), 353–391.

Grosjean, F. (1982). *Life With Two Languages: An Introduction to Bilingualism.* Cambridge, Mass.: Harvard University Press.

Gumperz, J. (1981). Conversational Inference and Classroom Learning. In J. Green and C. Wallat, eds., *Ethnography and Language in Educational Settings.* Norwood, New Jersey; Ablex.

Gumperz, J.J. (1975). Sociocultural Knowledge in conversational inference. In M. Saville-Troike, ed., *Twenty-eighth Annual Round Table-Monograph Series on Language and Linguistics.* Washington, D.C.: Georgetown University Press.

Gumperz, J. and Cook-Gumperz, J. (1976). Context in children's speech. In J.

Cook-Gumperz, eds., *Papers on Language and Context*. Working Paper number 46. Language Behavior Research: Laboratory, University of California, Berkeley, Ca., 94720.

Gumperz, J.J. and Hymes D., Eds., (1972). *Directions in Sociolinguistics*. New York: Holt, Rinehart & Winston.

Hymes, D. (1972). Models of the interaction of language and social life. In J.J. Gumperz & D. Hymes (Eds.), *Directions in Sociolinguistics: The Ethnography of Communication*. New York: Holt, Rinehart & Winston.

Hymes, D., (1980). *Language in Education*. Washington, D.C.: Center for Applied Linguistics.

Hymes, D.H. (1982). Ethnolinguistic Study of Classroom Discourse. Final Report to the National Institute of Education, April. (ED 217 710).

Karmiloff-Smith, A. (1979). Language development after five. In P. Fletcher & M. Garman (Eds.), *Language acquisition: Studies in first language development*. New York: Cambridge University Press.

Keating, Daniel P. (1983). The emperor's new clothes: the "new look" in intelligence research. In R.J. Sternberg (Ed.), *Advances in the psychology of human intelligence,* (Vol. 2). Hillsdale, N.J.: Lawrence Erlbaum Assoc.

King, L. and Rentel V.M. (1981). How Children Learn to Write: A Longitudinal Study. Final Report to NIE-G-79-0137 and NIE-G-79-0039 Columbus, Ohio: The Ohio State University Research Foundation.

Labov, W. (1972). *Language in the Inner City*. Philadelphia: University of Pennsylvania Press.

Labov, W. and Waletsky, J. (1967). Narrative analysis. In J. Helm (Ed.) *Essays on the Verbal and Visual Arts*. Seattle, University of Washington.

Lipset, D. (1980). *Gregory Bateson: The Legacy of a Scientist*. Englewood Cliffs, N.J.: Prentice-Hall, Inc.

Loban, W. (1976). Language development: Kindergarten through grade twelve. No. 18 in a series of research reports sponsored by the NCTE Committee on Research. Urbana, Illinois: National Council of Teachers of English.

Mace-Matluck, J., Hoover, A., and Dominguez, D. (1981, April). Variation in Language Use of Spanish-English Bilingual Children in Three Settings (Classroom, Home, Playground): Findings and Implications. Paper presented at the Annual Meeting of the American Educational Research Association, Los Angeles, Calif.

Maratsos, P. (1979). Learning How and When to Use Pronouns and Determiners. In Paul Fletcher and Michael Garman's (Eds.) *Language Acquisition,* New York: Cambridge University Press.

Mayer, M. (1974). *Frog goes to Dinner*. New York: The Dial Press.

Mayer, M., & Mayer M., (1975). *One Frog Too Many*. New York: The Dial Press.

Mehan, H. (1979). *Learning Lessons: Social Organization in the Classroom*. Cambridge, Mass.: Harvard University Press.

Messick, S. (1981, Nov.). Evidence and Ethics in the Evaluation of Tests. *Educational Researcher* 10:9. pp. 9–20.

Michaels, S. & Cazden, C.B. (1986). Teacher/Child Collaboration as Oral Preparation for Literacy. In B.B. Schieffelin (Ed.), *Acquisition of Literacy: Ethnographic Perspectives*. Norwood, N.J.: Ablex.

National Institute of Education. (1981). Report of the National Institute of Education on the testing and assessment implications of the Title VI Language minority proposed rules. Washington, D.C., U.S. Department of Education.

Nevo, D. & Shohamy, E. (1984, April). Applying the joint committee's evaluation standards for the assessment of alternative testing methods. Paper presented at the annual meeting of the American Educational Research Association, New Orleans, Louisiana.

Northwest Regional Educational Laboratory. (1980). Assessing Speaking and Listening Skills. *CAPTRENDS: Clearinghouse for Applied Performance Testing. 6*(2), November.

Ochs, E. and Schiefflin, B.B. (1979). *Developmental pragmatics.* New York: Academic Press.

Parishi, D. and Giannelli, W. (1974). *Language and Social Environment at Two Years.* CNR, Institute of Psychology, Rome.

Penalosa, F. (1981). Some Issues in Chicano Sociolinguistics. In Richard Duran (Ed.) *Latino Language and Communicative Behavior,* Vol. V in Advances in Discourse Processes. Norwood, N.J.: Ablex.

Peterson, P.L., Wilkinson, C., Spinelli, F., & Swing, S.R. (1983). Merging the process-product and the sociolinguistic paradigms: Research on small-group processes. In Peterson, P.L., Wilkinson, C., & Hallinan, M.T. (Eds). *Instructional groups in the classroom: Organization and processes.* New York: Academic Press.

Poplack, S., (1981). Syntactic Structure and Social Function of Codeswitching. In Richard Duran (Ed.) *Latino Language and Communicative Behavior, Vol. V in Advances in Discourse Processes.* Norwood, N.J. Ablex.

Powers, S. (Ed.). (1985). *Language Proficiency Measure: Technical Manual.* Unpublished manuscript, Tucson Unified School District, Bilingual Education Department, Tucson.

Powers, S., Johnson, D.M., Slaughter, H.B., Crowder, C. & Jones, P.B. (1985). Reliability and Validity of the Language Proficiency Measure. *Educational and Psychological Measurement, 45.*

Rosansky, E. (1981, March) Future perspectives on research in oral language proficiency assessment. Paper presented at the Language Proficiency Assessment Symposium Program, Warrenton, Virginia.

Slaughter, H.B. & Bennett, A.T. (1982, March). A sociolinguistic-discourse alternative for language proficiency assessment. Paper presented at the annual meeting of the American Educational Research Association, Washington, D.C. (ERIC Document Reproduction Service No. ED 222 500)

Slaughter, H.B., Bennett, A.T., Arrieta, O., Santa Ana-A, O., Garcia, B., & Prather, M.B. (1982). Methods of analyzing samples of elicited discourse in English and Spanish for determining student language proficiency. (NIE Grant No. 400-79-0042). Final Report to InterAmerica Research Associates and the National Institute of Education, U.S. Department of Education.

Slaughter, H., Crowder, C., Campuzano, C., Dickelman, N., Garcia, B., Ortega, M., Ortega, M., Ortiz, A., Reyes, F., Sanchez, O., & Tompkins, C. (1982). LPM Manual for Discourse Analysts to Use in Documenting Behaviors for the Communicative Competency Inventory—Preliminary Version. Tucson, AZ: Tucson Unified School District.

Slaughter, H., Crowder, C., Campuzano, C., Dickelman, N., Garcia, B., Ortega, M., Ortiz, A., Reyes, F., Sanchez, O., & Tompkins, C. (1983). Language Proficiency Measure Discourse Evaluation Handbook. Tucson, AZ: Tucson Unified School District.

Snow, C.E. (1979). Conversations with Children. In P. Fletcher & M. Garman (Eds.), *Language Acquistion.* New York: Cambridge University Press.

Stubbs, M. (1980). *Language and Literacy: the sociolinguistics of reading and writing.* Boston: Routledge and Kegan Paul.

Sulzby, E. (1981, August). Kindergarteners Begin to Read Their Own Compositions: Beginning Reader's Developing Knowledges About Written Language Project. Final Report to the Research Foundation of the National Council of Teachers of English.

Valdes, G. (1981). Codeswitching As Deliberate Verbal Strategy: A Microanalysis of Direct and Indirect Requests Among Bilingual Chicano Speakers. In Richard Duran's (Ed.) *Latino Language and Communicative Behavior,* Vol. V in Advances in Discourse Processes. Norwood, N.J.: Ablex.

Wald, B. (1981). Topic and situation as factors in language performance. In *Working Papers,* National Center for Bilingual Research, Los Alamitos, CA

Wallat, C. & Green J.L. (1980). Social Rules and Communicative Contexts in Kindergarten. *Theory Into Practice, 18* (4), 1980.

Wells, G., Bridges, A., French, P., MacLure, M., Sinha, C. Walkerdine, V., and Woll, B. (1981). *Learning through interaction: The study of language development.* Cambridge: Cambridge University Press.

Wiig, E.H. & Semel, E.M. (1980). *Language Assessment and Intervention for the Learning Disabled.* Sydney: Charles E. Merrill Publishing Co.

Wilds, C.D. (1975). The oral interview test. In R.L. Jones and B. Spolsky (Eds.) *Testing Language Proficiency.* Arlington, Vir.: Center for applies Linguistics.

Appendix A

Analysis of Elicited Student Discourse:
Documentation of Judgments of Language Proficiency

Directions for coding audiotaped data* as a prerequisite to analyzing student discourse:

Part I. *Analysis of Interactive Discourse About Global Topics Discussed by Student and Adult Examiner*

In this section the coder uses a series of slashes or tallies, e.g.,////, to indicate the frequency of occurence of student discourse. Slash marks are placed under Column One for student utterances *below* the level of a clause, such as one-word or phrase eliptical responses to examiner questions. The clause can be conceptualized as an oral language sentence. However, unlike the terms sentence or utterance, the term clause can be precisely defined. A clause is an expression of a single predicate with its accompanying complement of nouns or noun phrases.

Coders mark tallies in Column Two for single clauses, not connected by "and, because," and so on. Column Three is used to record all clauses interrelated serially by *and, and then, because,* and so on, or more complexly using *if-then, while,* etc. Coders should refer to the indicators in Part III for recording the types of connectors used.

Each topic discussed should be named in abbreviated form, (e.g., if the examiner asks "do you ride home on the school bus," coders list bus, E) with an E indicating that the Examiner initiated the topic and an S indicating the Student initiated the topic.

Interactional variables are to be noted if the coder recognizes that a negotiation of topic or conversational context is occurring between adult examiner and student. Brief notes may be written in to help the coder in checking the indicators in Part III or in writing a brief narrative about the student's response to the assessment situation, and/or examiner characteristics influencing the discourse which should be considered in judgments of language proficiency. Questions to be used for developing a profile or final analysis of the student's language proficiency found in Part III should be considered in coding the Interactional Discourse (ID) Column in Part I.

Coders should also note the clarity of student's use of reference. Does the student provide enough background information so that a listener who does not share the same context as the speaker can understand what is being said? Are the objects referred to by pronouns specified? After coding the topic by turn sheet, mark the most representative item under the category, Contextualization.

---

* For direct coding without a transcription Winter 1981 Helen Slaughter, copyright.

Part II. *Analysis of Student's Rendition of Wordless Book*

This section provides a procedure for listening to the child's handling of the wordless book situation. Some students complete this task independently, telling a coherent narrative that can be understood without seeing the book itself. Others wait upon direct examiner promptings before saying anything about the story. Even then, they may respond only in one-word answers or if using clauses, for example, oral language sentences, they may simply describe the objects in the picture but never develop a plotline that relates one event to another.

For Items One and Two, the coder should note, by slash marks and written comments if necessary, (1) examiner backchannel feedback such as *umhum* after the student finishes the page (because this seems to encourage the child to go on) and (2) examiner questions such as "what's happening now" and other probes. The coder should also note, if the examiner waits for the child to respond or goes on, and if the examiner allows the child time to develop the narrative independently, for example, using *umhum* as a nonverbal way of indicating the child is proceeding correctly, or continually uses examiner questions to elicit the narrative.

Regarding documentation of student discourse, Items One-Five, coders should indicate with slash marks (///) the frequency of one-word, phrase level elipsis, single clauses and interrelated clauses as described in Part I. In Item Four the frequency of indirect dialogue, e.g., he told the man to give him back his frog, or quotative speech, e.g., "he said, 'Give me back my frog!'" should be noted.

Item Five refers to conversational code switching involving mainly loan words, or a word from the child's other language, but not a complete switch into talking in the other language. Item Five B refers to switching entirely into another language. An example of this is if after the examiner finishes the English discussion of global topics and asks the student to tell the story, the student begins the story in Spanish.

Coders should also mark Item A-C referring to macro-level variables regarding the student's narrative or storytelling proficiency. In Item A, the coder marks a judgment regarding the degree to which the student independently produced a coherent narrative with a plotline. The coder selects the response which is most representative of the student's use of narrative form. For example, if a child used two simple clauses but otherwise only labeled the objects in the picture, choice five would be appropriate. Item B, *Narrative Style,* will only apply if the child was checked off on Items One-Three or possibly Item Four in Item A. The styles are defined on the Procedure for Coding sheet. Also taped examples of styles will be used in training coders. Item C, *Reference,* indicates whether the child defined pronouns specifically so that it was clear just who or what was being referred to without visual observation to see the picture being referred to. Deitic reference refers to pointing words, for example, here, there, this, that, which utilize context sensitive tools. It may be produced independently by the child or it may be produced by examiner deitic elicitation. In that case it is not an indication of lack of ability if more complex reference is not observed.

Note: Analysts should comment on the prosody of the child's language on either section of the assessment if this dimension enters into the determination of language proficiency. Prosody refers to modulations of the speech stream in terms of pitch, rhythm, tempo, and loudness.

PART I

Tape _____
Lang _____
Coder _____

Procedure for Coding: Analysis of Interactive Discourse About Global Topics Between Student and Examiner

TOPIC Write in, note E for Examiner, S for Student Initiation	STUDENT TURNS*			INTERACTIONAL VARIABLES** (ID)
	Word/phrase eliptical responses (1)	Snapshot/ single clause (2)	Inter- related clauses (3)	

* Use one line or more for each topic. Slash or tally marks indicate number and types of clausal level units used by student. This is a topic by clausal type analysis upon which reliability checks can be made.

** Check if a *negotiation* is occurring between examiner and student beyond the two step elicitation/response that should be noted in the final analysis.

NOTE: If additional sheets are needed, use lined paper indicating, T, 1, 2, 3, and ID for headings.

Procedure for Coding: Interactive Discourse

**Student's Provision of Background Information and
Use of Reference in Interactive Discourse**

A. *Contextualization:* Mark the most representative:

_____ 1. High decontextualized; background information provided to listener including defining pronouns specifically so the reference is clear.

_____ 2. Mixture of decontextualized/context embedded discourse appropriate to conversation.

_____ 3. Speaker does not provide adequate background information; pronoun reference unspecified.

PART II

Tape _____
Lang _____   **Procedure for Coding: Analysis of Student's**
Coder _____   **Rendition of Wordless Book**

Directions: Use slash or tally marks to indicate frequency of occurrence; write in or circle connectors, add comments.

Examiner (Do this only if student language is scanty, e.g., few instances of 2-4 below.)

1. Backchannel feedback (i.e., umhum) _____

2. Prompting with questions: _____

Student (Do this first, return to Examiner indicators if language is scanty.)

1. One-word phrase elipsis: _____

2. Snapshots/single clause: _____

3. Interclausal relations
   a. "and," "and then," "because," etc.: _____

   b. Juggling (while, if-then, etc.): _____

4. Indirect dialogue or quotative speech: _____

5. Code switching
   a. Within clause (use of loan words): _____

   _____

   b. Between clauses (topical, etc.): _____

   _____

Overview of Student's Narrative:

A. Use of Cohesive Narrative Form: Check the most representative

___ 1. Plotline from beginning to end
___ 2. After beginning launches into narrative styles to end
___ 3. Segments of narrative only
___ 4. Page-by-page picture description
___ 5. Responds with elipsis after prompting
___ 0. No judgment possible

B. *Style:* Check all that apply

___ 1. Eyewitness style (an oral, present tense style)
___ 2. Reading style (a nonfiction, past tense style)
___ 3. Oral reading style (litera-ture). A literacy style, using dialogue, may name characters, has oral reading prosody.

Procedure for Coding:
Analysis of Student's Rendition of Wordless Book

Overview of Student's Narrative:

C. Reference
   ___ 1. Infrequent or no deitic reference used, minimal use of book as a tool
   ___ 2. General mixing of deitic and nondeitic reference
   ___ 3. Maximal use of deitic reference, i.e., pointing words that utilize the book as a prop. Little context independent reference
   ___ 4. Note here if the examiner used any deitic elicitation

D. Perspective
   ___ 1. Indentifies motives or conditions
   ___ 2. Describes character's feelings

PART III

Overall or Final Analysis/Interpretation

Narrative Profile of Student Language Proficiency

After listening to the entire elicitation in one language, both the Interactive Discourse of Global Topics and the Student Rendition of the Wordless Book, the analyst writes a short narrative statement about the child's performance on each task leading to describing the student's proficiency. Select relevant topics from the following series of questions in writing this short analysis (adding additional concerns or topics as they arise in the data):

1. Is there mutual development of topics between examiner and student? _____ Yes _____ No

2. Does the child build on topics suggested by the examiner or simply give eliptical and/or one-word responses? _____ Yes _____ No

3. Did the student initiate and develop new topics during the discourse? How did this happen? _____ Yes _____ No

4. Did the student attempt to change the topic during the discourse? How was this negotiated? _____ Yes _____ No

5. Is there evidence of misunderstanding between examiner and student? _____ Yes _____ No

6. What happens when the examiner encourages the child to further extend his/her responses to the topics after the initial responses? _____ Yes _____ No

7. When the child goes beyond the "necessary" response, how does s/he develop topics? _____ Yes _____ No

8. Are there chunks of discourse indicating that the child is developing a strategy or proficiency? _____ Yes _____ No

9. Did the student provide adequate background information and use reference appropriately so that the examiner and coder could comprehend the meaning of what was being talked about? _____ Yes _____ No

Appendix B

Proficiency Levels: DEFINITIONS

PROFICIENT (P): A proficient student is one whose speaking and listening proficiency is equivalent to that of a native speaking monolingual or bilingual student of his/her age. Proficient students can interact and elaborate on a variety of topics. The term "native speaker" includes varieties of, and/or regional dialectal differences in, the language acceptable in the home and school speech community for this age student.

MODERATE (M): A moderate student is one whose speaking and listening proficiency is equivalent to that of a native speakling monolingual or bilingual student in nonacademic or informal situations. This student uses less elaborated discourse and fewer strategies for clarification than the proficient student. If a student is proficient in the home or native language and moderate in the second language, assessment of cognitive functioning or other language involved skills may not be considered complete and/or completely valid if carried out only in the less proficient language.

FUNCTIONAL (F): A functionally proficient student is one whose speaking and listening proficiency are equivalent to that of someone who is acquiring but has not yet achieved proficiency in a second language. This student usually comprehends the broad nature of spoken requests, but may miss nuances or complexity. His/her speech may be characterized by hesitations, brief responses, elaborate responses that are difficult to comprehend, and little variation (or irregular variation) in use of verb tenses and sentence structures.

LIMITED (L): This student cannot carry on a genuine conversation in the language, although she/he may be able to respond with words and phrases or formulaic expressions ("How are you?" "Fine, Thank you.") These students do not initiate conversation in the limited language.

NONE (N): The student neither indicates understanding nor gives any response in the language being assessed.

X: Is used to indicate that no assessment is available in the student's "other" language.

Appendix C

LPM Manual for Discourse Analysts to Use in Documenting Behaviors for the Communicative Competency Inventory (Slaughter et al, 1982)

I. *The Examiner's Performance Variables*—Interpretation of Item 1, Examination Context of LPM

In judging proficiency, it is necessary first to determine the context in which the student's language is assessed. Research on the LPM (Slaughter, Bennett, and others, 1982) and on children's language acquisition (Snow, 1982; Wells et al., 1981), has shown that adult responses to children's language have a determinant effect upon the quality of the language produced by children. A context in which (1) the adult establishes a relaxed, unhurried, and informal conversational tone with children; (2) the adult asks open ended questions of children and builds on the child's responses by adding to topics talked about; and (3) the adult topic shifts or changes are infrequent and transitions from one topic to another are not abrupt, tends to be the most favorable context for demonstrating language proficiency.

1. By which method did the examiner elicit conversation from the student generally? (Examiner's Performance Item 1)

    _____ conversational approach
    _____ interview
    _____ examination

Definition. The method used by the examiner to elicit conversational discourse will depend partly upon the student's responses to various probes. If the student does not respond, or responds only minimally to the opening elicitations, this will have an effect since a conversation is by definition a two-way interaction. However, an adequate elicitation procedure will minimally be that of the interview and preferably that of the conversation. An examination context is not appropriate to the LPM.

An *examination context* is one where (1) the examiner asks the student a series of questions for which specific answers are required, (2) the examiner's tone of voice and repeated follow up responses in an evaluative mode to the child such as "that's good," "OK," 'good," etc., suggest to the student that this is a test-like situation and that his responses are being evaluated, (3) the examiner rarely builds on the child's responses except to ask further limited response questions or give evaluations, (4) the examiner changes topics frequently and often abruptly, (5) the examiner does not attempt to be an equal and facilitating conversational partner with the child (e.g. s/he does *not* give the student time to respond, does *not* provide vocabulary elicited by the child, does *not* honor the student's attempt to change or initiate topics), (6) the examiner does *not* attempt to provide background information for the student to establish a basis for topics of conversation, and (7) the examiner gives negative evaluations to what the child says.

Examples

Example A—Examination Context: Examiner Changes Topic

E: What have you been doing today?

C: Nothing

Negative   E: Nothing? What do you mean nothing? What do
Evaluation   you do when you get home in the evening?

C: Working.

E: Working? Can you tell me what you were working on?

C: Spelling.

E: Did you get a hundred?

C: Yeah.

E Topic   E: What do you like to do during your recess? When you
Change   have your break?

C: Play jump rope.

Not building   E: What else?
on Child's
response   C: Ah, swing in the bar and a a (   )*
E Topic   E: What do you like to do after school?
Change

---

* Note: the symbol of an empty bracket (   ) indicates audiotaped speech that was inaudible to the transcriber (but which may have been understandable to the examiner).

Example B—Examination Context: Examiner narrows student's response options

E: Ahh/Can you tell me how.. some. a little. something about baseball//

C: Well//.they get to hit the ball/catch the ball//

E: Mhm

C: ....(use the   )/ (7 secs.) put something like a (bat th-).. on you

E: Mhm

C: And and....and you run to the bases/
     (   )/

E: Which base do you run to//

C: First//

E: And then//

C: Second//

E: And then//

C: Third//

E: And then//

C: Home//

E: And what happens if you run to all the bases at one time//..

C: Homerun//

An *interview context* (to be encouraged) is one where the examiner asks the child open-ended questions and gives the child ample time to respond. If at first the student does not respond, the examiner attempts further probes on the topic before trying out a new topic. Follow-up to the child's responses are on the topic and related to what had already been said, or asks the student to expand on the information given. The examiners themselves do not provide much new information in an interview context and are not conversational participants in the mutual exchange of information. The Interview context usually occurs where (1) the child can respond at length to open-ended questions or (2) the child's responses are very minimal.

Example of an Interview Context:

E: What kind of games would you like to play?
C: Valentine games
E: Like what?
C: eh Just some games that I know that you can play with hearts, and the the words on the hearts and you make two lines and they have to run up and get the heart and they have to do what it says.
E: Like what? What would the heart say?
C: Like um if it says heart you have to run up and get the heart and if it says hop you have to hop back.
E: Oh what else would you play?
C: . . nothing

A *conversational context* (to be encouraged) is one where several or all of the following occurs: (1) the examiner builds on the student's utterances, (2) the examiner indicates a personal interest in what the child is saying, (3) a "give and take" context where both interactants provide information, initiate topics, etc., (4) the examiner attempts to establish topics of conversation that the student will be comfortable talking about (e.g. where the child may know more than the examiner about the topic), and (5) the examiner follows the student's lead when the student initiates new topics.

Examples of Conversational Context:

Example A: Grade 1
E: Do you like movies?
C: The nasty ones
E: The nasty ones
C: umhum
E: Oh that's good, what kind do you like?
C: One time
    I went to the movies and we saw Jaws
E: You saw Jaws, did you like Jaws? What happened to Jaws? I never saw that.
C: He he he's a big shark and and he jumps like that and eat people.
E: Eats people umm. Did it scare you sometimes? What did you do?
C: When he jumped ( ) cause it scared me, cause it's scary.

Example B: Conversational context developing out of informal talk about ice cream, Grade 5

C: Está cerquita de Caborca. Y es que Caborca, es sí está grandecito. No es no es como Tucsón pero es más chiquito y pue p m. Me mhm qusta ir a esta tienda que se llama la PH. Y allí vive mi tía. Es que mi tío se casó co n una señora esta verano. Y, y vive mhm donde, vive ah x vive cerquita de, una parte donde hacen nieve. A mí me gusta ir much allí a comer nieve.

It is very near Caborca. And its *that* Caborca, is it is a little big. It is not like Tucson but is smaller and wel-m. I mhm like to go to this store called the PH. And my aunt lives there. It's that my uncle got married with a woman this summer. And, mhm and lives where, lives ah x lives near by, a place where they make ice cream. I like to go there very much to eat ice cream.

E: La nieve mexicana es
muy sabrosa   ¿verdad?
                Mexican ice cream is
very delicious,   isn't it true?

C: Y los raspados.
               And the snowcones.

E: Y los raspados también, especialmente durante el verano verdad?
And the snowcones also, especially during the summer, isn't it true?

S: mhm

Directions for marking. This item refers to the general character of the elicitation of conversation from students, that is, to the *best characterization* of the whole stream of interactive discourse which occurred between examiner and student. For example, if the beginning of the elicitation contains a few interview or examination type probes but a conversational context constitutes the main part of the elicitation, check "cooperative conversation."

Appendix D

Excerpt from the *Language Proficiency Measure,* Discourse *Evaluation Handbook.* (Slaughter, H., Crowder, C., Campuzano, C., Dickelman, N., Garcia, B., Ortega, M., Ortiz, A., Reyes, F., Sanchez, O., & Tompkins, C., 1983)

CONVERSATION
1. *Discourse Level*
    1. Student responded with *one or two words*
    2. Student responded with *one or two clauses*
    3. Student *elaborated on one topic,* using 3 clauses or more
    4. Student *elaborated on more than one topic*

    Level 1. Mark this level if the most the student did was produce one or two word responses that were meaningful and "fit into" the preceding question or utterance of the examiner. It is normal for even a very proficient speaker to give one or two word responses to questions requiring specific (closed-ended) responses. If the interviewer only asks such questions, the assessment is invalid.

    Level 2. While many responses may have been one or two words, the student also gave short responses of one or two clauses.

    A *clause* is defined as an expression that contains a subject and a verb, along with accompanying descriptive words.

    Level 3. The student elaborated on one topic, using at least three clauses within a "turn" in the conversation.

    Level 4. The student elaborated on at least 2 topics using at least 3 clauses within a turn in the conversation about each of the topics.

2. *Complex Meaning-Relationships*
    Definition. Complex meaning - relationships involve showing how two events, people, responses, etc., are related. Complex grammar may or may not be evident here.

    Kinds of complex meaning relations include, but are not restricted to the following adult-like examples.
    a. *Causes and effect:*
       My arm brushed the glass and knocked it off the table.
    b. *Event and result:*
       The glass fell off the table, hit the floor, and broke.
    c. *Event and human response* or vice versa:
       The glass broke and Mary got angry at me.

NARRATIVE (WORDLESS BOOK)
3. *Narrative Level*
    1. Labels/names objects in pictures
    2. "Snapshots" (no connectors)
    3. Tells event on each page separately
    4. Partially develops narrative
    5. Develops narrative throughout

Level 1. Labeling or naming objects is the lowest level marked. No clause used, and no description or connection of events is attempted.

Level 2. "Snapshots" are the use of short, simple clauses and/or phrases with no conjunctions used to connect one event to another.

Level 3. The student describes the events page by page, perhaps omitting some pages. Ideas may be connected *within* a page, but connections between one page and the next are not established.

Level 4. A connected narrative is developed in some segments of the story, but there is no coherent narrative from beginning to end. Younger children will sometimes begin a page-by-page manner, and develop a connected narrative in the middle of the book.

Level 5. The student told a narrative that extended from the beginning of the book (with possible exception of the first few pages) to the end.

The quality or richness of the narrative is not important for Level 5, rather it is the connectedness of the narrative which is crucial.

Appendix E

Excerpt from the *Language Proficiency Measure, Discourse Evaluation Handbook.* (Slaughter, H., Crowder, C., Campuzano, C., Dickleman, N., Garcia, B., Ortega, M., Ortiz, A., Reyes, F., Sanchez, O., & Tompkins, C., 1983).

Complex Grammatical Relationships (using subordinate clauses)

Definition. A subordinate clause is defined for our purposes as a dependent adverbial or adjectival clause. Subordination usually makes possible a more coherent organization of related statements than simple, parallel statements connected by *and* or *but*. Adverbial clauses are likely to be more common in the language sample than adjectival clauses. Loban (1976) stated that the use of subordination distinguishes between high and low proficiency at all ages, Grades K-12.

Subordinating conjunctions used to introduce a *adverbial* clauses and make it clear exactly what the relation is between clauses are as follows: *while, where, if, until, because, instead, so that, though, since, before, after,* and *unless. Adjectival* clauses used to modify a noun or pronoun may be introduced by: *who, whose, whom, which, that, when,* and *where.*

Examples of subordinating conjunctions in Spanish include *que, porque, ya que, hasta que,* antes *que,* and others with *que:* also, *si, cuando, donde, mientras,* (que), *aunque,* and others that express a complex or conditional relationship between the clauses of a sentence. (Credit is not given for simple conjunctions such as *y, y luego, ni, o,* etc.)

Directions for Marking. Mark this item "characteristically" if the student uses five (5) or more different subordinating conjunctions. Mark this item "sometimes" if two to four different subordinating conjunctions are used. Mark this item "rarely" if only one subordinating conjunction is used regardless of how often it is used.

Example (Grade 2)—Seven different subordinating conjunctions:
Before (1) we ate the cake, we ate—we had chicken and then we ate eggs.
I didn't eat the ice cream, *because* (2) my grandma never let me eat ice cream.
When (3) I'm in third grade, I'm gonna have the communion.
My grandma said that *after* (4) it fits me, I can save it for my cousin Sandra, *if* (5) she has a baby.
(Shoes) It has diamonds on the front right here, *where* (6) you buckle it.
And then some other kids, they would knock her down, *so* (7) I had to hold her.

Appendix F
Language Proficiency Measure Discourse Evaluation and Summary

Tape # _____

Last name_____ First name_____ Matric # _____

School _____ Grade _____ Date of Assessment _____

Use X to indicate levels reached in Spanish, Cirle for English

| | | | | | | Summary Profile | | Examples: |
| | | | | | | Spanish | English | |

Conversation	1	2	3	4	5		
1. Clause Level	1 or 2 words	1 or 2 clauses	Elaborates one topic	Elab. more than one			
2. Complex meaning Relationships	None	Rarely	Sometimes	Character-istically			
3. Complex Grammar Relationships	None	1 (or 2 isolated)	2 to 4 different	5 or more different			
4. Contextual Information	None	1 topic	Sometimes	Character-istically			
5. Explanation	No			Yes			
5a. Initiates, Shifts, Changes Topic							
Narrative							
6. Narrative Level	Labels	Snap-shots	Pages sep.	Partial nar.	Total nar.		
7. Complex Meaning Relationships	None	Rarely	Sometimes	Character-istically			
8. Complex Grammar Relationships	None	1 (or 2 isolated	2 to 4 different	5 or more different			
9. Verb Tense Variation	None	Once	Sometimes	Character-istically			

(continued)

138

Summary: **Spanish**   **English**

_____/9 for Proficient   (7)   _____/9 for Proficient   (7)

_____/9 for Moderate   (7)   _____/9 for Moderate   (7)

_____/9 for Functional (6)   _____/9 for Functional (6)

If student meets minimum for Moderate rating, yet is Functional in your judgment, in which area(s) does proficiency need to be developed further?

Spanish   Verb tense usage _____   English: Verb tense usage _____

Pronoun usage _____   Pronoun usage _____

Specific vocabulary _____   Specific vocabulary _____

Comments:

	Span.	Eng.
Recept.		
Expres.		

ANSWER SHEET   **LEVEL I**
Language Proficiency Measure   **Grade K-6**

Name _____ Matric _____ Birthdate _____

School _____ Grade _____ Examiner _____

Date of Assessment_____   Tape No. _____

Responded to Spanish Orientation?   Responded to English Orientation?
_____ Yes   _____ No   _____ Yes   _____ No

Part 1. SIGUIENDO Instrucciones   *Part 3. Following Directions*

1. página   _____   1. ear   _____
2. libro/mesa   _____   2. funny face _____
3. lápiz   _____   3. door   _____
4. nariz   _____   4. blink   _____
5. ojos   _____   5. knock   _____
6. luz   _____   6. turn around _____
7. siéntate   _____   7. hand behind _____

Examiner stopped Spanish   Examiner stopped English
portion after Part 1?   portion after Part 3?
_____ Yes   _____ No   _____ Yes   _____ No

Please comment on any aspects of the situation that might have affected the student's language production:

_____

_____

_____

_____

	SPANISH	ENGLISH
RECEPTIVE		
EXPRESSIVE		

Appendix G

Applying the Criteria for Proficiency

The typical performance profiles for functional, moderate, and proficient levels are given for each grade level grouping. Use the following procedure for determining student expressive proficiency in each language:

1. Listen carefully to the taped LPM interview. Note examples for each category to document level attained.
2. For each language, mark the level attained for each of the nine categories. Refer to the manual as necessary.
3. Use the proficiency level key to determine the overall level reached by a student. For each of the nine categories, compare the student's *actual* performance with the levels on the key. On the lines given to the right of the marking area on the student form, enter "P", "M", "F", etc. as appropriate for the level corresponding to the student's actual performance. For example, if a kindergarten student "elaborates on more than one topic" (Category #1: Clause level), enter a *P* on the line to the right of the marking area, since on the rating guide, this level of response falls in the "Proficient" profile.

If a third grade student uses 1 (or 2 isolated) example(s) of complex grammar in the conversation, an *F* is entered on the line for that category since that performance level is part of the "Functional" profile.

This procedure is followed for each of the nine categories. When a level of performance is found in two different columns (P and M, for example), enter the letter for the *higher* proficiency level.

When this has been done for all nine categories in each language, so that a letter representing a proficiency level is entered in each blank:

if *7* or *more* are P, the student receives an expressive proficiency rating of *P* for that language

if fewer than 7 are P, and *more* than 7 are M or P, the student receives a rating of M. (the exception to this is when the evaluator believes that the student is actually *Functional,* and needs further development in verb tense usage, pronoun usage, or specific vocabulary in order to be considered "M")

if fewer than 7 categories are P or M, *and* 6 or more are F, the student receives an overall expressive rating of F.

to receive an expressive rating of *L,* the student must meet the minimum criteria of giving one and two words *comprehensible* responses in the conversation, and labels or snapshots in the narrative.

The judgment regarding receptive language is made as follows:

1. The receptive rating will always be equal to or higher than the expressive, as understanding precedes production.
2. The seven screening items, to which nonverbal responses are given, allow for a distinction between a receptively *functional* and *M*oderate student. That is a student who responds appropriately to all these questions, yet shows *no higher levels* of understanding in the conversation could be given a maximum rating of F.
3. To be rated *M* or *P* receptively, a student would have to demonstrate a general understanding of what is being asked, even if complete and appropriate responses are given in the other language.

Appendix G
Proficiency Criteria Keys

		KINDERGARTEN			GRADES 1 & 2	
	F	**M**	**P**	**F**	**M**	**P**
Conversation						
1. Clause Level	1 or 2 clauses	Elab. 1 topic	Elab. more than 1 topic	1 topic or 1-2 clauses	Elab. more than 1 topic	Elab. more than 1 topic
2. Complex meanings Relationships	None	Rarely	Charac. or Sometimes	Rarely	Sometimes	Charac. or sometimes
3. Complex Grammar Relationships	None	1 (or 2 isolated)	1 (or 2 isolated)	1 (or 2 isolated)	2-4 dif	2-4 dif or more
4. Contextual Information	None	One topic	Sometimes or Charac.	1 (or 2 isolated)	One topic	Sometimes or Charac.
5. Explanation	No	Yes	Yes	No	Yes	Yes
5a. Initiates, Shifts, Changes Topic				No	Yes	Yes
NARRATIVE						
6. Narrative Level	Pages Sep.	Pages Sep.	Total or part Nar.	Pages Sep.	Part Nar.	Total Nar.
7. Complex Meaning Relationships	None	Rarely	Charac. or Sometimes	Rarely	Sometimes	Charac. or Sometimes
8. Complex Grammar Relationships	None	1 (or 2 isolated)	1 (or 2 isolated)	None	1 (or 2 isolated)	2-4 dif or more
9. Verb Tense Variation	No	Yes	Yes	None	Once or Sometimes	Charac-teristic

F = Functional
M = Moderately proficient
P = Proficient

(continued)

GRADES 3 & 4

	F	M	P	L
Conversation				
1. Clause Level	1 topic or 1-2 clauses	Elab. more than 1 topic	Elab. more than 1 topic	1-2 words
2. Complex meanings Relationships	Rarely	Sometimes	Charac.	None
3. Complex Grammar Relationships	1 (or 2 isolated)	2-4 dif	2-4 dif. or more	None
4. Contextual Information	None	One topic or Sometimes	Charac.	None
5. Explanation	No	Yes	Yes	No
5a. Initiates, Shifts, Changes Topic				
Narrative				
6. Narrative Level	Pages Sep.	Part Nar.	Total Nar.	Labels or Snapshots
7. Complex Meaning Relationships	Rarely	Sometimes	Charac.	None
8. Complex Grammar Relationships	1 (or 2 isolated)	1 (or 2 isolated)	2-4 dif or more	None
9. Verb Tense Variation	Once or None	Sometimes	Charac.	None

F = Functional
M = Moderately proficient
P = Proficient

Introduction to Chapter 6

In the following chapter, Canale and his colleagues focus on writing in a second language, an area of second language acquisition that is often neglected. The authors are interested in the cognitive foundations of writing in a second language but are also forced to deal with how writing is to be assessed. That is, the measures of writing ability in the first and second languages are related to the underlying cognitive abilities of the second language learners and to how different writing tasks require different cognitive processes. The authors start with hypotheses of what variables make writing difficult and then explore how to assess discourse by examining the writing produced by groups of subjects in their native and second languages.

The chapter's cognitive theory is based on two hypotheses: (a) that proficiency in language may rely almost completely on linguistic information with few if any hints from the situation of the language use (cognitively demanding and context-reduced) or on great reliance on the situation for hints of meaning (cognitively undemanding and context-embedded) and (b) the proficiency to perform cognitively demanding and context-reduced tasks underlies the subject's performance in both first and second languages. The authors extend these two hypotheses to the examination of writing in the first and second languages.

To compare writing in two languages, measures must be used that are not dependent on the specific languages involved, that can be interpreted in terms of the hypotheses of cognitive processing, and that are valid in terms of the reader's appreciation of the text. Two methods of scoring are used. Holistic scoring is based on a "rapid impression" of students' writing which in its nature depends on some undetermined combination of factors that impinge on the reader. Although the specific factors and their relative importance cannot be specified, this type of score probably resembles the kind of assessment readers make in nonclassroom situations. On the other hand, analytic scoring attempts to identify components of written text that can be judged separately. By grouping these separate components, general cognitive processes that may underlie more than one specific analytic measure can be discerned. A factor analysis is presented that demonstrates these groupings.

The methods of scoring are strongly related to each other, although from both the statistical data and in terms of nonclassroom situations the holistic scoring would seem to be more valid. The quality of writing in the first and second languages is shown to be related; however, the different scoring methods produce this result to varying degrees. The method of scoring itself is important in determining the strength of the relationship between first and second language writing. This situation suggests that more work is necessary to determine the salient components that make up communicatively effective writing and how those components are weighted relative to each other.

The work of Canale and his colleagues points in a number of directions. In terms of practical assessment of second language writing, they present tasks, reliable methods of assessment, and an indication of which skills are related in first and second language writing. In terms of cognitive processing, the authors provide evidence for a common proficiency that underlies first and second language writing in context-reduced tasks. Methodologically, the chapter suggests the value of factorial studies across subject groups and different kinds of tasks to help identify the focus of further research. The induction to cognitive processing should be compared to the work of Walters and Wolf who use experimental techniques to examine the processing of semantic information in two languages.

CHAPTER 6

Evaluation of Minority Student Writing in First and Second Languages

Michael Canale
Normand Frenette
and Monique Bélanger

The Ontario Institute for Studies in Education

Introduction[1]

This paper reports on a recent project in which we examined the teaching and testing of writing composition skills in French as a first language (FL1) and English as a second language (EL2) at grades 9 and 10 in French language secondary schools in Ontario. Under study were writing programs, samples of student writing, and samples of teachers' procedures and standards for grading student writing. The project's main goals were to better understand these three areas, to provide teachers with relevant feedback, and to encourage more collaboration in writing pedagogy between first and second language teachers. To these ends, we undertook a variety of studies.

The main study described below focused on the extent to which strengths and weaknesses in Franco-Ontarian minority students' writing in FL1 are reflected in their writing in EL2. Of particular interest was the Language

[1] This study was first presented, in a slightly different form, at the Fifth Annual Language Testing Research Colloquium held at the University of Ottawa, March 13 and 14, 1983; it is to appear under the title "On the interdependence of L1 and L2 in student writing in a minority setting" in the proceedings edited by Margaret DesBrisay, Stan Jones, and Sima Paribakht. The research reported here was carried out on the project "Writing evaluation at the intermediate level in Ontario's French language secondary school." We are grateful to O.I.S.E. for its financial support of this project and to all of the Franco-Ontarian educators and students who participated. We are also grateful for the assistance in data analysis provided by members of the O.I.S.E. Statistical Services Group (Bill Postl and Daphne Tucker, in particular) and by Lyle Bachman and Grant Henning. Of course, we are solely responsible for all opinions and errors herein.

Interdependence Hypothesis (Cummins, 1979, for example) which asserts that certain aspects of bilinguals' language skills are manifestations of a common underlying proficiency rather than of separate underlying ones. The following sections briefly describe some of the relevant aspects of Cummins' research, the methodology of our study and some of our tentative findings. Although no firm conclusions can be drawn from this study, some suggestions for more rigorous research in this area do emerge.

Cummins' Research

In a number of recent studies Cummins (1979, 1981, 1983) has advanced two main hypotheses supported by a variety of research.

The first hypothesis distinguishes two fundamentally different types of language proficiency. One type allows what he terms "cognitively demanding" and "context-reduced" language use, that is, performance of tasks that require active processing of much complex information and almost total reliance on linguistic rather than situational clues to meaning. An example of such a task would be reading a scholarly article on an unfamiliar topic. The other type of language proficiency suffices for "cognitively undemanding" and "context-embedded" language use, that is, tasks that require little active processing of information and allow greater reliance on situational rather than linguistic clues to meaning. An example of this kind of task would be talking with a close friend about a familiar topic. While noting that degree of cognitive demand can be just as great within as outside an academic setting, Cummins nonetheless claims that "clearly, context-embedded communication is more typical of the everyday world outside the classroom, whereas many of the linguistic demands of the classroom reflect communication that is closer to the context-reduced end of the continuum" (1981:12).

The second main hypothesis, the Language Interdependence Hypothesis (also stated by Cummins as the Common Underlying Proficiency Model), claims that the type of language proficiency required to successfully perform cognitively demanding and context-reduced language tasks underlies a bilingual's (or multilingual's) performance in any of his or her languages. In his words, "the literacy-related aspects of a bilingual's proficiency in L1 and L2 are seen as common or interdependent across languages" (1981:23–24). It might be noted in passing that he also allows for the possibility that cognitively undemanding and context-embedded language use may also reflect a (separate) type of common underlying proficiency (1981:25, footnote 13).

Two points are worth noting about the current status of these hypotheses. First, both have had a major influence on the planning and evaluation of bilingual education programs across the world—for example, on heritage language programs for immigrants to Canada and on Title VII programs for language minority students in the United States (see Cummins, 1983, for example). The second point is that both hypotheses have been developed and examined largely on the basis of evidence from measures of reading comprehension, listening comprehension and, to a lesser extent, oral expression. Measures of written expression have not been considered in much detail in his work.

For a number of reasons it seems particularly worthwhile to begin filling this gap in research bearing on Cummins' hypotheses. Consider three such reasons.

First, many recent studies have argued that the cognitive processes involved in writing are qualitatively different from those involved in reading comprehension, listening comprehension, and oral expression. Bereiter and Scardamalia (1982, 1983), Donaldson (1978), Olson (1977), and others argue for important differences between oral and written expression. For example, Bereiter and Scardamalia conclude "that the oral language production system cannot be carried over intact into written composition, that it must, in some way, be reconstructed to function autonomously instead of interactively" (1983:21).

Second, other researchers have suggested that written expression is not only different but also more demanding than other skill areas. For instance, Wells (1981:254) claims that the "creation of written text" is generally more cognitively and linguistically demanding than reading comprehension since the former but not the latter requires: (a) assembling and organizing relevant meanings in a manner appropriate to the genre and purpose of writing; (b) tailoring these meanings to the background and expections of the reader; and (c) encoding these meanings in language forms that clearly, grammatically, cohesively and elegantly convey one's message. Additionally, Bereiter and Scardamalia (1983) and Smith (1982) point out that composition and transcription processes in writing are generally slow, physically demanding, and often in conflict with one another.

Finally, there is a body of research that suggests that writing skills do not necessarily transfer smoothly from one language to another. Especially compelling work in this area is reported by Devito (1970), Kaplan (1972) and Schachter and Rutherford (1979). On this same point one might also note that certain bilinguals may choose to do certain types of writing in L1 and other types in L2; such seems to be the case with recognized writers such as Samuel Beckett, Joseph Conrad, Jerzy Kosinski, and Vladimir Nabokov (see Grosjean, 1982:284–288 for some discussion).

In view of these three reasons it is clear that a study of bilinguals' writing in L1 and L2 might provide different and interesting perspectives on the important hypotheses Cummins has advanced. In particular, the Language

Interdependence Hypothesis can be explored further by examining the extent to which bilinguals' written performance in L1 and L2 is similar (consistent with the hypothesis) or different (not consistent with it). The following section reports on such a study.

Methodology

Before reporting on the present study it is perhaps worth summarizing two pilot studies on which it was based.

Pilot study 1. In Canale, Bélanger, and Frenette (1982) we examined first-person narratives (of about 250 words each) in French and English written by 106 bilingual Franco-Ontarian students at grades 9 and 10 in four French language secondary schools located in geographically and demographically different areas of the province. It is important to point out that although French is the language of instruction in these schools (except in EL2 classes presumably), English may sometimes be a student's dominant language, particularly in those areas where francophones are few in number; see Mougeon and Canale (1979) for further discussion.

This sample was selected from a larger group of participating students (N = 427) on two criteria: (a) each student had written on the assigned topics in both French and English and (b) each was enrolled in the advanced-level French and English classes at the same grade level (where placement in advanced-level classes had been made previously on the basis of students' academic achievement in both language arts and other subject areas). The choice of first-person narrative and the particular topics—in English, "The most unfair thing that ever happened to me" and in French, "Alone at home on the night of a blackout" (translated here)—was based on teachers' input to us on the most common genres and most popular topics in the writing programs during the previous few years (see Frenette, Canale, Evans & Bélanger 1983).

Scoring of the narratives was done independently by three trained project members. Following the procedures outlined by Cooper (1977), a holistic (global and impressionistic) score on a scale of 1 to 10 was assigned by each scorer to each piece of writing and then the two closest scores were averaged. (At no time did the two closest scores differ by more than two points on the scale.)

A general analysis of the data revelaed little evidence for a relationship between student writing in FL1 and EL2. In only one of the schools was there a significant correlation ($r = .27$, $p < .05$, N = 56) between students' writing scores in French and English. Moreover, the overall Pearson Product Moment correlation was also quite modest ($r = .34$, $p < .01$, N = 106).

However, we viewed these data and results as very tentative given the limits of the pilot study (discussed further in Canale, Bélanger, & Frenette, 1982).

Pilot study 2. In a follow-up study (Canale, 1982) we randomly selected 20 students from the previous (nonrandom) subsample of 106 students in order to refine our scoring procedures. Our main goal was to examine the reliability and construct validity of analytic (fine-grained) scoring procedures to complement our holistic (global) ones. To this end we fleshed out the general comceptualization of writing composition we had used for the earlier holistic scoring into a set of 20 analytic scoring criteria (presented in Appendix A). Four trained project members then independently scored each of the 20 first-person narratives (without knowing the holistic scores previously assigned) on each of the 20 analytic criteria using a scale of 0 to 4 for each criterion.

Analysis of these analytic scoring procedures suggested that they were generally reliable and valid. Concerning reliability, the overall inter-rater reliability coefficient was very high (Hoyt Estimate of Reliability R = .92 for four scorers) while the reliability coefficients for the individual criteria ranged from .44 to .95, with the average coefficient in the .65 range (see Appendix B for details). As for validity, factor analysis of the scores on our 20 analytic scoring criteria suggested that certain of these criteria were related to one another and could in fact be grouped into five general aspects (or factors) of writing (see Appendix C for details). These five general factors are represented as A through E in Table 1 below. It should be noted that in anticipated of the major study reported below, these five factors were inter-

Table 1.   The Five General Factor Groups

A. *Standards of language usage* (SLU)
- spelling and capitalization
- grammar and vocabulary
- lexical and structural cohesion

B. *Standards of written documents* (SWD)
- genre: elements and layout suitable to mode of writing
- presentation: neatness, punctuation, and paragraphing

C. *Effectiveness for the reader* (ER)
- appropriate formality: language register, length, and subject matter
- effectiveness of ideas: arguments, examples, and depth of discussion
- effectiveness of language: choice and variety
- effectiveness of literary devices: e.g., imagery and sentence rhythm
- clarity of purpose and desired response

D. *The image of the writer* (IW)
- ease, confidence, and maturity of expression

E. *Quality of the message* (QM)
- originality and interest
- coherence of ideas: e.g., development, continuity, balance, and completeness

preted and labeled so as to reflect participating teachers' scoring concerns and preferences.

The major study. Several design changes were incorporated into the major study based on the two pilot studies. Many of these changes reflect the valuable suggestions of Jacobs, Zingraf, Wormuth, Hartfiel, and Hughey (1981). After summarizing these changes we will turn to the results.

First, a new sample of Franco-Ontarian minority students (N = 1407) was drawn. These students represented 43 general and advanced FL1 and EL2 classes at grades 9 and 10 in twelve French language secondary schools throughout the province. Furthermore, participating teachers were instructed (see the sample procedures in Appendix D) to have all students in a class write on two topics in each language. In FL1 classes the assigned topics dealt with a wasted Sunday afternoon at a relative's home (to elicit a first-person narrative) and a letter to a friend describing how the student repaired a bicycle, a snowmobile, or whatever (to elicit exposition of a procedure). Students were encouraged to prepare a draft and consult reference texts (e.g., a dictionary) before preparing the final version. The narratives were to be a maximum of one page and the expositions to be about a half-page. Teachers were to allow at least an hour for each narrative and a half-hour for each exposition. All writing took place over a period of four weeks; most students wrote the French essays first and most also wrote narratives before expositions.

Of the 1407 students who wrote essays, 230 of them from six schools did so in both genres and in both languages. From this subset we randomly selected 32 students for the present study.

The 128 student essays in this subsample (four essays for each of the 32 students) were scored in two ways. First, all essays from the 1407 students were scored holistically by participating teachers. Each essay was rated independently on a scale of 1 to 10 by at least two teachers; the recommended scoring procedures are in Appendix E. When teachers' ratings differed by more than two points on the scale, a third rater (any one of the project staff) independently rated the essay and the two closest scores were kept. Second, each of the 128 essays in the subsample was scored analytically by three trained project members. We independently rated each essay using a scale of 1 to 5 for each of the five factors A to E in Table 1. Before the holistic and analytic scoring was done, essays were coded, grouped (by genre and by language), and ordered differently for each rater; raters were free to choose the order in which the different groups of essays were evaluated.

Results

Since the main purpose of this study was to examine the interdependence of student writing in a first and second language, the main results reported below deal with comparison of student writing in FL1 and EL2. However, since the strength of this comparison rests on the strength of our measures of student writing, it is first necessary to consider two other types of results: (a) general data on inter-rater reliability and student performance and (b) validity of our scoring procedures. (All data analysis has been carried out through SPSS statistical programs.)

General data. Table 2 presents the inter-rater reliability estimates, mean scores, and standard deviations for the holistic and analytic scoring procedures. As can be seen, reliability is quite high for holistic scoring (ranging from .83 to .92) and generally high for analytic scoring (ranging from .59 to .90); this suggests that there was consistency in scoring from one rater to another. As can also be seen, mean scores on the four essays are similar both for the holistic scoring procedures and for the analytic ones; this suggests that as a group, the students in the subsample are not weaker in writing in one language nor genre than in the other. At the same time, the

Table 2. General Data (N = 32)

Measure	Inter-rater Reliability	Possible Max. Score	Mean	S.D.
Holistic French Narrative	.85	20	9.97	3.21
Holistic French Exposition	.92	20	10.34	4.29
Holistic English Narrative	.90	20	9.46	3.82
Holistic English Exposition	.83	20	9.41	3.15
Analytic French Narrative				
SLM	.87	15	8.53	2.84
SWD	.80	15	9.12	2.66
ER	.73	15	8.62	2.35
IW	.59	15	8.66	2.39
QM	.61	15	8.78	2.47
Analytic French Exposition				
SLU	.86	15	8.09	2.25
SWD	.86	15	9.19	3.37
ER	.89	15	9.22	2.99
IW	.90	15	8.25	2.99
QM	.83	15	9.03	2.75
Analytic English Narrative	.90	15	8.00	2.93
SLU	.81	15	9.23	2.77
ER	.78	15	7.78	2.48
IW	.80	15	7.69	2.49
QM	.75	15	7.84	2.71
Analytic English Exposition				
SLU	.87	15	8.75	2.68
SWD	.71	15	8.44	2.26
ER	.79	15	8.12	2.46
IW	.75	15	8.50	2.56
QM	.71	15	8.44	2.63

standard deviations indicate that within this subsample there is a fairly wide range of writing performance in both languages and both genres. If the range of performance were restricted, then our subsample would not reflect a normal distribution of the population.

Validity concerns. We carried out two analyses bearing on the validity of our scoring procedures. First, Pearson Product Moment correlations among analytic scores were calculated to examine the extent to which each of the five revised analytic criteria was distinct (in our scoring) from the others; as shown in Table 3, all five were highly intercorrelated. We thus combined them (using the Fisher z Transformation to disattenuate the correlations).

Also of relevance to our validity concerns was the extent to which, for a given essay, analytic and holistic scores are related to one another, that is, the extent to which these different scoring procedures measured the same thing. We thus calculated Pearson Product Moment correlations among the combined analytic scores and holistic scores. These are presented in Table 4.

Table 3.   Intercorrelations Among Analytic Scoring Criteria (N = 32)

	Narrative					Exposition				
	SLU	SWD	ER	IW	QM	SLU	SDW	ER	IW	QM
FRENCH										
Narrative:										
SLU	—									
SWD	.66	—								
ER	.77	.70	—							
IW	.84	.71	.83	—						
QM	.75	.77	.73	.73	—					
Exposition:										
SLU ·	.74	.71	.66	.80		.56	—			
SWD	.55	.66	.55	.71	.44	.83	—			
ER	.69	.57	.58	.74	.50	.87	.84	—		
IW	.70	.61	.68	.76	.55	.85	.78	.91	—	
QM	.63	.52	.52	.67	.41	.85	.79	.93	.86	—
ENGLISH										
Narrative:										
SLU	—									
SWD	.76	—								
ER	.75	.87	—							
IW	.78	.86	.90	—						
QM	.76	.83	.92	.90	—					
Exposition:										
SLU	.82	.84	.75	.79	.74	—				
SWD	.66	.63	.66	.58	.63	.64	—			
ER	.80	.80	.75	.77	.73	.72	.81	—		
IW	.71	.80	.82	.83	.76	.74	.72	.81	—	
QM	.73	.70	.76	.72	.69	.66	.78	.85	.89	—

Table 4 reveals that analytic and holistic scores are quite strongly related to one another both for essays in FL1 (with correlations of .78 for the narratives and .88 for the expositions) and for the essays in EL2 (with correlations of .77 for the narratives and .68 for the expositions). Also worth noting in Table 4 is the finding that scores for narratives and expositions are more strongly related to one another when analytic scoring rather than holistic scoring is done; this holds both for FL1 (with correlations of .77 for analytic scores and .64 for holistic ones) and for EL2 (with correlations of .94 for analytic scores and .64 for holistic ones). This suggests that even though analytic and holistic scores for a given essay are quite strongly related to one another, the analytic scoring procedure is itself reflected in the essay scores more than is the holistic scoring procedure. Hence, analytic scores would appear to be less valid than holistic ones in our study. (See, for example, Bachman & Palmer, 1981 for discussion of the notion "method effect," which refers to the different effects that different test methods can have on measurement of the same language skills.)

Comparison of writing in FL1 and EL2. Our examination of the relationship between the students' writing in FL1 and EL2 revealed two main sets of findings.

First, we found that while there is a relationship between the students' writing in the two languages, the strength of this relationship is influenced heavily by method of scoring and slightly by the modes of writing compared. This first set of findings is suggested by the correlations across languages in Table 4. For instance, the correlations between analytic scores in

Table 4.   Correlations Among Analytic and Holistic Scores (N = 32)

	French				English			
	Narrative		**Exposition**		**Narrative**		**Exposition**	
	Analytic	**Holistic**	**Analytic**	**Holistic**	**Analytic**	**Holistic**	**Analytic**	**Holistic**
FRENCH								
Narrative								
Analytic	—							
Holistic	.78	—						
Exposition								
Analytic	.77	.64	—					
Holistic	.76	.64	.88	—				
ENGLISH								
Narrative								
Analytic	.77	.61	.80	.68	—			
Holistic	.42	.43	.50	.32	.77	—		
Exposition								
Analytic	.70	.64	.78	.68	.94	.65	—	
Holistic	.36	.26	.51	.34	.72	.64	.68	—

FL1 and EL2 are quite high for both narratives (.77) and expositions (.78), thus suggesting a strong relationship between writing in the two languages. However, the correlations between holistic scores in FL1 and EL2 are much lower for both narratives (.43) and expositions (.34), thus suggesting a weak relationship between writing in the two languages. Similarly, the correlations between scores on different modes of writing—for example, French narrative and English exposition—are quite high for analytic scores (.70 and .80) but quite low for holistic scores (.26 and .32).

Second, even though there is a strong relationship among analytic scores for the four types of writing, each type is nonetheless in some way distinct from the others. Thus, a student's analytic score on an English narrative, for example, is not necessarily an accurate predictor of the same student's analytic score on a French narrative. This second set of findings is suggested by factor analysis of the analytic scores. As revealed in Table 5, four factors are distinguishable; furthermore, each factor seems to correspond to one of the four types of writing examined (as indicated by the factor loadings enclosed in boxes).

Table 5. Factor Analysis of Scores on Individual Criteria (N = 32)
(Factor pattern, SPSS PA2-oblique rotation)

Criterion	1	2	3	4	h^2
French Narrative					
SLU	.05	.60	.22	.14	.75
SWD	.13	.71	.20	.13	.73
ER	.02	.77	.03	.16	.79
IW	.06	.58	.30	.15	.85
QM	.09	.87	.10	.02	.79
French Exposition					
SLU	.02	.20	.69	.17	.90
SWD	.11	.13	.82	.08	.77
ER	.03	.02	.95	.01	.95
IW	.13	.18	.77	.07	.86
QM	.12	.11	.90	.03	.90
English Narrative					
SLU	.44	.18	.36	.32	.79
SWD	.58	.10	.22	.15	.85
ER	.72	.20	.02	.14	.91
IW	.84	.10	.09	.02	.94
QM	.77	.20	.02	.05	.88
English Exposition					
SLU	.41	.007	.43	.17	.78
SWD	.13	.18	.10	.82	.79
ER	.21	.10	.19	.70	.89
IW	.43	.09	.09	.58	.85
QM	.19	.003	.02	.83	.89
PF Eigenvalues	13.66	1.52	1.10	0.54	

Table 6.   Correlations Among Factors (N = 32)

Factor	1 (E.N.)	2 (F.N.)	3 (F.E.)	4 (E.E.)
1	—			
2	.51	—		
3	.61	.58	—	
4	.69	.43	.59	—

Finally, as would be expected from the strong relationship among all analytic scores that we witnessed earlier in Table 4, the relationship among the four factors in Table 5 is moderately strong. The correlations among the four factors are reported in Table 6.

Concluding Remarks

In summary, our study of minority students' writing in FL1 and EL2 bears on Cummins' Language Interdependence Hypothesis in three interesting ways. First, the writing data we have gathered are of interest since few data on written expression have been considered in evaluating Cummins' hypothesis and since writing is viewed by many psycholinguists as a different and generally more demanding cognitive activity than reading, speaking, or listening. Second, our major finding is that, in line with this hypothesis, there is a significant relationship between writing performance in FL1 and EL2 at the grade 9 and 10 levels in Ontario. Third, we have also found that the strength of this relationship varies considerably according to method of scoring, that is according to whether analytic or holistic scoring procedures are used. On this third point, we think that our holistic scoring procedures represent a more valid measure of student writing than do our analytic ones.

Several suggestions can be offered for more rigorous research and practical applications in the area of comparison of writing in a first and second language. First, it is obvious that scoring procedures must be carefully selected and validated. Regarding our own procedures, it is possible that the weaker relationship we observed between holistic scores as opposed to analytic ones for first and second language writing is due to failure of the analytic criteria to capture the important elements, and their proper weighting, that comprise a written text. In other words, our general impression of the quality of a piece of writing is likely more valid than are our more explicit theories of such quality. Second, similarities and differences in writing tasks must be carefully considered and controlled. For example, it is not clear just how different topics, different genres, order in which texts are written, presentation of tasks, time allowed on task, and the like may influence the relationship between writing in a first and second language; however, there are certainly effects of this sort (see Quellmalz, Capell, & Chou 1982, for example). Third, examination of various written products is really no substitute for study of the various writing processes and process problems that bilingual writers may exhibit in their first and second languages (see Jones, 1985 and Scardamalia & Paris 1984, for example). Finally, it is crucial for further research and classroom applications to consider writer variables such as age, degree of bilingualism, previous writing instruction in each language, and the different preferences in writing in one language or another that individuals may express. Because our own understanding of all of these various points is quite limited, the study and findings reported here are of a very preliminary nature. Nonetheless, we hope to have provided some indication of why it may be of theoretical and practical significance to devote more attention to writing in a first and second language and of how further work in this area might profitably be undertaken.

References

Bachman, L. and Palmer, A.S. A multitrait-multimethod investigation into the construct validity of six tests of speaking and reading. In A.S. Palmer, P.J.M. Groot and G.A. Trosper (Eds.) *The construct validation of tests of communicative competence.* Washington, D.C.: TESOL, 1981.

Bereiter, C. and Scardamalia, M. From conversation to composition: the role of instruction in a developmental process. In R. Glaser (Ed.) *Advances in instructional psychology, Vol. 2.* Hillsdale, N.J.: Lawrence Erlbaum Associates, 1982.

Bereiter, C. and Scardamalia, M. Does learning to write have to be so difficult? In A. Freedman, I. Pringle and J. Yalden (Eds.) *Learning to write: first language, second language.* New York: Longman Inc., 1983.

Canale, M. Evaluating the coherence of student writing in L1 and L2. Paper presented at the Colloquim on Discourse Analysis and Language Teaching, TESOL, Honolulu, 1982.

Canale, M. Bélanger, M. and Frenette, N. Analyse préliminaire de de l'interaction L1-L2 à l'écrit. In G. Alvarez and D. Huot (Eds.) *Interaction L1-L2 et stratégies d'apprentissage.* Québec: Laval University Press, 1982.

Cooper, C.R. Holistic evaluation of writing. In C.R. Cooper and L. Odell (Eds.) *Evaluating writing: describing, measuring, judging.* Urbana, Ill.: National Council of Teachers of English, 1977.

Cummins, J. Cognitive/academic language proficiency, linguistic interdependence, the optimum age question and some other matters. *Working Papers on Bilingualism,* 1979, 19, 197–205.

Cummins, J. The role of primary language development in promoting educational success for language minority students. In The California State Department of Education (Ed.) *Schooling and language minority students.* Los Angeles, Ca: California State University, 1981.

Cummins, J. Language proficiency and academic achievement. In J.W. Oller, Jr. (Ed.) *Issues in language testing research.* Rowley, Mass.: Newbury House, 1983.

Devito, J. *The psychology of speech and language: an introduction to psycholinguistics.* New York: Random House, 1970.

Donaldson, M. *Children's minds.* Glasgow: Collins, 1978.

Frenette, N., Canale, M., Evans, P.J. and Bélanger, M. *Writing evaluation at the intermediate level in Ontario's French language secondary schools.* Final project report. Toronto: O.I.S.E., 1983.

Grosjean, F. *Life with two languages.* Cambridge, Mass.: Harvard University Press, 1982.

Jacobs, H.L., Zingraf, S.A., Wormuth, D.R., Hartfiel, V.F. and Hughey, J.B. *Testing ESL composition: a practical approach.* Rowley, Mass.: Newbury House, 1981.

Jones, S. Problems with monitor use in second language composing. In M. Rose (Ed.) *When a writer can't write: studies in writer's blocks and other composing process problems.* New York, Guilford Press, 1985.

Kaplan, R.B. *The anatomy of rhetoric.* Philadelphia: The Center for Curriculum Development, 1972.

Mougeon, R. and Canale, M. A linguistic perspective on Ontarian French. *Canadian Journal of Education,* 1979, 4.4, 59–65.

Olson, D.R. From utterance to text: the bias of language in speech and writing. *Harvard Educational Review,* 1977, 47, 257–281.

Quellmalz, E.S., Capell, F.J. and Chou, C.-P. Effects of discourse and response mode on the measurement of writing competence. *Journal of Educational Measurement,* 1982, 19.4, 241–258.

Scardamalia, M. and Paris, P. *The function of explicit discourse knowledge in the development of text representations and composing strategies.* Occasional Paper No. 5. Toronto: Centre for Applied Cognitive Science, O.I.S.E., 1984.

Schachter, J. and Rutherford, W.E. Discourse function and language transfer. *Working Papers on Bilingualism,* 1979, 19, 1–12.

Smith, F. *Writing and the writer.* New York: Holt, Rinehart and Winston, 1982.

Wells, G. *Learning through interaction: the study of language development.* Cambridge University Press, 1981.

Appendix A: Analytic Scoring Criteria

A. *Writing as a reflection of community standards*
   — *Standards of language usage*
   1. Spelling and capitalization
   2. Grammar and vocabulary
   — *Standards of written documents*
   3. Neatness (e.g. handwriting, spacing, and margins)
   4. Punctuation
   5. Paragraphing
   — *Standards of appropriate formality*
   6. Appropriate language register, purposes, subject matter, length
   — *Standards of mode or genre of writing*
   7. Elements and layout (e.g., address, date, and salutation in a business letter)

B. *Writing as a reflection of individual personality*
   8. Originality and interest of ideas presented
   9. Ease, confidence, and maturity of expression

C. *Writing as unity of form and ideas*
   — *Cohesion devices to unify sentence forms*
   10. Lexical cohesion devices (e.g., use of pronouns, synonyms and conjunctions or transition expressions such as *however, on the one hand...on the other hand, in addition,* and *finally*)
   11. Structural cohesion devices (e.g. use of ellipsis, parallel sentence structures)
   — *Coherence elements to unify ideas*
   12. Development: the sense of direction and the order of presentation of ideas
   13. Continuity: the consistency of facts, opinion and writer perspective, as well as the reference to previously mentioned ideas and the relevance of newly introduced ideas
   14. Balance: the relative emphasis accorded each idea
   15. Completeness: the degree to which all ideas in a piece of writing work together as an integrated, thorough discourse

D. *Writing as an effective act of communication*
   16. Clarity of writer's purpose and desired response from his or her audience
   17. Sense of audience (e.g., suitable degree of detail or background provided)
   18. Effectiveness of ideas (e.g., arguments, examples, analogies, and depth of insight)
   19. Effectiveness of the choice and variety in language (e.g., precise vocabulary and varied sentence structure)
   20. Effectiveness of literary devices (e.g., effective use of imagery and sentence rhythm)

Appendix B

General Results of the Four Measures of Student Writing

Measure	N	Judges	Maximum Score	Mean	S.D.	Inter-rater Reliability (R)
English Holistic	20	4	40	23.55	3.55	.65
English Analytic	20	4	320	194.90	30.78	.92
English Coherence	20	5	25	14.95	3.46	.77
French Holistic	20	4	40	19.05	4.65	.76

Appendix C

Factor Analysis of Scores on Individual Criteria (N = 20)
(Factor pattern, SPSS PA2—orthogonal rotation)

Criterion	First Unrotated Factor	After Varimax Rotation*				
		1	2	3	4	5
1. Spelling and capitalization	.14				.75	
2. Grammar and vocabulary	.56				.70	
3. Neatness	.31			.50		
4. Punctuation	.52			.57		
5. Paragraph	.31					.85
6. Appropriate formality	.68	.58				
7. Genre	.58	.50				.76
8. Originality and interest	.70	.67				
9. Ease and confidence	.84		.62			
10. Lexical cohesion	.74			.57	.57	
11. Structural cohesion	.67		.44	.46		
12. Development	.80	.88				
13. Continuity	.83	.69		.60		
14. Balance	.87	.70		.49		
15. Completeness	.90	.81				
16. Clarity of purpose	.80		.83			
17. Sense of audience	.84	.68	.53			
18. Effective ideas	.78	.58				
19. Effective variety of language	.80		.72	.54		
20. Effective literary devices	.62		.75			

* Factor loadings less than .50 have been omitted except where of interest.

Appendix D

Writing Tasks for Anglais/English (Grades 9 and 10)

General Instructions for Teachers

The following instructions apply for both assignments described below.

1. Ask students to write their final draft with a ball point pen on the multi-copy paper provided. If students make any errors when writing the final copy, they should simply cross out the error and continue with the correct text. Students should *not* try to *erase* errors!

2. Ask students to write their name, teacher's name, school, grade level, and group at the *top* of the final draft copy. This information will be kept *anonymous* for our reporting.

3. Ask the students first to prepare an outline, then a rough draft. They may use their grammar reference books and dictionaries.

Special Instructions

A. *First assignment - narrative mode*

1. Ask the students to write a one-page story about someone who has the knack of making people laugh. The title of the story should be: "Everything goes wrong when _____ is around."

2. Students have a maximum of 70 minutes to work on the story. If it is necessary to use two class periods, please collect all student work at the end of the first period and redistribute it at the beginning of the second.

3. *Ten minutes* before the end of the 70-minute time limit, please advice students that they should complete their story as best they can. At the end of the alloted time, all students *must* hand in their copy whether it is completed or not.

B. *Second assignment - expository mode* (process/procedure)

1. Ask the students to write a maximum of half a page telling a friend how to prepare for selling an item of their choice. The title of the paragraph should be: "How to sell a _____."

2. Students have a maximum of 35 minutes to work on the paragraph. *Five minutes* before the end of the 35-minute time limit, please advise students that they should complete their paragraph as best they can. At the end of the alloted time, all students *must* hand in their copy whether it is completed or not.

Thank you very much for you cooperation.

1. *Narratve mode:* 3rd person   Time limit: 70 minutes

Write a one-page story about someone you know who has the knack of making people laugh. He or she might do it on purpose or might not even be aware of doing it. The title of you story should be:

Everything goes wrong when _____ is around.

Fill in the blank of the title. You might write about a younger brother or sister, a girlfriend or boyfriend, a bully, or the classroom smart aleck.

The story doesn't have to be completely true. You may want to exaggerate it a bit; you may even want to invent it completely.

You might choose to begin by describing the main character briefly, referring to past occasions when he or she was the cause of laughter. Move as quickly as possible into a particular incident. Don't try to get a whole lot of people in your story, and don't get sidetracked into a particular incident that you want to tell. Make sure the story has an outsome or conclusion.

2. *Exposition mode:* Process/procedure   Time limit: 35 minutes

Often when we have an unaccustomed task before us, it is useful to think about what we have to do beforehand. Such a task would be selling an item, whether it be a car, a stereo, a worn-out pair of shoes, or a diseased parrot. As you can see from the examples, the task can be very serious or very frivolous.

Write a maximum of half a page telling a friend how to prepare for selling an item of your choice.

The title of your paragraph should be:

How to sell a _____.

You can make your paragraph either very serious or very lighthearted. Your approach will depend to a certain extent on your choice of the item to be sold, but you could choose a serious item and try a serious approach to it.

Appendix E

Holistic scoring

Steps to follow

1. Score all 80 essays in one mode of writing before going on to essays in the other mode.

2. Use the scale of 1 to 10, where 1 is the lowest and 10, the highest. Please try to use *all* of the points on the scale.

3. Read each essay rapidly *once only* and give it a holistic (global) score.

4. Each student has been assigned a number, thus guaranteeing anonymity for the student and for the school. Write this number (which contains eleven (11) digits) on the sheet provided; write your score in next to the number. Please make certain that you keep the narratives separate from the expositions.

5. Please note that a score of 5 is not a "pass" or 4 a failure. Rather, essays should be rated in relation to the others in the same mode. In other words, an essay is simply better or worse than the others which you read in the same mode.

6. We ask you *not* to circle, underline, comment on, or correct "errors." The evaluation should represent your general impression of the essays; please try to give equal attention to the major components of writing (e.g., language conventions, interest, organization, and effectiveness).

7. You are not expected to score equal numbers of essays at each point on the scale, that is, seven essays scored at one (1); seven scored at two (2); seven at three (3), etc. You need not worry about the distribution of the scores unless a large number of essays begins to pile up at one or two points.

8. Work rapidly, taking as few breaks as possible between essays. If, however, you begin to feel tired, it is best to stop for a time and to start up again when you feel refreshed.

9. Faced with all these essays, you probably thought "This will take forever!" Holistic scoring is truly "rapid impression" scoring. In fact, judges can achieve a rate of one essay (250-300 words) a minute (more or less). If you find that it is taking you much longer than that to do one essay, you might be spending too much time on particulars rather than trying to get a general impression of the essay.

Introduction to Chapters 7 and 8

In the following two chapters, Walters and Wolf are concerned with the psycholinguistic processing of the second language learner when that learner is in a situation that requires of the learner more information about the second language than he or she has. How does such a learner go about finding the right information? What are the strategies involved and which ones are relatively more important than others?

In the first of their chapters, Walters and Wolf provide a detailed review of psycholinguistic models of second language processing. They then propose their own model for how to study and interpret the process of second language comprehension. Comprehension occurs at a specific time and under specific conditions. Walters and Wolf want to study what information the second language learner draws on given different possible sources of information.

As with other papers in this volume, Walters and Wolf insist on being able to focus on more than one factor at a time. Their theory of information integration requires that experimental designs be set to equally focus on two factors (theoretically, more are possible) and allow for the study of the interaction of the factors as well as the main effects. That is, the concern for the multiple sources of second language usage must be matched with the appropriate experimental design. This methodological point is important not only for the specific area of second language learning studied by Walters and Wolf, but for many other studies concerned with the processing and use of a second language. For example, studies of the influence of the first and second language between speakers in conversation would have to follow the experimental design requirements of Wolf and Walters.

In the second of their chapters, Walters and Wolf present an example of their experimental design and show how information from different sources (in their case from hints in the first and second language) is assessed by language learners and native speakers. Although the specific task is admittedly not realistic in terms of everyday language use, it establishes the value and stability of the method. Given this evidence about the method, more ecologically valid tasks could be constructed based on the outlines of other papers in this volume (for example, Wolfson, Pica and Doughty, Fanselow).

The first experiment of Walters and Wolf shows that native speakers think they depend more on first language than second language information in dealing with a difficult problem of interpretation. In the second experiment this finding is extended to high and low proficiency second language learners when confronted with an unknown idiom in the target language.

The high proficiency subjects do not regard themselves as depending on their knowledge of the target language, but rather have integrated information from the two languages and so can use first language information to a greater extent in solving a comprehension problem in the second language.

The Walters and Wolf work is similar to other studies in this volume in searching for the factors involved (causally or collaterally) with second language learning. However, they focus on the psycholinguistic processing involved. This psycholinguistic processing itself is dependent on features of situation, and Walters and Wolf investigate the proficiency of the second language speaker as well as the semantic relations of clues they give their subjects. Like Pica and Doughty and Canale, Walters and Wolf follow an experimental approach in an area where there is sufficient theory to formulate hypotheses that can be quantitatively tested.

CHAPTER 7

Second Language Comprehension Processes: Theories and Methods

Yuval Wolf
Joel Walters

*Department of English
Bar Ilan University*

Let's imagine a person who watches a movie in which the actors speak a language the viewer acquired after he was already quite proficient in his native language (call the latter L1 and the former L2). The viewer, presumably, is not familiar with all of the linguistic components presented in the movie, be they elementary structures such as verbs, nouns, adverbs, and the like or more pragmatic forms such as metaphors and idioms. Is there any reason to assume that he can comprehend and understand all of these elements strictly within the limits of the language of the movie? Certainly not, since movies are produced for L1 users. So, how would our L2 user cope with the problem of incomplete information needed to comprehend the utterances of the movie? Would he give up whenever there is an unrecognizable linguistic component within the sentences or texts in the movie, or would he make do with a partial understanding of what is going on? Such a passive approach is unreasonable, both from a motivational perspective and from the viewpoint of learning theories. From the former perspective, this person's cognitive operating system is expected to be motivated to do something to complete the needed information.

Assuming that some active approach would be taken, however, learning theories would predict that our L2 user would do what he is used to. Now, even without knowing him personally, we are left with the conclusion that he is accustomed to using his first language. To exemplify how this mechanism works in such cases, let us present another typical situation, that of code switching. Who of us does not recognize the situation in which he is chatting with someone from an L1 background not his own? In such situations one of the two conversants uses an unfamiliar language. Furthermore, it seems that we occasionally listen to utterances in L2 and automatically switch to our own language to consider the matter, and many times, to give an answer. With this background, if we return to our movie viewer, there is an implied prediction that he would be motivated to complete information by integrating the L2 linguistic components with the most recognizable ones which happen to serve as substitutes for the missing information. The most likely (if not only) linguistic substitute is L1 information.

These situations are exemplary of the psycholinguistic universe that this chapter focuses on. They are states in which a language user is exposed to verbal material in L2 and is required to do something to arrange the material in a way which will enable him first, to understand, and then, to demonstrate his understanding through a regular mode of communication or through a test of achievement.

The paper is divided into four sections. The first examines contrastive analysis and its offspring, error analysis. The second presents three models for which L2 use is a primary target of investigation. After a summary and synthesis of this earlier work in the third section, we present a framework which may permit an integration of prevailing modes of thought on L2 processing within a single theoretical and methodological approach.

Contrastive Analysis: First Generation Theoretical Thought

No volume on second language comprehension would be complete without reference to the Contrastive Analysis Hypothesis (CAH). Nor would any paper in the field be placed in the proper historical context without mention of CA's offspring, Error Analysis (EA).

A number of overviews of the L2 field (Brown, 1980; Dulay, Burt, & Krashen, 1982) indicate that CAH had its origins in behavioristic psychology and structural linguistics. In one of the earliest proposals, Fries (1945) described learning a second language as very different from first language learning, its problems stemming not from the second language but from the "set" created by L1 habits. Similarly, the oft-quoted remarks of Lado (1957) claim that:

> ...we can predict and describe the patterns that will cause difficulty in learning, and those that will not cause difficulty, by comparing systematically the language and the culture to be learned with the native language and culture of the student. (p.vii)

While several papers (Ritchie, 1967; Wolfe, 1967; Wardaugh, 1970) attempted to put CAH to rest, Wardaugh's (1970) now classic review ironically gave the field a new, albeit short-lived, breath of life. In that paper he distinguished between the Strong Version of CAH, which claimed that a structural comparison of two languages could predict a learner's errors, and a Weak Version of the theory, which maintained that a comparison of L1 and L2 could account a posteriori for observed learner difficulties.

CAH's assumptions about the nature and extent of linguistic theory brought about the theory's eventual demise. First, CAH assumed that comparisons of L1 and L2 could be fully specified (or at least specified to the extent necessary to describe learner difficulties). Second, it assumed that such a comparison could explain (forwards or backwards) degree of difficulty. And finally, CAH presupposes a valid and reliable measure of learner difficulty. We need not belabor these points here, since our interest is not in the purely linguistic implications of CAH, but in what it has to say about psycholinguistic processes of L2 use.

In that light, CA's origins in the structural linguistics of the 1940s and its association with behaviorism was a major source of criticism as linguistics became more mentalistic and more generative. Critics of CAH (Brown, 1980; Dulay, Burt, & Krashen, 1982; Ritchie, 1967; Wardaugh, 1970) attack the theory for its assumption that L2 learning results primarily from the acquisition of appropriate "new habits." Such habits are said to include new phonological, morphological, syntactic, and semantic patterns as well as new lexical items. It is also conceivable that they would include the match between meaning and context. This criticism reflects an inherent dissatisfaction with notions of transfer and interference. In early CAH terminology, when two languages share habits, positive transfer occurs. Where linguistic interference is found, negative transfer (read: learner difficulty) is the result. Our reading of the history of this dispute is that it derives from a lack of clear boundaries between linguistic and psychological claims within CAH. That is to say, CAH has both linguistic and psychological underpinnings and applications. However, the questions and the methods are not necessarily the same, and most of the criticism of CAH is linguistic in nature, not psychological.

First let us defend CAH's association with behaviorism by claiming that L2 studies should never have been a battleground for the innatist-behaviorist dispute. Carroll (1968) expresses this position succinctly when he states: "I am not convinced...that there is any real difference between a "habit" and a "rule," or between a "response" and a "rule-governed performance." (p. 114) A similar terminological parallel is pointed out by James (1980) when he compares transfer theory to Gestalt psychology's notion of 'set.' Finally, a 1968 paper by Lado entitled "Contrastive Linguistics in a Mentalistic Theory of Language Learning" suggests that the behaviorist/cognitivist distinction may not be real.

While most post-Chomskyan discussion of CAH has remained at this terminological level, Carroll (1968) and James (1980) stand out as notable exceptions. Both center on transfer/interference theory and its role in L2 learning. Carroll concludes that this psychological theory and its accompanying research have little to offer the L2 field. Most transfer experiments have examined how a new set of habits comes to replace an old one while the phenomenon of interest for the study of second language use is "transfer from a very highly learned system of habits to a new and different set" (Carroll, 1968:117). James (1980), a major proponent of CA, describes its psychological bases as S-R and Transfer Theory. Basing his work on Jacobovitz (1970), he identifies environmental conditions antecedent to linguistic utterances as the stimulus information, further specifying mental conditions as belonging legitimately to this domain. The utterance, then, becomes the response in this S-R framework. In his examination of transfer, James cites Corder whose approach remained consistent while at the same time undergoing changes in its superficial psychological dress. Corder (1971) depicts the learner as carrying out mother tongue habits in L2 while Corder (1975:411) states that the "sense we make of environment depends on what we already know about it...the relevant existing cognitive structures may be those of the mother tongue."

We recall that Corder's (1967) seminal paper marked the beginning of Error Analysis (EA) studies, an approach which was intended to replace CA as the major proposal in the L2 field. EA did, in fact, accomplish this substitution, at the same time creating a more abstract terminology (see Tarone, Cohen, & Dumas, 1976). The phenomenon for study, however, remained essentially the same as the one investigated by CA, namely, the utterances produced by the L2 user.

Second Generation Psycholinguistic Models in Second Language Use

In this section we treat questions which concern the nature of theories intended to describe and explain L2 processing. In particular, Krashen's (1982) Monitor Hypothesis, McLaughlin, Rossman and Mcleod's (1983) information processing approach, and Bialystock's, (1981, 1984a) model of analysis of knowledge and control of cognition will be considered. This work seems to be most representative of the thought which has emerged in the field of L2 studies after CAH. For each approach we will first look at the issues these theories address and then treat their accompanying methods.

Krashen's Model of Acquisition and Learning

In recent work (Dulay, Burt, & Krashen, 1982; Krashen, 1982) a three-part model, consisting of a filter, an organizer, and a monitor is presented. The latter two components encompass a basic distinction between acquisition and learning, as proposed in Krashen's earlier model (Krashen, 1977).

In an attempt to explain the processing distinctions between acquisition and learning, Krashen (1977) specifies two differences: (a) time and (b) attention. In the case of the former, the model states that amount of processing time available controls whether the L2 user will perform in an acquisition mode (limited time) or will use "conscious grammar" in a learning mode. The other process mentioned, attention, is claimed to be necessary to invoke the monitor's operation. Other earlier discussions of the model (Krashen, 1977; Krashen & Pon, 1975) emphasize processing time while the most recent presentation of the Monitor Model (Krashen, 1982) presents time, attention, and rule knowledge as necessary conditions for operations of the monitor system, that is, for involving conscious rule use.

In the later version, a great deal more is specified about the processing functions of these two systems. In that elaborated model (Krashen, 1982: 15–20) acquisition processes are said to be involved in initiating utterances in a second language and for controlling fluency. Learning is limited to a single purpose, namely, as an editor for making changes in the form of an utterance after it "has been 'produced' by the acquired system." (p. 15)

Among the processes mentioned above, initiating and fluency would seem to involve a complex system, including mental operations such as planning, selecting, retrieving, and ordering among others. However, the model does not specify all of the details concerning this complexity. Even though this variety of terms promises an explicit analysis from a perspective of higher mental functions, the dominant attempt is to provide an explanation for functioning in L2 in the context of previous experience. Of the different domains of psychology which are purported to deal with linguistic functioning, this approach fits primarily in the psychology of learning. This in and of itself is not a shortcoming. It, nevertheless, generates a commitment on the part of the authors to deal with questions of processing. Such is the problem with any attempt to explain linguistic functioning beyond the level of single words in terms of previous experience (learning).

On the methodological side, an important issue emerges from an examination of Krashen's work. In that regard, the model relies primarily on elicitation of grammatical morphemes (Bailey, Madden, & Krashen, 1974; Dulay & Burt, 1974; Larsen-Freeman, 1976; Krashen, 1977) and individual case studies (Krashen, 1978; Krashen & Pon, 1975) for assessing monitor use. Some of the problems with this work concern the elicitation procedures, learning environments, and scoring methods.

The 1982 version of the model is notable with respect to its emphasis on individual/group differences. In that book, Krashen discusses over-users, under-users, and optimal users of "conscious rules," concluding that only "acquisition" can assist in L2 performance. Implicit in this distinction among monitor-users is the notion that under-users of conscious rules are somehow "better" than over-users and that optimal users are likewise better off than the other two. However, within this post-facto type of analysis, one is not able to answer the question of whether monitor use is determined (explained) by individual differences. That is, one cannot determine whether the individual is an overuser or an underuser or whether situational/processing differences (i.e., overuse or underuse in specific controlled conditions) account for the findings. This latter possibility can strengthen the explanatory power of such hypotheses because it frees the researcher from the obligation to control events in the history of the individual L2 user—events which by their very nature are uncontrollable. An excellent basis for claims against reliance on individual differences is presented in Schoenfeld (1974). There he states:

> We are a culture that dotes on differences among people. In our universities we multiply courses on group and individual differences, never on group and individual similarities. Of course, one implies the other, but it is notable that we drum away on the differences. The similarities are casually derived from the differences and are presented as the overlapped portions of individual score distributions. We do not train our students to conceive of the similarities as a negation of the differences.... We ask some types of questions rather than others. None of this is 'scientific' in itself, but only personal...

The work described above suffers from all of the problems raised by Schoenfeld here as well as in other parts of his paper. It represents a type of thinking that finds expression in the construction of models of individual and group differences. Nevertheless, we are still left with the question of whether individual differences alone can provide insight into the study of L2 processing. In other words, are distinctions between over-users, under-users, and the like a sufficient source of knowledge of how an L2 user attends, selects, retrieves, plans, identifies, discriminates, classifies, comprehends, and understands information in his non-native language?

This is essentially a question of the quality of the knowledge accumulated by an individual differences approach. Schoenfeld points to a basic oversight relating to individual differences as a source of scientific knowledge. The necessary summary and conclusion of this approach leads one to recognize that a researcher ought to be as cautious as possible with respect to the assumptions he makes. The untested assumptions in our case are essentially similar to those to which Schoenfeld refers, namely, that the samples compared are matched, that we are reliable managers of our own research, and that our measures are consistent. By saying this, we do not mean that the search for individual differences in L2 processing is methodologically unsound. Rather, we accept Schoenfeld's approach and the significance it implores. That is to say, a research question ought to be separable into its core components such as its basic time units, simplest relevant (explanatory) variables, simplest measures, and so on. Thus, in order to validate an answer to a specific L2 question one cannot be satisfied only with individual differences. Rather, it is also necessary to perform some strict experimental analysis concerning the same L2 questions. That should lead to knowledge of a more basic nature.

McLaughlin, Rossman, and McLeod (1983): Information Processing in L2

Another approach to the question of L2 processing happens to take into account the aforementioned distinction between individual and situational differences. It does so by distinguishing between individual L2 users according to the quality of their learning experience and their previous achievements, that is, between users who are new at a skill and users who are well-trained, or between users who perform on the basis of formal rule learning and those who base performance on implicit analogic learning. At the same time, the model encompasses domains of cognitive psychology in addition to learning.

This approach has been brought to the field of L2 learning from that branch of cognitive psychology known as information processing. McLaughlin, Rossman, and McLeod (1983) distinguish two types of processes: focus of attention, which they say can be either "focal" or "peripheral," and information processing ability, which is labeled controlled and automatic. The distinction between focal and peripheral focus of attention is further characterized as a distinction between intentional and incidental performance.

This model encompasses two domains of cognitive research. They are the psychology of perception (focal/peripheral) and the psychology of learning (new skill/well-trained skill). (See Table 1: Cells A and C vs. Cells B and D.) The information-processing distinction between controlled and automatic is collapsed into this same distinction between new and well-trained skills. In other words, the distinction between controlled and automatic information

Table 1. Possible Second Language Performances as a Function of Information-Processing Procedures and Attention to Formal Properties of Language

Attention to Formal Properties of Language	Information Processing	
	Controlled	Automatic
Focal	(Cell A) Performance based on formal rule learning	(Cell B) Performance in a test situation
Peripheral	(Cell C) Performance based on implicit learning or analogic learning	(Cell D) Performance in communicative situations

(from McLaughlin, Rossman, & McLeod, 1983:141)

processing finds no explicit expression in the cells of the model. Thus, the dimension of information processing is left without a suggstion for operationalization. Nevertheless, one cannot ignore the fact that the model intentionally establishes the construct 'information processing' as a basic one. That construct, following our biased reorganization of the model, gives expression to a third domain: the psychology of thinking. The above analysis also seems to hold for the version of the model which incorporates the terms and contructs of L2 learning. We can see from Table 1 that here the term *learning* is explicit in the two cells labeled "controlled" information processing in a way which supports the claim that the terms within the cells naturally belong to the domain of learning.

McLaughlin et al.'s model apparently adopts the terminology of the three basic subfields of cognitive psychology. However, one should distinguish between the phenomenon that a model deals with and the explanations that it proposes. In the model in question, the explanatory factors treat only two of the three basic subfields, that is perception and learning. The remaining domain, thinking, finds no explicit expression in the explanatory-oriented terms of the model. Rather, this dimension is evident in what is intended to be explained: problem solving in L2. Within the cells, only the term "performance" represents what is intended to be explained. Thus, one who attempts to understand the model must rely on the observational definitions the authors have used. Those definitions were expressed in the variety of tasks reviewed, including measures of reaction time, recognition, recall, and categorization and only the categorization task is suggestive of the thinking/problem-solving domain. However, that phenomenon is not clearly housed within the conceptual and observational framework of the model. That the model does not clearly formulate the phenomenon it intends to explain is a distinctive deficit, since everything can be included or excluded as an observational definition, according to the speculations of the reader.

Bialystock (1981): Analysis of Knowledge and Control of Cognition

Bialystock (1981) is quite clear in the structure of her model. The model attempts to explain variability in L2 learner speech and progressive mastery of the target language. That model, which has envolved and undergone several modifications since its original inception in 1978 (Bialystock 1978, 1983, 1984a), is also characterized by a multidimensional approach. It recognizes the complexity of language processing and attempts to explain two aspects of that complexity in a single experimental framework. In the following sections we will consider the elements of processing which Bialystock's model addresses as well as the methods appropriate for testing that model.

In Bialystock's (1981) model two dimensions are distinguished: analysis of knowledge and access to information. In a later presentation of her research, Bialystock (1984a) includes both of these skills in a single framework she calls metalinguistic awareness. Analysis of knowledge is described as "the skill responsible for making explicit those representations that had previously been implicit or intuitive." Specific types of knowledge referred to include: knowledge of the unity of speech (words, syllables, phonemes), the relationship between form and meaning, and syntactic awareness. Bialystock's other dimension, which she labels access to knowledge, or control of cognition, is said to involve processes of attention and switching. In a more explicitly theoretical statement about the model, Bialystock (1984b) views this dimension as a continuum running from "controlled" at one end to automatic processing at the other.

As with the two previous models, the emphasis here lies in the domain of learning. One dimension (analysis of knowledge) attributes explanatory power to the level of skill an L2 user has already acquired. The other (control of cognition) deals with storage and retrieval, terms which are also part of the domain of learning. In this model, as in the other two, there are no indicators that thinking processes may be core elements. These higher level processes were not explicitly postualted in Bialystock's model. The model, however, need not be judged on these terms. The phenomenon to be explained by the model is clearly enough declared as the product of learning (i.e., mastery of the target language). The tasks used to test the predictions of the model include: (a) grammaticality judgments, (b) location of grammatical deviance, (c) correction of syntactic errors, (d) judgements of meaningfulness, (e) awareness of words, and (f) solution of sentence anagrams (Bialystock, 1981, 1984a, 1984b). The first four assess the processes involved in an analysis of knowledge; the last two address questions of how information is accessed. In any case, all of them are consistent with the primary purpose of the model: to explain learning, or in Bialystock's own terms, mastery of the target language.

Summary and Synthesis

Three models have been purposefully selected to represent what we label second generation theoretical thought in L2 studies. They were selected for review because of their relevance to our locus of interest in comprehension processing during L2 use. The perspectives from which this work has been reviewed suggest two issues which deserve mention at this point: one methodological and one theoretical. The methodological issue relates only to the second generation models, since, as compared to the theoretical orientation of the first generation approach, they demonstrate an empirical as well as theoretical orientation. In the discussion which follows, the methodological and theoretical implications from our review are incorporated into a single framework. This synthesis rehabilitates the contrastive analysis construct and extracts the problem-solving element from the complexity of the second generation models. Methodologically, it is based mainly on the factorial modeling which emerges from the empirical approach of this generation.

The main criticism of the second generation models results from an inconsistency between intended purposes of the three models (both explicit and implicit) and the way they have been implemented. Another criticism relies on the distinction between personal (individual) and situational (experimental) explanations for L2 processing while still another addresses the distinction between unifactorial and multifactorial explanations for L2 processing.

All three models reviewed above were aimed at predicting L2 performance which is expected to be learned. In Krashen's model the ultimate goal is to predict the conditions under which the L2 user will employ acquired or learned material. In McLaughlin et al.'s proposal, "learned material" is the central explanation for L2 performance. The same can be said about Bialystock's model, which attempts to explain L2 performance by means of what is known to the L2 user and the extent to which that knowledge is available. In all of these models a gap exists between that which they postulate as core elements and the expectations they generate in their readers concerning higher mental processes such as problem solving. All three models generously use the term processing, which by its very nature is devoted to a class of phenomena defined as including additional mental operations. The additional element reflected in these mental operations cannot be handled by any conceptual or methodological framework from the subfield of learning. Learning explains how associations, habits, and so on are formed, maintained, and retrieved. The subfield of thinking explains how acquired associations are processed. That is, types and rules of processing are part of the definition of the domain labeled thinking and problem solving.

Establishing a framework which focuses on a term such as processing means that the phenomenon in question is situational by its very nature. That is, processing is conceived as something which occurs within relatively narrow boundaries of space and time. Its time limit can be captured within an observational unit which, in rare cases, extends for several minutes but usually is a matter of seconds or even milliseconds. This clarifies what we mean by calling processing a situational phenomenon. For such a phenomenon one would have expected that models built around it would use situational terms for descriptive and explanatory purposes. However, we find this practice only in one of the models we analyzed, that is, Bialystock's. In fact, her model is the only one that happens to validate its assumptions by experimental design. This is not to say that individual characteristics of processing (invariance among processing events of a single individual) are not of great importance. The opposite is true. Identification of individual differences could help reveal crucial properties of processing as a phenomenon. However, such differences ought to be combined with situational factors in order to receive a more complete explanation of L2 processing. For example, the comparisons embodied in Bialystock's (1984a) model relate to whether subjects are unilingual or bilingual. This is accompanied by two types of metalinguistic tasks (grammaticality judgements and sentence error correction) which could be viewed as situational. In this light Bialystock's work is exemplary in that it involves use of both personal and situational modes of investigation within the boundaries of the same conceptual framework, albeit not within the same experimental design. (This will be discussed later on.)

However, like the other work reviewed, there is a further demand which is not met by her model as well. That is the demand for integrity between the overall methodological framework and the specific designs for carrying it out. The point is that the intent of Bialystock's model (1984a) is bifactorial, that is, the overall explanatory framework consists of two classes of relevant variables: analysis of knowledge and control of cognition. These are presented in a way that involves the assumption of a main effects model as well as an interactive model. The former model tests for the independent effect of one or both of two variables, the latter for the mutual effect of both of them. The bifactorial nature of the overall plan should be expressed in a design which affords equal weight to each condition (cell). These are designs which place all of the combinations of the different levels of each variable (in Bialystock's case, $2 \times 2 = 4$ conditions) in a unified framework and give each of them the same opportunity in terms of the instructions, task, scale of measurement, and so on. Actually, the ideal means to accomplish this is a bifactorial experimental design. Only if a researcher uses such a design can he or she benefit from trying to relate the observed differences to individual ones. Bialystock's work has not taken advantage of this potential, since the model has not been examined by means of a single bifactorial design including four conditions. The relevant variables of task (grammatical judgements and corrections) as well as those of text (anomolous and nonanomolous sentences) are nested within her basic bifactorial design. Thus, the comparisons were made between nonequalized conditions. From a purely methodological perspective this means that the actual explanatory attempt was unidimensional and not bidimensional as intended.

Toward a Processing Model in L2 Use

The literature reviewed demonstrates that, beyond minor differences among models, they all share the same concern with the term processing. As we saw above, however, their primary goal is related to phenomena of a wider scope, which include, by definition, many events each of which reflects processing. In sum, all of the models focus on processes such as learning.

At this point a clear distinction must be made between two connotations of the term "process." It is possible to use this construct to describe the repetition of observable behaviors and their contiguities with rewards, punishments, and so on. From this viewpoint, the principal concern lies in change of behavior which occurs as a function of such reinforcing experiences. The main interest is on some entity which is beyond any specific occurrence of this sort. Another scientific connotation of the term "process" is of a more problem-solving nature. That is, "process" can be a label for something which characterizes a single mental event. A problem-solving perspective conventionally focuses on distinctions and changes within each such event as opposed to changes from one event to another. This problem-solving connotation belongs to the domain of thinking, the other perspective to the domain of learning. We take as our baseline the problem-solving connotation of the term process.

Up to this point we have attempted to establish the boundaries for treating the issue of processing from our own perspective. Now we will directly address the question of processing and its role in L2 use. We begin with a consideration of the meaning of this term in the three models.

Wherever learning of linguistic material exists, processing of that material is expected. However, one who focuses on processing should go beyond a terminology which is typical of the subfield of learning. That processing terminology should include, at least in its simplest form, a distinction among several types of mental operations which serve to connect linguistic units with each other. There is no doubt that what we have called higher mental operations is a matter of great complexity. However, when one wishes to make distinctions in a field which lacks them, it is most proper to begin with distinctions which are as simple and central as possible.

Some indication of such desired distinctions can be found in McLaughlin, Rossman, and McLeod (1983). They speak about information processing procedures which are based on formal rule learning and analogic learning (see Table 1, Cells A and C). In an extension of this work, we choose somewhat different distinctions, since they are perhaps the most basic semantic properties of a text. One property is the notion of vertical relations (subordinate and superordinate), that is, the relations between a category and its special cases. The other property can be labeled horizontal and concerns relations within and across semantic categories. These two are simple and central relations between semantic nodes. The process of forming these relations within the language user's mind is collapsed into a simple and central distinction concerning mental processes. Actually these distinctions are largely treated in the psychological literature under the labels synthetic/analytic and analogic, respectively. At this point we have arrived at the core of our porposal. Thus, we prefer to go beyond the three models sampled, bringing to bear literature from different areas of cognitive psychology. To that end we will review briefly some of the literature on these concepts.

From the field of intelligence testing and evaluation, Guilford and Hoepfner (1971) define synthesis as organizing parts into wholes, further specifying it as an ability to maintain logical or meaningful order. Operationally, the authors define synthesis by means of tasks requiring completion of verbal and figural elements which demand closure on the part of the subject. On the verbal side, which is of most interest to us, synthesis is evaluated by finding a class in a set of symbols. Analysis, the polar opposite of synthesis, is defined as a facility to break things down into their natural components.

The second concept of interest to us, analogy, is also treated by Guilford and Hoepfner (1971). However, it appears there in semantic dress which does not help to clarify our own view of the concept. They distinguish between divergent and convergent operations within the context of their concept of creativity. This complex of creativity and divergent/convergent operations makes it difficult to determine the correspondence between these conceptualizations and analogic operations. This could be done by demonstrating the similarity between the definitions of divergence and analogy. Since our aim is to clarify our own view, however, we turn at this point to writers who provide a more explicit treatment of the concept of analogy.

Sternberg (1977a) makes the following general statements: "Reasoning by analogy, is pervasive in everyday experience and would seem to be an important part of what we commonly refer to as intelligence... Analogical reasoning is of the utmost importance in a variety of intellectual disciplines." (p. 99) He further specifies that whenever one encounters a new experience and draws a parallel to an old one, one operates in an analogic fashion. He goes on to define analogy as "a hierarchy of relations taking the form A is to B as C is to D" (1977b: 134). This formula is used in various parts of IQ tests: verbal, figural, quantitative, geometric, pictures, and so on. (see Guilford and Hoepfner, 1971, for examples). With reference to language, Verbrugge (1977) claims that "it is likely that most of what we learn through language is a result of analogic references to the relations made available by our earlier experience" (p. 382).

Rumelhart and Norman (1981) claim that analogies are very useful in learning new bodies of knowledge, though not everything can be studied by this process: addition and subtraction are easily learned through analogies; multiplication and division are more difficult. "The perfect analogy is one in which the learner is already able to reason within the source domain with ease and in which *all of and only* the operations of the target domain are represented in source domain..." (Rumelhart & Norman, 1981:341).

Up to this point we have referred the reader to the relevant literature concerning the centrality of synthesis and analogy within the conceptual framework of human intelligence. We should also note that synthesis and analogy are relatively comprehensive concepts, cutting across the entire range of the terms and operations of that field. However, the logic we follow in borrowing literal and operational terminology from the field of intelligence might still not be clear enough. As a matter of fact, intelligence is of most interest to us, since we are essentially interested in the question of how good and bad language performance is processed. The main question of that field can be formulated as: "Who is a good or bad performer?" This formulation clarifies the similarity as well as the distinction between their question and ours. The similarity lies in the common focus on psycholinguistic (verbal) performance. The difference is that we are attempting to deal with situational perspectives of this sort of performance, while the "intelligence" field is directed towards invariant performance above and beyond a specific situation, that is, performance which characterizes a good or bad performer. (Following this analysis, it is clear that we are actually dealing with specific situations of "intelligent" functioning in a foreign language). Thus, constructs as well as operations taken from the field of intelligence are most legitimate for addressing our own problem.

Returning now to the main line of thought in this section, we remind our patient reader that we began by sampling indications for centrality and comprehensiveness of synthesis and analogy within the domain of intelligence. Then we justified the legitimacy for borrowing from that domain. Now, we shall attempt to justify our choice of the specific conceptual framework—synthesis/analogy.

Our first criterion is the simplicity of the basic conceptualization. A desired theoretical framework is one which contains the least number of constructs and premises (Law of Parsimony). It follows, then, that research in a field such as L2 processing, which is only in its infancy, should begin with the simplest (although not simplified) distinctions possible, and later on proceed toward more specific or complex terminology and distinctions.

So far we have tried to justify our choice of the reference field, that is, the psychology of intelligence, and our choice of the conceptual framework taken from this field. Assuming the proposed logic to be sound, the reader should next ask what essential features of this framework make it useful for the field of L2 processing. Our answer lies in the very central feature of L2 as a secondary set of linguistic processes. It is well accepted (i.e., in both first and second generation models) that any new linguistic system (L2, in our case) operates on the basis of generalizations from an already acquired and functioning system (L1, in our case). On this basis L2 processing can be characterized by a great reliance on L1 knowledge and on the L1 processing modes discussed above, namely, synthetic and analytic processing. Language use is assumed to operate within a single generalized framework. On the basis of this assumption we might hypothesize that these two modes of processing involve the use of L1 during L2 processing. That is, the L2 user searches for similar L1 linguistic units (nodes, properties, etc.) and integrates information from both languages to produce understanding in L2. Similarly, he or she abstracts properties and features or analyzes concepts from L2 and applies them to L1 semantic categories, integrating information from both languages.

At this point we would like to return to CAH, a first generation theory concerning L2 use, and to reconstruct its fundamental idea. This idea may be summarized in the following form: Insofar as L2 material corresponds to L1, L2 use will be successful. A strong 'mentalistic' implication can be derived here, that is, L2 use is characterized by the process of comparison between the features of L2 material that the user is exposed to and the relevant elements of his already established L1 linguistic structures. Essentially, this restatement provides a theoretical basis for our assumption that L1 knowledge is incorporated into L2 processing.

Following this logic, the basic notion of CAH is revived by means of the fundamental construct implied in second generation models, that is, processing. Due to the problem-solving nature of this construct, our interpretation of the CA approach permits actualization of the processing concept. This brings us closer to the psychological meaning of this concept than do the second generation methods. The CAH is inherently suggestive of the very process of L2 comprehension by virtue of the term "contrastive." This term implies that we are dealing with a process of contrasting between two linguistic systems in order to validate one of them, namely, L2. In other words, new information from L2 is integrated with what is known in L1. It can be viewed as if the L2 elements that are compatible with L1 components are integrated with the latter by the process of L2 comprehension. The integration rule may add compatible elements or may eliminate incompatible L2 elements from those in L1. These possibilities will be discussed later on.

Remaining on the theoretical level, the notion of contrastive or integrative processing can be combined with the "access of processing" notion that we speculatively derive from Bialystock's second generation theorizing. We adopt the hypothesis that an L2 user would integrate information available to him about semantic special cases in L1 with information about L2 concepts while he is comprehending L2 material. Similarly, he would integrate information from concepts in L1 with information about special cases in L2 in comprehending L2 material. Following the same principle, it is assumed that an L2 user would integrate information about special cases from both L1 and L2, or he would integrate information about concepts from both L1 and L2. Finally, we assume that the L2 user would integrate information about L2 concepts and its L2 special cases with information about special cases or information about concepts in L1. Later on we present examples of how these hypotheses might be tested.

The conceptual framework we have attempted to describe should be coordinated with a methodological framework. To this end, we return to second generation methodologies. The literature review of the second generation models was addressed, among other things, to the problem of fair and balanced empirical comparisons. This problem might emerge from the reality in which the conceptual frameworks (models) are not accompanied by methods which require balanced comparisons. The best case would be to work with a model that demonstrates consonance between its conceptual and methodological parts. The ideal model should be factorial to allow tests for the role of each of the sources of information (in our case, L1 and L2 elements) which the model assumes to be involved in the process of L2 comprehension (main effects is the classical term for these tests) as well as a test for integrative processing (interaction, in classical terms).

To sharpen this distinction we claim that the "latent" factorial models (e.g., Bialystock, 1984a) make a crucial assumption which remains untested due to the ad hoc nature of the methodology chosen from the examination of the explicit assumptions. This is the assumption that the process of L2 comprehension is multidimensional and that multiple dimensions are involved in the very same psycholinguistic process. However, these models could not test for such an assumption, since they did not programmatically and systematically use factorial designs. Consequently, they are not able to address a basic question involved with factorial modeling, namely: Are the (two) relevant factors interactively involved in language comprehension?

To illustrate our point, let us assume that some researcher follows this factorial design and finds that the different explanatory linguistic variables are involved in the process in question (i.e., he finds two significant main effects) and that the interaction model which is included in the factorial design is empirically supported. It is undoubtedly a significant step forward, since the researcher can conclude that the two factors are interactively involved in the process.

Now that we have satisfactorily adjusted our methodology to the requirements of the theoretical multidimensional orientation, we still need to resolve one fundamental question: Do the relevant factors interact with each other (outside the reader's mind) or are they integrated within the mind of the language processor? A simple factorial model is not able to provide an answer to that question. As a matter of fact, factorial modeling conventionally assumes that the relevant factors interact with each other. However, one who is "processing-oriented" should remain unsatisfied, since he is not able to determine, even with minimal confidence, what the fundamental nature of the comprehension process is, that is, is it integrative or is it simplified? Furthermore, let us assume that using a factorial design, a researcher finds two main effects and no significant interaction. Would he conclude that the two sources of information are not integrated within the readers mind? The classical factorial modeling does not allow a rejectable test of such a conclusion.

We think that answers to the relevant questions of L2 processing can be provided by adopting Anderson's (1981, 1982) Information Integration

Theory (IIT). This theory incorporates factorial modeling while at the same time making innovative use of its procedural and statistical potential. Conceptually it is most striking for our subject in its implementation of the term "integration." Integration occurs, according to this theory, within the reader's mind. In our case, it is the basic characteristic of the process in question, namely, comprehension in L2. The theory is based on the assumption that "all thought and behavior has multiple causes, being integrated resultants of multiple sources of stimulus information" (Anderson, 1981:4). Its methodology allows one to show how different sources of information are integrated within the reader's mind into a single choice made by him.

IIT has been applied to a variety of problems in psycholinguistics (e.g., Anderson, 1981; Greunich, 1982; Leon, 1982; Oden & Anderson 1974; Oden 1977, 1978). The psycholinguistic work with IIT, through manipulation of relations between sentence parts, has examined how different bits of semantic information are integrated into a single judgment (see Oden & Anderson, 1974). The reader is presented with sentences, in each of which there exists a combination of a particular level of one source of information with a particular level of a second source. The reader responds to these sentences consecutively on a rating scale. The complete design is factorial, that is, it includes all combinations of the levels of each source of information. These data are arranged by a variety of statistical means, both descriptive and inferential, which are constructed to provide answers to the following basic questions: Does the cognitive process in question involve integration of different sources of information? And if so, what rule does that integration follow? The information subjected to integration has included different bifactorial (and sometimes tri-factorial) combinations of a person's sociableness, interestingness, trustfulness, dependableness, gregariousness, and pleasantness (Oden & Anderson, 1974). It has also included work on the integration of intentions with consequences and regrets (Greunich, 1982; Leon, 1982); relative truthfulness of premises involving category membership (Oden, 1977); and relative sensibleness of the readings of ambiguous sentences (Oden, 1978). Findings of the experiments cited above are unequivocal regarding the multidimensional nature of the processes in question. With respect to the form of the integration rule, multiplicative and additive rules were found to play a central role in the processes of attribution and sensibleness evaluation, respectively.

The IIT paradigm is constructed to examine objectively the compatibility of its own tools. It tests the validity of its measurement scale as well as its choice of the levels of the stimulus dimensions. This part of the theory, labeled functional measurement, "reverses the traditional approach and makes measurement theory an organic component of substantive investigation" (Anderson, 1981: 12). It follows from this logic that only if the trend in a multifactorial design obeys a predicted (simple) algebraic function will the measures as well as the sampling procedure of the levels of the stimulus dimensions be valid ones. This theory and its accompanying method also has the unique power to reject its own assumptions concerning the nature of the process in question: that it relates to several sources of information and that it is integrative.

Since the methodology proposed by IIT is an integral part of the theory, it might be helpful to present here the work of Oden and Anderson (1974). Their subjects were provided with sentences which combined varying compatibilities of agent-verb and verb-recipient constraints. For example:

> Mr. X is *very sociable*. How likely is it that he will socialize with *very sociable* people?

This sentence contains two bits of information, one concerning an agent and one concerning a recipient. Each one represents a particular level of sociableness. Since the authors decided to establish four levels for each of these two sources of information, there are a total of 16 sentences, fifteen in addition to the above example. In each one a different combination of two specific levels of each source of information is presented. The reader is required to make his likelihood judgment on a 20 point rating scale. In contrast to the first example above, which presents a strong complex of information concerning sociableness, the following example presents a weak complex of information.

> Mr. X is *very unsociable*. How likely is it that he will socialize with *very unsociable* people?

In the first example it is most reasonable to expect the reader to attribute a high level of sociableness while the second example is likely to elicit a low likelihood. Another sentence from among the 16 could include a high level of agent sociableness and a low level of recipient sociableness, as follows:

> Mr. X is *very sociable*. How likely is it that he will socialize with *very unsociable* people?

In an example of this type, if the subject takes into account the sociableness of both the agent and recipient information, he will make a likelihood rating in the middle of the scale. The entire set of examples is composed of the factorial combinations of the agent-verb and verb-recipient information in the following sentence.

> Mr. X is *very sociable (or moderately sociable, moderately unsociable, very unsociable)*. How likely is it that he will socialize with *very sociable (or moderately sociable, moderately unsociable, very unsociable)* people?

The agent-verb constraint here is represented by the combinations of adjective information (very sociable, etc.) related to one character with a verb (socialize), while the verb-recipient constraint is constructed from the combination of that same verb and the adjective related to a second character (very sociable, etc.).

An example from Oden and Anderson's (1974) findings is illustrative of the different types of answers to the questions the theory is intended to address. The slope of all the curves in Figure 1 from the lower-left to upper-right-hand corner of the graphs indicates the impact of the "recipient" information while the distances between the various curves indicates the impact of the "agent" information. The fan-shape of the curves in Figure 1a represents a multiplicative-type rule of integration between agent and recipient information. A left-to-right survey of the curves reveals that, at any level of agent sociableness, the distance of mean judged likelihood related to the corresponding level of receipient sociableness is greater. This implies that the increase in the judged likelihood as a function of both dimensions is greater than the simple summation of them as represented by the parallel relations between the curves in Figure 1b. The fan-shape is, according to the theory, a result of a multiplicative process in the mind of the reader. That part of the theory, labeled functional measurement, postulates that such an inference regarding the mental rule of integration is the most parsimonious. It can be attained only if the scale of measurement is psychometrically sound and the sampling procedure of the levels of information of both dimensions is valid and representative.

IIT is presented here as a possible tool for comprehensive examination of theories and assumptions concerning the nature of processing in L2. A useful application of such a paradigm requires careful construction of L2 sentences or texts which involve L1 elements, that is, in a way that allows manipulation of L1 and L2 information in a manner that may provide answers to the following general question: Is L1 information integrated with information from L2 during the process of L2 comprehension? Following an IIT method this question might be investigated through a series of experiments. Each experiment would present to the reader a specific combination of instances and categories, asking that reader for a judgment of the sensibility (or truthfulness) of the text. Each instance and category would appear in different combinations of L1 and L2, allowing examination of the question raised.

From Oden and Anderson's (1974) and Oden's (1977) results (dealing with the information integration rule in processes of attribution and sensibleness evaluation), two competing hypotheses emerge: (a) that the rule is multiplicative and (b) that it is additive. The first hypothesis means that information from L1 is integrated with L2 information in a gestalt-like fashion. If that is the case, the TV viewer described at the beginning of this

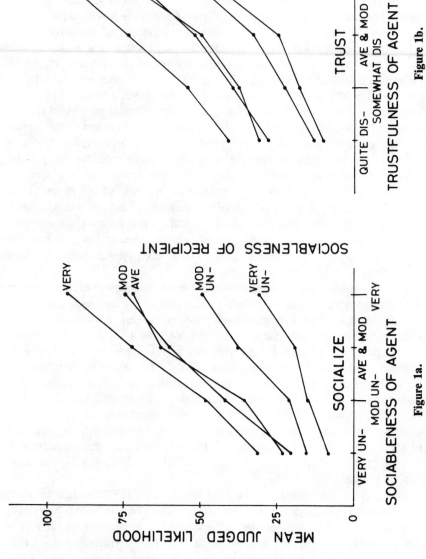

DEPENDABLENESS OF RECIPIENT

TRUST

Figure 1b.

SOCIABLENESS OF RECIPIENT

SOCIALIZE

Figure 1a.

chapter gains more from integrating L1 information with the L2 information provided in the movie than if the rule of integration is additive. Moreover, this gain is expected to be of a higher quality than if the rule of integration is additive.

Systematic experimentation in this direction will relate to several crucial problems, one of which concerns the extent to which the task requiring integration of L2 and L1 material is approached volitionally. This is important since the proposed methodology forces the L1 information on the L2 user. That is, the researcher would do well to design a task (other than the IIT forced choice method) which will allow the reader to turn willingly to L1 information while comprehending an L2 text. Another problem lies in the notion of individual differences, especially the question of whether people more proficient in L2 tend toward less integration of L1 with L2 information. Alternatively, those who are more proficient in L2 might use a multiplicative rule of integration while those who are less proficient might use an additive rule of integration. Such systematic experimentation can contribute a great deal to the understanding of the nature of L2 comprehension processes.

References

Anderson, N.H. 1981. *Foundations of Information Integration Theory.* New York: Academic Press.

Anderson, N.H. 1982. *Methods of Information Integration Theory.* New York: Academic Press.

Bailey, N., Madden, C. and Krashen, S.D. 1974. Is there a natural sequence in adult second language learning? *Language Learning, 24,* 235–243.

Bialystock, E. 1978. A theoretical model of second language learning. *Language Learning 28,* 68–83.

Bialystock, E. 1981. The role of linguistic knowledge in second language acquisition. *Studies in Second Language Acquisition 4,* 1, 31–45.

Bialystock, E. 1984a. Cognitive dimensions of metalinguistic awareness. Paper presented at the annual meeting of the Canadian Psychological Association, Ottawa.

Bialystock, E. 1984b. Factors in the growth of linguistic awareness. Manuscript, York University.

Brown, H.D. 1980. *Principles of Language Learning and Teaching.* Englewood Cliffs, NJ: Prentice-Hall, Inc.

Carroll, J.B. 1968. Contrastive linguistics and interference theory. *19th Annual Georgetown Roundtable.* Washington, D.C.: Georgetown University Press.

Corder, P. 1967. The significance of learners' errors. *IRAL 5,* 161–170.

Corder, P. 1971. Idiosyncratic dialects and error analysis. *IRAL 9,* 2, 147–160.

Corder, P. 1975. The language of second language learning: The broader issues. *Modern Language Journal 59,* 8, 409–413.

Dulay, H., Burt, M. and Krashen, S. 1982. *Language Two*. New York: Oxford University Press.

Dulay, H. and Burt, M. 1974. Natural sequences in child second language acquisition. *Language Learning 24*, 37–53.

Fries, C. 1945. *Teaching and Learning English as a Foreign Language*. Ann Arbor: University of Michigan Press.

Greunich, R. 1982. The development of children's integration rules for making moral judgments. *Child Development 53*, 887–894.

Guilford, J.B. and Hoepfner, H. 1971. *The Analysis of Intelligence*. New York: McGraw-Hill.

Jacobovitz, L.A. 1970. *Foreign Language Learning: A Psycholinguistic Analysis of the Issues*. Rowley, MA: Newbury House.

James, C. 1980. *Contrastive Analysis*. London: Longman.

Krashen, S.D. 1977. The monitor model of adult second language performance. In M. Burt, H. Dulay, and M. Finocchiaro (eds.) *Viewpoints on English as a Second Language*. New York: Regents.

Krashen, S.D. 1978. Individual variation in the use of the monitor. In W. Ritchie (ed.) *Second Language Acquisition Research: Issues and Implications*. New York: Academic Press.

Krashen, S.D. 1982. *Principles and Practice in Second Language Acquisition*. New York: Pergamon Press.

Krashen, S.D. and Pon, P. 1975. An error analysis of an advanced ESL learner. *Working Papers on Bilingualism 7*, 125–129.

Lado, R. 1957. *Linguistics Across Cultures: Applied Linguistics for Language Teachers*. Ann Arbor: University of Michigan Press.

Lado, R. 1968. Contrastive analysis in a mentalistic theory of language learning. *19th Annual Georgetown Roundtable*. Washington, D.C.: Georgetown University Press.

Larsen-Freeman, D. 1976. An explanation for the morpheme acquisition order of second language learners. *Language Learning 26*, 125–134.

Leon, M. 1982. Rules in children's moral judgments: Integration of intent, damage and rational information. *Developmental Psychology 18*, 6, 835–842.

McLaughlin, B., Rossman, T., and McLeod, B. 1983. Second language learning: An information processing perspective. *Language Learning 33*, 2, 135–158.

Oden, G.S. 1977. Fuzziness in semantic memory. *Memory and Cognition 5*, 2, 198–204.

Oden, G.S. 1978. Semantic constraints and judged preference for interpretations of ambiguous sentences. *Memory and Cognition 6*, 1, 26–37.

Oden, G.S., and Anderson, N.H. 1974. Integration of semantic constraints. *Journal of Verbal Learning and Verbal Behavior 13*, 138–148.

Ritchie, W.C. 1967. Some implications of generative grammar for the construction of courses in English as a Foreign Language. *Language Learning 17*, 45–69, 111–131.

Rumelhart, D.E. and Norman, D.A. 1981. Analogical processes in learning. In J.R. Anderson (ed.), *Cognitive Skills and Their Acquisition*. Hillsdale, New Jersey: Lawrence Erlbaum Associates.

Schoenfeld, W.C. 1974. Notes on a bit of psychological nonsense: Race differences in intelligence. *The Psychological Record 24,* 17-32.

Sternberg, J.R. 1977a. Component processes in analogical reasoning. *Psychological Review 84,* 4, 353-378.

Sternberg, J.R. 1977b. *Intelligence, Information Processing and Analogical Reasoning: The Componential Analysis of Human Abilities.* Hillsdale, New Jersey: Lawrence Erlbaum Associates.

Tarone, E., Cohen, A.D., and Dumas, G. 1976. A closer look at some interlanguage terminology. *Working Papers in Bilingualism 9,* 76-90.

Verbrugge, R.R. 1977. Resemblances in language and perception. In: R. Shaw and J. Bransford (eds.), *Perceiving, Achieving and Knowing: Toward an Ecological Psychology.* New Jersey: Hillsdale.

Wardaugh, R. 1970. The contrastive analysis hypothesis. *TESOL Quarterly 4,* 123-130.

Wolfe, D.L. 1967. Some theoretical aspects of language learning and language teaching. *Language Learning 17,* 173-188.

CHAPTER 8

Integration of First Language Material in Second Language Comprehension

Joel Walters
Yuval Wolf

Department of English
Bar Ilan University

Introduction

This chapter intends to advance the notion that second language comprehension involves an integration of information from two different linguistic sources: first language (L1) and second language (L2). Our orientation is empirical-experimental. Since this notion has not been systematically treated, a rather artificial task was created to demonstrate that the hypothesized integration is observable and reproducible. Following the methodological tradition adopted in such experimentation, we make no pretenses about the realism of the experimental task and its external or ecological validity. Rather, we leave it to further experimentation which ought to be conducted and designed on the basis of this study's results.

Following a brief introduction, we present a paradigm within which two experiments were conducted. The focus here on the methodology and on the results of the experiments introduces Anderson's (1981, 1982) Information Integration Theory and its paradigm as an analytic tool which naturally fits issues such as integration of L1 information within L2 processing.

As discussed in Wolf and Walters (earlier this volume), a person who is exposed to L2 material but who is not familiar with all of the linguistic components presented in that material cannot satisfactorily comprehend it using only the information given by the L2 text. Presumably, he is accustomed to using information from his first language and to integrating the L2 linguistic components with the framework of the L1 information. This L1 information is assumed to serve as a substitute for the missing L2 information.

Fries (1945) and Lado (1957) consider L1 habits as a viable source for the prediction of L2 performance. These writers are considered the founders of the contrastive analysis hypothesis (CAH). Wardaugh (1970), among others (Ritchie, 1967; Wolfe, 1967) refined the original proposal, distinguishing between a Strong Version of CAH, which claimed that a structural comparison of two languages could predict a learner's errors, and a Weak Version of the theory, which maintained that a comparison of L1 and L2 could account a posteriori for observed learner difficulties. While CAH was severely criticized from a number of perspectives (Brown, 1980; Dulay, Burt, & Krashen, 1982; Ritchie, 1967; Wardaugh, 1972), its principal underlying conception is appropriate for a multidimensional approach to the study of L2 comprehension processes.

Such a multidimensional paradigm which is intended to experimentally examine the relative contribution of several dimensions of information as well as the rule for their integration is Anderson's (1981) Information Integration Theory (IIT). The IIT paradigm (Anderson, 1982) seems to be able to supply our field with a powerful multidimensional tool (see a detailed review in Wolf and Walters, earlier this volume), which allows the systematic examination of whether and how an L2 user integrates information from several relevant dimensions while he comprehends L2 material. It allows simultaneous exposure of the reader to both L1 and L2 information during comprehension of an L2 text. We accomplished this in two different experiments which are described in the next part of the chapter. These experiments were intended to test the assumption that L2 users integrate L1 and L2 information during L2 processing. In more operational terms, it is hypothesized that both L1 and L2 bits of information which are presented as hints for the L2 user will be involved in his comprehension of unfamiliar L2 material.

The study was run in Israel where Hebrew is generally considered to be L1 and English is considered L2. Thus, the linguistic material subject to comprehension was in English (defined here as L2) and the hint words were in Hebrew (defined as L1) as well as in English. The subjects in the experiments were sampled from two different linguistic subpopulations who live in Israel: Hebrew native speakers (HNS) and English native speakers (ENS) who have lived for several years in Israel and speak Hebrew. The latter group is characterized by the use of Hebrew for daily purposes and fluency in English. For the ENS, terms from the two languages are expected to be more equally balanced than for the HNS group. These subjects, then, are expected to integrate English and Hebrew information more coherently. In methodological terms, they are expected to adopt an interactive rule of integration between the two sources of information while the HNS subjects are expected to use a non-interactive—additive—rule of integration. (For a comprehensive review of the different integration rules Anderson's 1981 and 1982 books are recommended).

Experiment 1: Integration of L1 and L2 Information
at the Lexical Level

Method

Each of 12 HNS and 12 ENS female subjects was examined individually. Proficiency was determined by a standardized English placement examination used by all Israeli universities. Each subject was shown the following sentence and asked whether she understood all the words: "A medlar is like an apple." The subject of this sentence—medlar (a small fruit about the size of a date with a mildly sour taste)—is, supposedly, unknown to those who are not native English speakers. Thus, the reader is left with some uncertainty concerning its exact nature. It is this very uncertainty that allows for a systematic presentation of several bits of information which differ from each other in their relevance to the lexical item in question. All subjects in the two groups reported not knowing the meaning of the word "medlar."

Next, the subject was told that she would be presented with a series of 16 cards, each consisting of a pair of words which would help her to understand the meaning of the word "medlar." Each pair consisted of an L2 word (English) and an L1 word (Hebrew). These were a 4 × 4 factorial combination of four English words (peach; bread; cat; love) and four Hebrew words ('agas' = pear; '?uga' = cake; 'kelev' = dog; 'sixma' = joy). The two series of words gradually shift from close similarity to the meaning of the target word (peach and 'agas') to a great semantic distance (love and 'sim-xa'). Peach and "agas" belong to the same semantic category as medlar. Bread and "?uga" are not fruits but they belong to the more general category of food. Cat and "kelev," in contrast, cannot (usually) be considered food. Rather, they are food consumers or, more generally, concrete animate objects. Love and "simxa" are abstract nouns which have a maximal semantic distance from the noun "medlar."

The subject was asked to evaluate the relative contribution of each of the two "hint" words on each card for the understanding of the meaning of the target item. She was then told that she would be asked to use a 20 point rating scale to judge the amount of help she received from each pair of hint words. At this point, the subject was provided with a graphic scale and asked to make several practice ratings. This was done in order to establish a close connection between the stimulus words and the response choices in the mind of the subject. The number of practice items ranged between 3 and 8, depending on the experimenter's assessment as to whether the subject was appropriately warmed up for the task. Following the practice items, the 16 stimulus pairs were presented sequentially in a random order, the subject making her ratings on a graphic scale from 1 to 20. Immediately following this set of items, the same 16 items were presented as a replication of the initial experiment. The entire procedure took approximately 15 minutes.

Results and Discussion

The data collected for each subject was organized in a 4×4 (English and Hebrew) factorial table. These data were averaged over the 12 subjects in each of the two groups, and the two graphs which result from the mean ratings are depicted in Figure 1. The two graphs seen in Figure 1 indicate that both English and Hebrew sources of information were considered by the subjects as meaningfully contributing to their understanding of the meaning of the target item in question. The effect of English information is evident by the wide bipolar spread of lines. (Bipolarity is relected in the pairing of the two upper curves and pairing of the two lower curves). The two lines representing the two terms which are semantically closer to the target term (peach and bread) are positioned higher in the graph, that is, these two terms are considered by the subjects as contributing more to their understanding than the other two terms. The impression concerning the general effect of the English hints is supported by the results of a two-way ANOVA for repeated measures. That analysis reveals significant main-effects for English information in both the HNS group ($F(3,11) = 80.23$, $p < 0.0001$) and and in the ENS group: ($F(3,11) = 97.94$, $p < 0.0001$). The impression con-

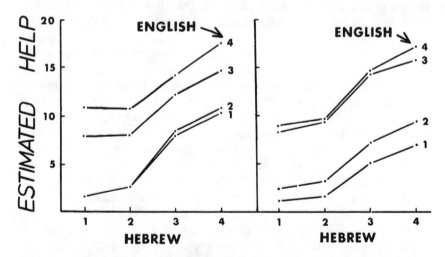

Figure 1. Mean estimates of the contribution of English and Hebrew information to the understanding of an English term, made by Hebrew Native Speakers (HNS) (left panel) and English Native Speakers (ENS) (right panel).

Legend

English	Hebrew
1 = love	1 = simxa ("joy")
2 = cat	2 = kelev ("dog")
3 = bread	3 = ?uga ("cake")
4 = peach	4 = agas ("pear")

cerning the bipolarity of the evaluations was tested by a Scheffe test, which isolates out each different effect from the entire F test. This test indicates that the terms "peach" and "bread" belong to one category (the upper one) and the terms "cat" and "love" belong to another category for the ENS group only (see right panel of Figure 1). In the HNS group, in contrast, the terms "peach" and "bread" significantly differ from each other. The terms "cat" and "love" belong to another category, a finding similar to the one for the HNS group (see left panel of Figure 1). The marginal means (collapsed across the two groups) for the terms "love," "cat," "bread," and "peach," are 3.7, 5.6, 11.9 and 12.6, respectively. This different spread of effect is quite difficult to explain, since those who are highly proficient in English (ENS) are expected to differentiate in English material at least as much as Hebrew speakers. In summary, the ENS group reflects a bipolar distinction while the HNS group reflects a three-way distinction among the English lexical item.

The effect of Hebrew information is evident by the left to right upward slope of the four curves. The closer the meaning of the Hebrew term is to the meaning of the target term, the more it is considered as contributing to understanding. This impression is inferentially supported by the main-effects of Hebrew information in the HNS group ($F(3,11) = 119.35$, $p < 0.0001$ and in the ENS group ($F(3,11) = 287.84$, $p < 0.0001$). The left to right upward slope starts only from the second term, "kelev," suggesting that the effect of English information in both groups is tri-polar (a tri-partite division among the four curves). This impression is supported by a Scheffe test. The marginal means for the terms "simxa," "kelev," "?uga" and "agas" are 5.2, 5.9, 10.3 and 12.2, respectively. Now that we see that the only bi-polarity was observed in the effect of English information on the ENS group, we may try to speculate about it. One clue may lie in the F value (287.84), which represents the effect of Hebrew information on the ENS subjects. One can interpret such a large effect in the following way: Those who are more used to functioning in two languages prefer, when the meaning of the target material is uncertain, to utilize hints from L2 than those in L1. Of course, such speculation should be tested in a further study designed to systematically examine its validity.

The similarity between the marginal means in Hebrew (5.5, 5.7, 10.9, 13.13) and English (5.6, 5.8, 10.5, 13.13) in the ENS group also deserves consideration. Since the HNS subjects represent the reference group, the similarity mentioned above together with the similar weights of these effects (as represented by the F values) can be accepted as validating the experimental manipulation.

Now that we know that both sources of information are meaningful for L2 comprehenders tested in this study, the crucial question is: What rule governs the integration of these informative hints? A descriptive answer to such a question can be obtained from an analysis of the relative trend of the four curves. A figural abstraction of the overall structure of the curves in the two graphs in Figure 1 reveals two different relative shapes of the curves in each graph. Since the visible difference is not ultimately convincing, we had better start from the relevant inferential statistics, namely the interaction terms. In the HNS group this term is not significant ($F(9,99) = 1.7$, $p = 0.1$) while in the ENS group it is significant ($F(9,99) = 2.45$, $p = 0.014$). The former result (HNS group) confirms that the curves in the HNS graph are parallel. Following IIT, such parallelism means that the two types of information are integrated in an additive fashion. As opposed to this, the significant interaction in the ENS group means that the subjects use a multiplicative rule of integration. Descriptively, use of such a rule should be expressed by a fan shape of the curves. A close inspection of the HNS figure reveals a fan shape within each of the two pairs of curves as well as between the pairs. This means that the Hebrew information given to the L1 comprehender on any trial is not simply added to the L2 (English) information (or vice versa). Rather, it indicates that the Hebrew information contributes more to the understanding process as the relevance of the information from both sources increases. These findings clearly fit our hypothesis that those who are more fluent in the use of both relevant languages will adopt a more compact rule of integration.

The results dealing with the lexical level of comprehension can be summarized as follows: Both Hebrew native speakers for whom English is a second language and English native speakers who have frequently used Hebrew for several years relate to both English and Hebrew hints when they comprehend an unfamiliar English term. However, the ENS tend to adopt a more compact (multiplicative) rule to integrate the English and the Hebrew hints while the HNS adopt a less compact (additive) rule of integration. The English native speakers give greater weight to the Hebrew information than the weight they ascribe to the English information; the Hebrew native speakers weight both sources of information equally. These findings seem to provide solid support for our integration assumption. At the same time they suggest that language users with different relative proficiency and experience in two languages approach the comprehension task in different ways. Specifically, it seems that those who are more equally proficient (bilingual) and more experienced in both languages (the English native speakers who currently and fluently use Hebrew) tend to make their (more compact) integrative comprehension on the basis of a bias in favor of information from a language (L1) other than the target language (L2).

To advance the matter further another experiment was conducted with two major changes. First, due to the limited nature of the lexical comprehension task, the focus of the comprehension task was extended to a more pragmatic linguistic unit. Thus, an idiom was chosen for the comprehension task in Experiment 2. Second, the ENS group was replaced with a group of high proficiency HNS subjects. This was done to clarify the role of L2 proficiency in the integration of L1 and L2 hints.

Experiment 2: Integrative Comprehension of an Unfamiliar Idiom in L2

Method

The IIT methodology was implemented in order to investigate the relative contribution of L1 and L2 in understanding the meanings of an unfamiliar L2 idiom. The same experiment was conducted with two groups (including both males and females), one of low L2 proficiency (LP) and one of higher L2 proficiency (HP). Proficiency was determined by a standardized English placement examination used by all Israeli universities. One group (HP) consisted of six advanced level students of English as a Foreign Language; the second group (LP) was comprised of four students at an intermediate level. Each student judged the extent to which a pair of words, one in English and one in Hebrew, helped them to understand the meaning of the idiom "hit it off."

The procedure was the same as in the previous experiment. Each of the subjects was examined individually. First, the subject was shown the idiom and asked whether he or she understood it. All subjects reported the idiom "hit it off" to be unfamiliar. (If anyone had indicated knowledge of the idiom, he or she would have been thanked and released.) Unfamiliarity with the target idiom is a common phenomenon in L2 processing. Due to the more complex nature of this comprehension task, only three levels of similarity of the hint words to the target idiom were established. The pairs of words consisted of the nine combinations of the following English items: "to like," "to tolerate," "to read," with the following Hebrew items: "l'hitxaver" = to socialize, "l'histader" = to get long, and "lashevet" = to sit. The two (English and Hebrew) series of words include: categorical similarity to the meaning of the target idiom ("to like" and "l'hitxaver"), a moderate similarity to the target item ("to tolerate" and "l'histader"), and a great categorical difference ("read" and "lashevet"). A series of nine cards comprising a factorial pairing of the different hint terms was prepared. The subject was told that each pair of words was intended to help him to understand the meaning of the idiom "hit it off." He was instructed to rate on a 20 point graphic scale the relative contribution of each of the two hint words on each card for the understanding of the meaning of the idiom. Then, after a period of careful explanation and practice, the nine stimulus pairs were presented sequentially in a random order, the subject making his ratings after each pair. Following a short break, this experiment was replicated, the nine items being presented in a different random order. From a simple methodological perspective the replication can be viewed as compensating for the relatively small number of subjects. The two measures in each experimental condition enables us to draw a graph of the averaged individual scores, each of which is already strengthened by being averaged over the two scores for each individual subject. This issue is treated in more detail in the general discussion.

Results and Discussion

The English and Hebrew graphs of the 3×3 factorial data averaged for both the LP and HP groups are presented in Figure 2. The two graphs seen in Figure 2 indicate that in the idiom comprehension task, as in the lexical task, both sources of information were judged to affect the comprehension process. The finding of the previous experiment concerning the relative weight of the two sources of information seems to gain support from the difference between the two structures seen in Figure 2. While the overall shape of these structures is quite similar (the lines seem to slightly diverge from lower-left to upper-right), the lines representing the different levels of

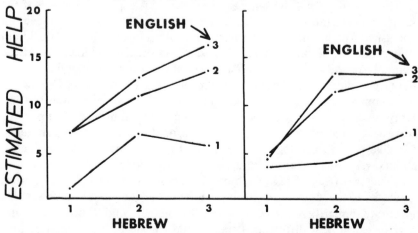

Figure 2.   Mean estimates of the contribution of English and Hebrew information to the understanding of an English idiom, made by low proficiency (LP) (left panel) and high proficiency (HP) (right panel) subjects.

Legend

English	Hebrew
1 = to read	1 = lashevet ("to sit")
2 = to tolerate	2 = l'histader ("to get along")
3 = to like	3 = l'hitxaver ("to socialize")

English information are somewhat more condensed in the HP group (see right panel). The data suggest that the LP subjects (left panel) ascribed a weight to Hebrew information (L1) which is smaller than the weight they attributed to English information (L2). This impression is confirmed by the inferential statistics. For the Hebrew information $F(2,5) = 54.7$, $p < 0.0001$ with marginal means of 5.2, 11.8 and 11.9. For the English information $F(2,5) = 4.9$, $p = 0.0329$ with marginal means of 7.3, 10.3 and 11.3. In the LP group both English and Hebrew information were rated quite similarly. For the Hebrew information $F(2,3) = 19.6$, $p = 0.002$ with marginal means of 5.0, 11.2 and 12.0. For the English information $F(2,3) = 15.6$, $p = 0.004$ with marginal means of 5.0, 10.7 and 12.5. The clear bi-polar effect means that the two terms which are closer to the target idiom are considered as if they belong to the same category. This effect mirrors the effect of grouping the two extreme terms seen in the previous (lexical) experiment. In other words, both experiments show evidence of a general trend to bipolarity.

With regard to the rule of integration between the Hebrew and the English information, the HP graph in Figure 2 is more of a fan shape. However, the descriptive difference between the HP and LP groups is not obvious. The interaction term, which serves as the inferential test in such cases, is as follows; for the HP subjects $F(4,20) = 2.41$, $p = 0.08$ and for the LP subjects $F(4,12) = 1.53$, $p = 0.26$. The fact that the p value for HP subjects did pass the limit of 0.05 may be due to the low power of the test (very few subjects). However, the noticeable difference between the two p values is support for the expectation that the HP language users tend to multiplicatively integrate L1 and L2 helping information.

General Discussion

The main line of findings can be viewed as encouraging for Anderson's (1981, 1982) Information Integration Theory and its paradigm as a framework for the study of L2 comprehension as an integrative process. This conclusion is based on the successful demonstration of how two bits of information, one from L1 and the other from L2, simultaneously presented to L2 comprehenders, are judged to be significantly involved in the comprehension of specific L2 material.

Different pairs of L1 and L2 information served as a means to systematically manipulate the semantic similarity between the information carried by them and the L2 target material. The required response was the subject's evaluation of the extent to which this information contributed to his understanding of the L2 target term or idiom. A two-factorial inferential statistical test of the results provided the answer that the observed response was determined by an integration of both sources of information.

The theoretical framework of IIT enabled us to identify two different rules of integration—additive and multiplicative. These rules, which follow a plausible psycholinguistic conceptualization, are utilized by two different sub-populations, that is, low proficiency and high proficiency L2 users, respectively. The latter adopted a more compact rule of integration. In comprehending English terms or idioms, subjects who are presumably more fluent in both Hebrew and English showed a tendency to rely on Hebrew more than on English hints. As a result of these findings, IIT seems to serve as a promising conceptual and methodological framework for the examination of the bi-dimensional nature of the process of L2 comprehension.

The replication of the main line of results using two different individual linguistic distinctions (Hebrew native speakers vs. English native speakers and low proficiency vs. high proficiency Hebrew speakers) in two different linguistic comprehension tasks (lexical and pragmatic) reinforce the external validity of our conclusions. However, the generality of our results is jeopardized by several limitations, the most striking of which are discussed below.

Substantive Considerations

The findings of the two experiments reported here relate to a metalinguistic approach to comprehension processes. The subjects' task was to evaluate the contribution of English and Hebrew information to the understanding of an English term. They were not required to demonstrate their logical understanding of material in L2. We might suppose that the predictions for the metalinguistic and the logical stages of comprehension do not differ and that it is harder to obtain such meaningful results in the former case than in the latter. Nevertheless, the pure (logical) understanding of L2 material remains the core of L2 comprehension.

The method of designing a test of logical understanding can be developed on the basis of the method used in this study. This will be demonstrated in terms of the lexical task. The same 4 × 4 design with the same terms may be used. The same pairs of Hebrew and English helping words can be inserted into the opening cover sentence in the following way: "Medlar" is something which is close to "agas" (or "?uga," or "kelev," or "simxa") as well as to "peach" (or "bread," or "cat," or "love")". A question such as "How likely is it that a medlar is like an apple?" should repeatedly follow each of the 16 items using a rating scale. This procedure establishes 16 different bilingual semantic relations for a certain unknown term. In this way the given semantic distance of "medlar" from "apple" is manipulated, allowing the adjacent question (i.e., How likely is it...) to determine the extent to which the subject located the unknown L2 term in the different semantic network that is defined for him by each item.

Our distinction between proficiency levels is considered necessary on the basis of the following prediction: Functioning in L2 is hypothesized to rely on complementary knowledge from the first language. Thus, the greater the proficiency in L2, the more this mechanism of reliance on L1 information should be manifested. In more operational terms, the high proficiency language users should rely more heavily on L1 hints in comprehending unfamiliar L2 material. This hypothesis, while gaining some support from our findings, still needs careful consideration on both the substantive and the methodological levels. It may lead to a more specific claim that the process in question has two stages. In the first stage the proficient L2 user comprehends L1 hints. Then he turns to the L2 hints and incorporates them into the former. The operationalization of such a complex hypothesis requires a series of experiments in which the order as well as the time of presentation of L1 and L2 hints must be carefully manipulated.

Methodological Considerations

To linguistically counterbalance the knowledge which has been accumulated through this line of experimentation, the same procedures that were used in this study and those proposed here are recommended for adaptation to Hebrew as L2 and English as L1. For reasons of homogeneity of task and of stimulus material, a strict translation of the current task can effectively be used in such a transitive study. The subjects should be sampled from a population of English native speakers who use Hebrew as a second language. Further, this transitive bilingual procedure can be applied to other pairs of languages whose differences are noticeable enough to polarize them, while their similarities allow for a transfer from L1 to L2.

The artificial nature of the results leaves the possibility that our findings can be generalized only to situations in which bilingual hints are presented to the L2 user and he is required to relate to both hints. At least two questions deserve careful experimental consideration in this respect: 1. Do L2 users integrate L1 and L2 information when this information is available in spite of the fact that they are not required to use it? 2. Do they look for such information aids when they are not available and when it is not required? And if so, do the L2 users gather such information on their own from available sources such as dictionaries, or do they recall relevant information from long term and short term memory?

Another more methodological comment may be in order here. The integration exemplified so far is between L1 and L2 hints. To identify its limits, a test of integration between two "same language" hints should be conducted. For this purpose, one series of experiments should manipulate two sets of equated but different L1 helping terms. Each pair of informative terms to be presented to the subject should contain a different combination of terms from both sets. Another series of experiments should also manipulate two sets of L2 helping terms.

Statistical Considerations

This study dealt with data averaged over the entire group. Those who maintain a highly conservative methodological approach would accept our conclusions as reductionist, since they are based on grouped data. According to this approach it could be claimed that we gained knowledge about an average comprehender or, in other words, a dozen-headed subject in the lexical experiment and about half a dozen-headed subject in the pragmatic experiment using idioms. We can draw a graph for each subject to describe the similarity among the different patterns. But one can still claim that each of the individual patterns does not perfectly fit the averaged structure and that any single subject has his own unique way of integrating L1 and L2 information during the process of comprehending L2 material. To bridge the gap between the group analysis and the individual nature of our topic, one ought to demonstrate that the group findings are reflected in the performance of the individual subject. That is, an inferential test should be conducted on each subject's data.

To accomplish this it is necessary to have several measurements on each individual subject in each experimental condition (i.e., for each of the $4 \times 4 = 16$ cells of the bifactorial "lexical" design). This is achieved, following IIT, by replicating the original experiment several times. The items in the replications should be presented to the subject in different random orders. Several measurements are then produced for each individual subject within each experimental condition. In statistical terms, these two measurements produce variance (a within-cell error term) within each cell of the original factorial matrix. The replication of the experiment with each of the subjects establishes two measures for each subject in each of the cells of the original factorial design. The variance that it produces within each cell is the very condition necessary to perform an F test for each subject. In statistical terms, the two measurements in each cell produce variance which allow for a within-cell error terms.

Summary

This chapter has attempted to present an innovative method for multifactorial study of second language comprehension. The purpose of the method is to detect whether the cognitive process that precedes an observed response can be integrative. The theory behind the method (Information Integration) assumes that the different sources that are available to the responder are integrated in his mind by simple algebraic rules. Only a simplified modification of the paradigm that derives from the theory has been adopted in this study. The aim of this study was to exemplify the conceptual and methodological opportunities that are embedded in the IIT framework and its power to operationalize substantial psycholinguistic issues concerning second language comprehension. One basic issue deals with the question whether second language comprehension by its very nature is multidimensional, that is, whether it relies on information aids from several sources. In terms of our specific hypothesis the two main sources are L1 and L2 hints. It was found that L2 comprehenders related to both sources of information while trying to understand either lexical or pragmatic L2 material. Another issue derives from the evidence that L2 comprehenders do combine L1 and L2 hints. It deals with the general question of whether the integration of these hints in the mind of the comprehender obeys simple algebraic rules, or whether the rules of integration are more complicated or even unidentifiable. The results decisively support the former hypothesis. These findings must be treated cautiously. They should be considered as an intriguing exemplification of the advantages of IIT as a comprehensive framework for a multifactorial study of second language comprehension.

References

Anderson, N.H. 1981. *Foundations of Information Integration Theory*. New York: Academic Press.

Anderson, N.H. 1982. *Methods of Information Integration Theory*. New York: Academic Press.

Brown, H.D. 1980. *Principles of Language Learning and Teaching*. Englewood Cliffs, NJ: Prentice-Hall, Inc.

Dulay, H., Burt, M. and Krashen, S. 1982. *Language Two*. New York: Oxford University Press.

Fries, C. 1945. *Teaching and Learning English as a Foreign Language*. Ann Arbor: University of Michigan Press.

Lado, R. 1957. *Linguistics Across Cultures: Applied Linguistics for Language Teachers*. Ann Arbor: University of Michigan Press.

Ritchie, W.C. 1967. Some implications of generative grammar for the construction of courses in English as a Foreign Language. *Language Learning 17*, 45–69, 111–131.

Wardaugh, R. 1970. The contrastive analysis hypothesis. *TESOL Quarterly 4*, 123–130.

Wolfe, D.L. 1967. Some theoretical aspects of language learning and language teaching. *Language Learning 17*, 173–188.

Author Index

Subject Index